300 Day Hikes To Take With Your Dog Before He Tires You Out

*...Trails where you won't be able to
wipe the wag off your dog's tail*

Doug Gelbert

HIKEWITHYOURDOG.COM BOOKS

There is always a new trail to look forward to...

300 Day Hikes To Take With Your Dog Before He Tires You Out

hikewithyourdog.com books
a division of Cruden Bay Books
crudbay@mac.com

International Standard Book Number   978-1-935771-39-5

Ahead On The Trail...

Grab That Leash and Hit the Trail

"They look like they are having the time of their lives." If you hike with dogs chances are you have heard sentiments like that from other trail users when they see your happy trail dogs. Dogs are happy on any trail but they become especially excited on new trails. New scents to sniff. New sounds to hear. New sights to see.

Every year an estimated 15 million people travel with their dogs. But our best trail companions are not always welcome where we most want to go. National parks ban dogs from trails for the most part and more than half of America's 1,500+ public beaches don't allow dogs. But let's not dwell on the negative - our dogs will not allow it.

Are these the 300 best hikes in America you can take with your dog? While there are many, many hikes described in this book that are on "best lists" and "must-do lists" and "bucket lists" the goal here is to emphasize the rich variety of hiking experiences that await you and your dog. There are canine hikes dusted in history, canine hikes to unusual destinations, and canine hikes that are notable just because. There is a mix of leg-stretchers and hikes requiring a full day on the trail.

All the day hikes are in the continental United States that can be reached by driving. The selected hikes are spread throughout regions so that you are never far from a special outing with your dog.

How do I use this book? The 300 day hikes are broken into 14 different regions of the country. In each section the trails are presented alphabetically by the park involved. In the index are all the parks, alphabetized by state.

Before each hike description is a symbol. They represent:

E   The hike is rated for difficulty; either E, M, or S. There is also a time estimate of the duration of the hike. Easy hikes and strenuous hikes explain themselves. Moderate hikes typically involve either several hours of relatively easy hiking or a short period of lung-busting effort that doesn't last long enough to be rated as strenuous. The time estimates can help distinguish the character of a moderate hike.

▲   The availability of a campground in the park or near the trailhead is indicated. This does not refer to primitive camping which may sometimes be available. These are day hikes.

🏊   The swimmer indicates the chance for your dog to have a swim on the hike. While this is usually full dog-paddling it may only be splashing for larger dogs.

$ This will tell you if an admission fee is required to take this canine hike.

🚙   If a hike has a jeep symbol it means that at least part of the trip to the trailhead will be on unpaved roads. All of the canine hikes in this book can be reached by low-clearance, two-wheel drive cars.

A Word About Seaman -
America's First Great Trail Dog

When writing a canine hiking guidebook the narrative can get choppy when constantly referring to "your dog." Many describers get around this tedious wordsmithing by assuming a generic-named dog, like Spot or Fido. I will adopt that same convention here using Seaman as the name for our generic trail dog.

Who was Seaman? In the summer of 1803 as he was rounding up supplies for his forthcoming Corps of Discovery exploration, Meriwether Lewis bought a dog in Pittsburgh. He paid $20 - half of his monthly captain's wage. He wrote in his journal, "The dog was of the newfoundland breed one that I prised much for his docility and qualifications generally for my journey." Lewis named his dog Seaman.

Seaman would make the entire trip to the Pacific Ocean and back with the Lewis and Clark expedition, serving as sentry, hunter, and companion. He had more than a few adventures on the trail as well, including being bitten by a beaver and performing an occasional rescue of Corpsmen trapped in the Missouri River.

A dog collar has been discovered with an inscription that reads: "The greatest traveller of my species. My name is SEAMAN, the dog of captain Meriwether Lewis, whom I accompanied to the Pacific Ocean through the interior of the continent of North America." If Seaman were around today he would be out tackling these trails.

Paying homage to Seaman in Montana, one of a dozen statues erected to America's first great trail dog.

New England

 ## ACADIA NATIONAL PARK

Jordan Pond Nature Trail
MOUNT DESERT, MAINE
Hiking Time: 1 hour

E ▲ $

Acadia National Park is one of the crown jewels in America's park system and hands down the best national park to hike with your dog. After Woodrow Wilson designated Acadia, then called Lafayette, the nation's first national park east of the Mississippi River, patron John Rockefeller, Jr. spent decades constructing carriage roads across the wooded island.

There are 45 miles of rustic roads and 100 more miles of hiking trails. And Seaman is welcome on practically all of them. The *Jordan Pond Nature Trail* circumnavigates a glacial tarn in an easy mile loop. The trailhead is at the Jordan Pond House that was built by the original landowners in the 1870s and has been a hub of social activity on the island ever since. Wooden boards help traverse the marshy areas on shore.

The adventure for Seaman at Jordan Pond comes on several trails that branch off the nature walk, including paths that lead to the top of two rounded mountains framing the pond known as the Bubbles. Unobstructed views of the park and Jordan Pond await with a delightful array of glacial erractics posing on the summits of the North Bubble (872 feet) and the South Bubble (766 feet).

The clear waters of Jordan Pond go as deep as 60 feet - the deepest in Maine. This is a drinking water supply and no dogs are permitted to swim here but the Atlantic Ocean is not far away.

 ## ARCADIA MANAGEMENT AREA

Ben Utter Trail
WEST GREENWICH, RHODE ISLAND
Hiking Time: 1-2 hours

E ▲ 🦢 🚙

Rhode Island has only 777,000 acres and 14,000 of those are managed at Arcadia, kept in a "more or less" natural state. For excitement many canine hikers pick their way up rocky ledges to the 360-degree views atop 430-foot Mt. Tom.

For an exceedingly peaceful Arcadia hike take Seaman to the *Ben Utter Trail*. **The soft dirt path under paw traces the lively Wood River amidst giant white pines and red maples that escaped logging due to their awkward location by the stream.** You pass foundations of old mills and moss-covered boulders decorate the water. This glorious stretch of woodland is a memorial to George Benjamin Utter, a pioneering member of the Narragansett Chapter of the Appalachian Mountain Club.

There is no canine universe where this hike could be considered taxing but log steps and wooden bridges smooth over any rough spots. Under an airy forest, the *Ben Utter Trail* is heading towards a climax at Stepstone Falls that make up in charm and bucolic beauty what they lack in large drops.

The trip is less than one mile and can be done as an out-and-back or combined with an old mill road known as Tanner Washout to build a canine hiking loop. There are continuous pools and shallows for Seaman to drop in for a dip - did that need to be mentioned?

BEAR MOUNTAIN

Undermountain Trail/Appalachian Trail

SALISBURY, CONNECTICUT

Hiking Time: 2-3 hours

M

The highpoint of Connecticut is on the slopes of Mount Frissell, whose summit is across the state line in Massachusetts. Bear Mountain, four miles away, is the highest *summit* in the Nutmeg State. Also a better adventure for your dog.

The blue-blazed *Undermountain Trail* links to the *Appalachian Trail*, to tag the peak in just under three miles. Bear Mountain is an honest mountain - there is scarcely a downhill step on the ascent to the top - no depressing drops into saddles and ravines that set tails to drooping when Seaman knows he should be headed up. You are gaining over 1,500 feet in elevation on this canine hike but the serious panting does not begin until the final half-mile.

Without the aid of any roads in 1885, Owen Travis spent three years hauling 350 tons of stone to the summit to build a pyramid 20 feet square and 22.5 feet high. **The tower has crumbled but Seaman can still scramble up ten feet of stabilized rubble and think about what it took to bring all these rocks to the roof of Connecticut**.

A return option is across the summit and down the 2.1-mile *Paradise Lane Trail* that crosses upland forests. The plunge on the north slope is steep, quick and rocky and will challenge the most cautious of dogs so take your time here. The full loop with a backtrack on the *Undermountain Trail* will cover about 6.6 miles.

BLOCK ISLAND GREENWAY TRAILS

Rodman's Hollow/Clay Head Nature Trail

NEW SHORHAM, RHODE ISLAND

Hiking Time: 4-5 hours

M 🏊

Most day-tripping canine hikers to Block Island arrive on the ferry carless and queue up with their dogs ready for some spirited walking. The ferry rate per person is less than $20 round trip and dogs ride free.

Once on the island there are two famous beach bluffs within walking distance: to the north is Clay Head, and to the south are the Mohegan Bluffs. To do both in one day on foot is quite an undertaking so you will be forced to pick a destination. This is not a win-lose proposition by any means - especially since your dog will demand to return to Block Island again.

To reach Mohegan Bluffs, you will cross through Rodman's Hollow, including miles of trails crafted in the tradition of walking the English countryside. **What is your dog interested in? Open fields? Sporty hills? Long vistas? A romp on the beach? A swim in a pond? Unique woodlands? The *Greenway* here has them all**.

Turning north, two miles on the Corn Neck Road leads to a trail system known as "The Maze." These grassy paths are unmarked but well-maintained and a delight for your dog - even when you are lost. You can pop out at a stone wall or one of the best views on the East Coast. The *Clay Head Nature Trail* runs for about one easy-going mile along the top of 70-foot bluffs. It may be one of the longest miles you've ever stepped with Seaman when you factor in frequent stops for watching crashing waves or charting the progress of a passing vessel.

BLUE HILLS RESERVATION

Skyline Trail
MILTON, MASSACHUSETTS
Hiking Time: 2-3 hours

M

In 1893, the Blue Hills became the first land in Massachusetts set aside for recreation. The framers of the Bay State parks found plenty to love in the shadow of Boston - hills and meadows, forests and wetlands, even a unique Atlantic white cedar bog. There's wildlife here not often associated with Boston Brahmins: timber rattlesnakes, coyote, and otter.

The *Skyline Trail* travels across the spine of the reservation for nine miles from east to west. The route breaks into two legs west of park headquarters and gives canine hikers a chance to complete a 4.5-mile loop to Great Blue Hill, at 635 feet the highest of the 22 hills in the Blue Hills Chain.

Narrow and twisting, the rocky route is well-marked as it crosses three hills before the steep ascent to your final destination. **The northern leg of the loop will set your dog to panting more than the southern leg so plan accordingly**.

The star of Great Blue Hill is the weather observatory that was founded in 1885 and is home to the oldest continuous weather record in America. Of more practical interest to Seaman on the summit is Eliot Tower, a 90-year old stout stone lookout that makes a fine resting spot in this canine hike.

There are 125 miles of trails in the park, including many in this vicinity so feel free to call an audible or two with map firmly in hand. One, down the *Houghton Path* to a spring-fed pond, winds up on a long beach with easy access to dog-paddling.

BLUFF POINT COASTAL RESERVE

Loop Trail
GROTON, CONNECTICUT
Hiking Time: 1-2 hour

E

Even Connecticut natives can be surprised by this slice of Cape Cod on the Nutmeg State's heavily developed Long Island shore. Bluff Point is the last remaining undeveloped public land of any size along the Connecticut coastline. Ironic, since it was one of the first to be developed - Governor John Winthrop made his home on the peninsula in the late 17th century. But during the Hurricane of 1938 every vacation cottage - over 100 - was destroyed. None were rebuilt.

Most of Seaman's trotting around Bluff Point will take place on a wide, level cart road that serviced the long-gone agricultural fields. The trip from the parking lot to Bluff Point in the Long Island Sound is 1.6 miles through alternating maritime forest and open shore land. Easy grades take Seaman up to his ultimate destination atop the pink granite rocks of the bluff.

A short detour leads to a one-mile wide sand spit that connects to the small Bushy Point Beach. Seaman will salivate at the chance to romp across the open sand but it is closed to dogs during the plover nesting season from April 15 to September 15.

The *Loop Trail* back travels along a forested ridge where stone ruins of the 300-year old Winthrop homestead can be explored. There are more nooks and crannies to explore on Bluff Point, including a cut-off to the full 3.6-mile loop for Seaman if too much swimming has left him tuckered out.

CAMDEN HILLS STATE PARK

Megunticook Trail

CAMDEN, MAINE
Hiking Time: 2 hours

M A 🏊 $

The *Megunticook Trail* climbs to the top of the highest mainland mountain on the Atlantic seacoast. Maine pioneering landscape architect Hans Heistad spent the better part of a decade shaping the rocky slopes and groves of Eastern white pine into a park on the shores of Penobscott Bay.

Camden Hills features ten named mountain peaks, with Mount Megunticook at 1,385 feet standing above them all. **The elevation gain on this hike is nearly 1,000 feet but the path takes a joint-friendly one mile to accomplish the summit.** The trail reaches open ledges at the Ocean Lookout which delivers sweeping views of the entire Penobscott Bay and the town of Camden, where the groundbreaking prime time soaper *Peyton Place* was filmed in the 1960s. On a clear day it is possible to glimpse New England's tallest mountain, Mount Washington, to the west. The cliffs offer prime nesting habitat for peregrine falcons, the world's fastest birds.

Heistad designed more than 30 miles of tail-friendly trails at Camden Hills, affording numerous options coming down. The descent on the *Tablelands Trail* leads to the 360-degree views atop 780-foot Mount Battie. The stone tower here was dedicated in 1921 as a remembrance to Maine's World War I soldiers. These ocean views can also be purchased by an auto road that can incorporated into your Seaman's exploration of the Camden Hills.

CAMEL'S HUMP STATE PARK

Monroe Trail

DUXBURY, VERMONT
Hiking Time: 3-4 hours

S 🏊

There is no mistaking the distinctive double-humped exposed peak in the center of Vermont's Green Mountains. It has long stirred the imagination of those who want to name it. The Waubanaukee Indians called it "Tah-wak-be-deece-wadso" that translates to "saddle mountain." To French explorers in the 1600s it was the "resting lion." When Vermont Founding Father Ira Allen sketched out a regional map in 1798 he colorfully called the unique mountain "camel's rump." By 1830 the name "Camel's Hump" was in common usage.

Camel's Hump is the only alpine peak in Vermont without a ski resort on it so it is a very popular canine hiking destination. Several well-marked routes lead to the 4,083-foot summit. The *Monroe Trail* takes about 2,500 feet of that elevation to climb up the east side of the mountain in 3.3 miles.

Rocks are a big part of your dog's hiking day here that begins in thick birches and past a reflective beaver pond. After clearing the tree line the boulders become more prominent and many dogs may require a helping hand once or twice. The windswept summit serves up a classic Vermont panorama.

Retreat on the *Monroe Trail* or make a loop with the *Long Trail* and *Dean Trail* that tacks another mile onto the journey. **Upon reaching the bottom cool down with an easy stroll on the *View Trail*, a wide swath of grass, to allow Seaman to admire what he has just accomplished**.

Cape Cod National Seashore

Great Island Trail

WELLFLEET, MASSACHUSETTS
Hiking Time: 2-4 hours

M 🏊 **$**

There are some who will argue that the *Great Island Trail* is the best National-Seashore hike in all of the national park service system. Seaman cannot participate in that debate because he is only allowed on part of the trail. But that is more than he was able to experience until 2015 so there is hope that one day your dog may see it all.

This is a hike on Cape Cod Bay, launching Seaman pleasantly onto a roomy path through a mature pitch pine forest. In just a few minutes the trail drops into the open grassy dunes on a still wide, hard-packed sand surface. That sand will become increasingly softer and more problematic as you close in on the bay beach. This area is known as "The Gut" where silt filled in to turn the once Great Island into an appendage of the mainland.

After hiking on the beach for a spell the trail heads inland towards the site of a 17th century tavern that was a favorite stop for whalers. This is where your dog is forbidden to go. Instead, Seaman must continue hiking down the sandy, likely deserted beach, for three miles to Jeremy's Point, a treeless sand spit that gets submerged at high tide.

There are far worse ways to condemn your dog. This stretch of beach is backed by bluffs and dunes, culminating in the Great Beach Hill, a 75-foot pile of sand. And of course there is easy swimming any time Seaman desires before retracing his steps to the trailhead.

Cedar Tree Neck Sanctuary

Loop Trail

WEST TISBURY, MASSACHUSETTS
Hiking Time: 1-2 hours

E 🏊 🚗

Just off the southern coast of Cape Cod, Martha's Vineyard is an extremely dog-friendly resort destination. For canine hikers, the Sheriff's Meadow Foundation has conserved over 2,600 acres of land on Martha's Vineyard in more than 150 separate parcels. From these protected lands the Foundation has created eight sanctuaries open to the public, including dogwalkers. **The largest trail system is at Cedar Tree Neck Sanctuary where two miles of paw-friendly trails await canine hikers on the shores of Vineyard Sound.**

Your dog's day at Cedar Neck begins in a dense maritime forest where the results of twisted trees battling decades of ocean winds are much in evidence. This is a rich arboreal tapestry, woven of red pines, American beeches, cedars, and tupelo trees. At bejeweled Ames Pond one of Martha's Vineyards' trademark memorial benches remembers the donors of these special places.

The trails, alternately sandy and sand-infused dirt, make gentle work of the dunescape. A narrow corridor through shrubby beach grass leads to a quarter-mile of dune-backed sandy shoreline dotted with glacial souvenirs. The gentle waves on the north shore of the island will lure any dog into the water for play.

Beyond the beach a final loop on the *Brown Trail* circles the headland along Cedar Tree Neck Pond where Seaman may meet a local goat introduced into the sanctuary to gobble invasive plants.

Cliff Walk

America's Finest Backyard Stroll

NEWPORT, RHODE ISLAND

Hiking Time: 1-3 hours

M 🏊

Newport's "cottages" are America's finest collection of Gilded Age mansions, built on spellbinding rocky bluffs overlooking the Atlantic Ocean. No matter how rich the owner, however, no one's property could extend all the way to the shoreline. By virtue of "Fisherman's Rights," first granted under British colonial rule and then enshrined in the Rhode Island constitution, the public is always guaranteed the legal right to walk along a small sliver of cliff. Hence, America's finest backyard stroll with your dog.

The *Cliff Walk*, named the first National Recreation Trail in New England, rambles for about 3.5 miles, about two of which are paved and easy to hike. Many folks choose to turn back after this park-like experience, satisfied with glimpses of the houses of the one percent of the one percent.

Continuing past the paved path, the *Cliff Walk* turns rustic with some walking on unprotected, open cliff faces and boulder hopping for your dog. It requires concentration but any level of canine hiker can negotiate the trip. It's not unusual to catch a bit of ocean spray on the tail out here.

At the end of the *Cliff Walk* you will drop to ocean's edge and Reject's Beach where Seaman can get in some ocean dog paddling. You now have the option of returning by the same route along the black Atlantic rocks or exiting into the town and walking back on the sidewalks in front of the mansions whose backyards you have just wandered through.

Dog Mountain

Overlook Trail

ST. JOHNSBURY, VERMONT

Hiking Time: 1 hour+

E 🏊

After surviving a coma following a fall down some stairs in 1994 sculptor/artist/author Stephen Huneck was struck by a vision to build a dog chapel on his property outside St. Johnsbury. He modeled the white-steepled wooden shrine after 1820s New England-styled churches. The exterior is festooned with Huneck's dog sculptures and the interior hand-carved dog pews are lit through stained glass windows telling stories of the familiar canine tropes of loyalty, trust, play, and most of all, joy. Tributes to dogs departed fill the Remembrance Wall inside.

Seaman is welcome, of course, in the dog chapel but he will likely be eyeing the series of grass trails that are cut though wildflower meadows up the side of Dog Mountain. **The grounds are always open for leash-free canine frolic - as the sign says, "Welcome all creeds, all breeds, no dogmas allowed."**

The *Overlook Trail* works gently to scenic views of the surrounding Northeast Kingdom. At the apex your dog is joined by Huneck's winged memorial to his Labrador retriever Sally and a red fire plug.

There are open fields for play time and an agility course for Seaman to try. Also on the 150-acre property of rolling hills are ponds whose only purpose is for dogs to splash and paddle. At any point an impromptu doggie beach party is apt to break out on the banks. Wagging tails are always all around on Dog Mountain.

Mount Greylock Reservation

Hopper/Mt. Prospect/Money Brook Trails
LANESBOROUGH, MASSACHUSETTS
Hiking Time: 6-7 hours

S Δ $

In 1844 Ralph Waldo Emerson urged his friend Henry David Thoreau to climb Mount Greylock, a place he described as "a serious mountain." More than 170 years later the climb up the highest point in southern New England (3,491 feet) is still the must-do major canine hike in the Berkshire Mountains.

At Mount Greylock you can hike longer with your dog (more than 70 miles of trails), higher with your dog (some canine hikes will gain over 2,000 feet in elevation) and see more of New England's oldest trees (200+ years old) than any place in Massachusetts.

The Hopper is a unique glacial-carved bowl on the western slopes of Mount Greylock. Studded with red spruce, some of it old-growth, the Hopper has been designated a National Natural Landmark. An 11-mile canine loop includes the *Hopper Trail*, the *Mt. Prospect Trail* and the *Money Brook Trail* and tags the summits of Mt. Prospect, Mt. Williams and Greylock. **Surrounded on three sides by steep slopes this is honest climbing for your dog with long, steady ascents.** Streams course down the slopes to keep this canine hike lubricated.

The first observatory tower was erected on Mt. Greylock in 1831; today's summit has a 93-foot stone lighthouse. Seaman won't need the War Memorial Tower to admire the long, open views. He can gaze out from the rock-studded slopes while you study the bronze model of the mountain to see what how far you have come.

 # Noanet Woodlands

Noanet Peak Trail
DOVER, MASSACHUSETTS
Hiking Time: 2-3 hours

M ⚞ $

You can't get there from here. Noanet Woodlands is a paradise for trail dogs; Caryl Park doesn't allow dogs. There is no parking for Noanet Woodlands, you have to park in Caryl Park. There are two lots at Caryl Park. One allows dogs and accesses a trail/road from the parking lot that leads behing the ballfields and into the woodlands. Just don't let Seaman stray off that golden path.

The quarry you are hunting is a classic New England canine hike with mature forests, rocky outcroppings, and postcard worthy millponds. **This is flat-out one of the best places in Massachusetts to hike with your dog.** The trails are wide and paw-friendly dirt and, especially in the early going, woodchips.

There are 17 miles of footpaths packed into 695 acres of former farmland. The *Noanet Peak Trail* takes 1.5 miles to reach the rocky summit of the 387-foot high "mountain." It may not summon nosebleeds but the open granite bluffs serve up a unique one-way view straight into downtown Boston.

The *Noanet Peak Trail* feeds into the 2.5-mile *Peabody Loop* that traipses past three millponds and the ruins where the Dover Union Iron Company once crafted barrel hoops and wheel rims from forged iron. There are over 45 trail junctions in these pleasant woods so to take a road less traveled with your dog - with a firm grasp on a park map.

 NOTCHVIEW
15 RESERVATION

Circuit Trail

WINDSOR, MASSACHUSETTS
Hiking Time: 2-3 hours

M $

In 1920, World War I hero Arthur Budd met and married the widowed Helen Bly in London. Back in Massachusetts on Bly family land the couple set about consolidating 20 homesteads in the Green Mountains into the 3,000-acre Notchview estate. Budd gave his property to the Trustees of Reservations for a park in the 1960s.

Notchview has evolved into one of the premier cross country skiing areas in New England. **The Nordic center was one of the first in the country to feature a separate trail system exclusively for skiing with your dog, a sport known as skijoring.**

For the nine months of the year when the trails are snow-free whatever you have in mind for a day hiking with your dog is at Notchview. The *Circuit Trail* loops back through the middle of the property on a wide swath through the trees and spends time in the open meadows. The 1.8-mile ramble travels just about the entire way on a pebbly farm road that is kind to the paw. Although these hills have long supported farming most of the open land has been reforested in red spruce and northern hardwoods.

After this easy ramble you can decide how much of the park's 15 miles of trails to chew off with Seaman. The highest point at Notchview is the 2,297-foot Judges Hill but the reserve elevation averages more than 2,000 feet so Seaman can keep his four-paw drive in reserve for most of the day.

 QUODDY HEAD
16 STATE PARK

Coastal Trail/Thompson Trail

LUBEC, MAINE
Hiking Time: 1-2 hours

M ≈ $

How would you like to stand with your dog on the easternmost point in the continental United States and experience the nation's first sunrise (at least part of the year, depending on the earth's tilt.) You can do just that at Quoddy Head State Park where a lighthouse guiding ships through the fog has perched on 80-foot black rock cliffs since President Thomas Jefferson signed the authorization papers in 1808.

The *Coastal Trail* rolls south from the West Quoddy Head Light for two miles along the clifftops. Seaman will thrill in this rollercoaster romp at land's end, eagerly bounding to the top of the many hillocks to see what awaits on the other side as the path dips and rises. Keep an eye on the waves crashing in from the Atlantic Ocean - tides can fluctuate as much as 20 feet. **The final drop is into Carrying Place Cove where Seaman can enjoy the shallow waters on a sandy beach.**

The return trip over the inland *Thompson Trail* rolls through maritime forests of shallow-rooted white spruce and hardy balsam trees battling the wind and salt spray. Many of these arboreal warriors remain standing after losing the fight, leaving spectral sculptures along the coast. A side trip leads to the Carrying Place Cove Bog, a National Natural Landmark, where the subarctic remnant houses carnivorous plants that survive in low temperatures and thin, non-nurturing soil by sucking nutrients from captured insects.

SANDY NECK BEACH PARK

Great Marsh Hiking Trail

BARNSTABLE, MASSACHUSETTS
Hiking Time: 2-5 hours

E 🏊 **$**

Seaman can certainly count on sand on this one. Sandy Neck is an appropriately named six-mile barrier island at the foot of Cape Cod Bay. The dune community here reaches back one-half mile to the Great Marshes draining Barnstable Harbor. Two sets of dunes, some as high as 100 feet, run the length of the park and shelter vernal ponds, maritimes forests and vibrant displays of hardy beach grasses.

This is about as far from civilization as your dog can get on Cape Cod - and it comes in a hurry from the trailhead. There is plenty of deep, soft sand on the *Great Marsh Hiking Trail* but there are also dune areas with grass and scrub pine and even a spot of shade in dense forest.

The views of the wetlands are the star on this trail; Great Marsh is the largest marsh on Cape Cod and you can decide how deeply to immerse your dog in this beautiful salt-sprayed world. You can use crossover trails 1, 2, 4, and 5 to the Sandy Neck beach for a return trip whenever you've had your fill of cordgrass and spike grass and blackgrass. Don't try and find Trail #3 - it was abandoned many years ago.

The full trek to Trail #5 will cover 12 miles but a satisfying sample of Sandy Neck can be accomplished in a 1.6-mile circuit on Trail #1. Out on the beach you will be sharing the rock-infused sand with off-road vehicles and on a busy summer weekend it can feel like you need a wide shoulder. Of course you can always cross back to finish up on the marshside path.

SLEEPING GIANT STATE PARK

Tower Trail

HAMDEN, CONNECTICUT
Hiking Time: 1-2 hours+

M **$**

Most of the basaltic ridges in Connecticut run predictably from north to south but one rogue two-mile band of hills runs east-west. If was called Mount Carmel but anyone with imagination looking at the isolated ridge could see a recumbent giant humanoid. The granite was especially fine on the mountain and quarrymen were enthusiastically blasting large holes in the giant's head until a horrified populace laid the foundation for the Sleeping Giant Park Association.

Just about any kind of canine hiking fare is on the menu in this cherished park. There are more than 30 miles of trails running from the feet to the head of the Giant, the first trails in Connecticut to be designated a National Recreation Trail. Most are rocky and tricky but even a novice trail dog can tackle the gently ascending road trail that makes up the 1.6-mile *Tower Trail*.

Surmounting 739-foot Mount Carmel is a four-story stone observation tower that looks as if the Knights of the Roundtable and their Irish wolfhounds will be walking out of any minute. Ramps inside allow Seaman multiple views through the arched openings.

Sleeping Giant is a tangle of short trails so adventurous dogs can opt for a final push to the summit on the rocky *Blue Trail*. Many of the ascents are pick-your-way passages and at some spots on the ridge around cobbles of jumbled boulders - like Hezekiah's Knob - the trail narrows enough to demand Seaman's attention.

Snake Mountain Wildlife Management Area

Carriage Road Trail

WEYBRIDGE, VERMONT

Hiking Time: 2-3 hours

M ≈•

Locals in the Lake Champlain Valley always called the long serpentine ridge along America's sixth largest freshwater lake Snake Mountain. In the 1870s when Jonas Smith built a fancy inn on the 1,287-foot summit he didn't think potential visitors would flock to a serpent-themed guest hotel. So it became Grand View Hotel and the mountain took that name until the inn burned down some 50 years later.

It is Snake Mountain once again and the lure here are some of the best views available of Lake Champlain, backed by the Adirondack Mountains in the distance. **Seaman purchases these open, 180-degree views of the 107-mile long lake courtesy of a roomy old carriage road constructed by innkeeper Smith**.

The three-mile canine hike takes its time gaining your objective; there is a spiderweb of walking trails across the property but signs point the route to the summit as you gain almost 1,000 feet in elevation. There are joys on offer beforehand, beginning with the lush northern hardwood forest.

Stands of hemlock and cedar have infiltrated the upland forest here as well. An open bog mat of sphagnum moss awaits along the route, ringed by a bog forest of black spruce and red maple. Near the summit, Red Rock Pond is small and shallow and Seaman will be excused for thinking he has happened upon his own private swimming pool.

Steep Rock Reservation

Steep Rock Loop

WASHINGTON DEPOT, CONNECTICUT

Hiking Time: 2-3 hours

M ≈•

Attractive woodlands, a sporty trail, a one-of-a-kind view, a long riverside ramble - Steep Rock Reservation has it all for your dog. The *Steep Rock Loop* leaves from the west side of the Shepaug River on a wide, switchbacking path into the hills. When the hemlocks give way to hardwoods the path gets rockier but is still easy on the paw.

The destination is the overlook of the Clam Shell, where the river loops back on itself. Seaman can stay well back of the fence and soak in the dramatic view from a rock outcropping. Heading back down the wooded slopes carriage roads, built by 19th century architect Ehrick Rossiter when this was his country estate, lead the way. A striking series of multi-trunked hemlocks are passed and at the river is the Hauser Footbridge, a cable-and-wood suspension bridge in the fashion of the Brooklyn Bridge.

The last half of this 4.2-mile loop follows the old rail bed along the Shepaug River. The Shepaug Valley Railroad had to blast through 238 feet of solid rock to bring vacationers here from New York City to the now defunct Holiday House. The tunnel seems barely large enough for Seaman to pass through, let alone a locomotive.

There is plenty of opportunity for Seaman to slip into the Shepaug River for a swim on this easy stretch. There are more trails that hug the tranquil river and elsewhere in the hills to extend your dog's hiking day in this magical place.

 UNDERHILL
STATE PARK

Sunset Ridge Trail
UNDERHILL, VERMONT
Hiking Time: 3-4 hours

S △ $

Mount Mansfield is Vermont's highest peak, noted primarily for its skiing and the resemblance of the ridgeline to an elongated human face. The geographic features of the mountain have subsequently been given corresponding human facial feature names.

Underhill State Park is a gateway to the 4,393-foot summit with several trails, including a paved road, to ascend busy Mount Mansfield, site of the Stowe Mountain Resort. The *Sunset Ridge Trail* conquers the 2,568-foot elevation gain in three miles. **This canine hike starts out low voltage on an old gravel access road for one mile but your dog's ears will perk up when you break in the open and begin to enjoy nearly continuous ridgeline views.**

The trail will be completely rocky under paw - in fact it will be mandatory to hike on the bare rocks since the last two miles will be across the largest patch of alpine tundra in Vermont. There will be a false summit or two but there will be no doubting being on the "Chin" of Mount Mansfield where Seaman can soak in extensive 360-degree views. You'll know you've caught a clear day if you can see the skyscrapers of Montreal.

Retrace your pawprints back down on the exposed ridge or opt for a shorter descent without the views (*Laura Cowles Trail*). Another choice is a longer hike back down the "face" along the *Long Trail*, the premier hiking route through Vermont's Green Mountains.

 WHITE MOUNTAIN
NATIONAL FOREST

Franconia Ridge Trail Loop
FRANCONIA, NEW HAMPSHIRE
Hiking Time: 6-7 hours

S △ 🏊

When *National Geographic* published an article on the "World's Best Hikes: 20 Dream Trails" there was only one day hike in the Lower 48 on the list and this was it. That's a lot to promise your dog.

Sooner or later all trail dogs make their way to Franconia Notch. The destination is 5,260-foot Lafayette Mountain and it will take crossing two others, Haystack (4,840 feet) and Lincoln (5,089 feet), to complete the loop. Most canine hikers opt to begin this classic New England journey on the *Falling Waters Trail*, boulder-hopping along and across several waterfalls. The ascent to Franconia Ridge is accomplished on the grueling "45," climbing 3,840 feet in only four miles. **Some of the rock formations may make Seaman think for a second but there is nothing insurmountable for him on this spectacular hike.**

Upon reaching the ridge Seaman meets the *Appalachian Trail* and the fabled Franconia Ridge knife-edge - exposed rock that dips and rolls for 1.7 thrilling miles. If you catch a clear day the views, including the entire Presidential Range, are the best in New England.

The leg back down is on the *Old Bridle Path* that will give a new appreciation of the sturdiness of horses before the coming of the automobile. When the long, rocky descent across open slopes dips into stunted pines the nine-mile loop is coming to its rewarding end. Seaman will go to sleep dreaming about this one.

White Mountain National Forest

Ammonoosuc Ravine Trail / Jewell Trail

BRETTON WOODS, NEW HAMPSHIRE
Hiking Time: 6-8 hours

S ⛰ 🏊

You say you've always wanted to hike with your dog in the snow in July? It can happen at Mount Washington. The weather here is considered the worst in the world; winds have been recorded at 231 miles per hour and hurricane force gales over 75 mph blow one day in three. Dense fog visits the 6,288-foot summit 315 days a year.

There are at least 15 long, rugged hiking trails up Mount Washington, the first of which was hacked out in 1819. Today it is the oldest continually used mountain trail in the United States. The *Ammonoosuc Ravine Trail* climbs up the western slopes. The route traces the plunging Ammonoosuc River through the woods with stream crossings and waterfall views. The hike begins in earnest with steep climbs up rock steps.

From the Appalachian Mountain Club Hut the original *Crawford Trail* climbs 1.4 open miles and nearly 2,000 feet to the busy top. Much of the way is boulder hopping but Seaman can make it without too much difficulty. The views are astounding but the price paid is likely exposure to that harsh weather. The hike to the weather station at the summit is about 7.5 miles.

If the weather is co-operating the *Jewell Trail*, that works along the cliffs with long exposed views, is a good option to come back down the western face of the mountain. Since Seaman won't be sniffing his scent keep a sharp eye out for trail markers across the open, rocky terrain.

MIDDLE ATLANTIC

MARYLAND
28. Catoctin Mountain Park

NEW JERSEY
32. Delaware Water Gap NRA
35. Higbee Beach WMA
42. Pyramid Mountain Natural Area
45. Stokes State Forest
47. Wharton State Forest

NEW YORK
24-26. Adirondack Park
27. Bear Mountain/Harriman
   State Park
29-30. Catskill Forest Preserve
33. Fillmore Glen State Park
36. Hither Hills State Park

37. Lake George Wild Forest
38. Letchworth State Park
39. Minnewaska State Park Preserve
44. Saratoga National Historic Park

PENNSYLVANIA
31. Delaware State Forest
34. Gettysburg National Military Park
41. Pennsylvania Game Lands #110
43. Ricketts Glen State Park
46. Tiadaghton State Forest
48. World's End State Park

WASHINGTON D.C.
40. National Arboretum

ADIRONDACK PARK

Tongue Mountain Range Loop
LAKE GEORGE, NEW YORK
Hiking Time: 5-6 hours

S A ≈

Canine hikers who complete the *Tongue Mountain Range Loop* above Lake George run out of superlatives to describe it. The journey begins in the middle of six summits on an isthmus that thrusts into the lake and crosses the three southern peaks - Fifth Peak, French Point Mountain, and First Peak.

Although these mountains never reach higher than 1,813 feet there are also several unnamed knobs that make the ascents and descents seem like your dog is climbing across the back of a stegosaurus. There are steep, rocky drops - nothing that Seaman can't handle - but canine hikers are best served by taking the loop clockwise.

Views from the lightly forested ridges are spectacular up and down the water, including memorable looks at some of Lake George's 365 islands, many clustered in the Narrows caused by the peninsula. Your destination is the very Tip of the Tongue, where the mountain range plunges into Lake George. **Here, wide rock perches make ideal diving boards for a well deserved doggie dip**.

The loop is closed with a 4.8-mile return trip along the sometimes-steep shoreline. The lower elevations of the Tongue Range invite a smorgasbord of vegetation to mingle and form a deeply green primoridial forest. The total distance for this invigorating exploration is about 13 miles. Bring plenty of water for Seaman as there is none aside from the lake.

ADIRONDACK PARK

Van Hoevenberg Trail
LAKE PLACID, NEW YORK
Hiking Time: 6-8 hours

S A ≈ $

Mount Marcy is the monarch of the 46 mountains that comprise the High Peaks of the Adirondacks, soaring 5,344 feet above sea level. A professor named Ebenezer Emmons led the first recorded ascent on August 5, 1837, naming the peak for New York Governor William Learned Marcy.

Today Mount Marcy can be tagged on well-marked trails from four directions. The shortest route comes in from the north on the *Van Hoevenberg Trail*. It is still 7.4 miles one way, with an elevation gain of 3,224 feet. **Despite those daunting numbers this hike is so popular you might think you are scaling a hill in a neighborhood park with your dog**. Some claim it is the most visited "remote" peak in the United States.

About two miles in the trail crosses Marcy Lake - a perfect refresher for Seaman on the way up and on the way back. Views are scant along the way as you work moderately through a dense spruce forest. The peak can experience snow eight months out of 12 and usually sits in low clouds so puddles are a common feature on the trail.

Nearing the summit, Mount Marcy is covered in dense stands of scrubby balsam fir and the trail narrows considerably. A bit of rock climbing is also introduced. A few hundred feet below the broad summit the treeline fades away and Seaman is left with a scramble on bare rock through rare New York alpine vegetation to the top. The views, suffice to note, are extraordinary in every direction from here.

ADIRONDACK PARK

Wilmington Trail

WILMINGTON, NEW YORK
Hiking Time: 5-6 hours

E △ ⫯ $

There are more than 2,000 miles of foot trails in America's largest park and this canine hike is one of its classics. The destination is Whiteface Mountain, one of the 46 4,000-footers that comprise the Adirondack High Peaks.

Lake Placid has twice hosted the Winter Olympic Games, in 1932 and 1980. When they hold the alpine skiing events the 4,867-foot Whiteface Mountain is where they come. The 3,430 feet of vertical drop is the steepest in eastern North America.

So it is fitting that a good part of your canine hike will follow the towline of a retired ski trail. You are off on an ascent of 3,578 feet and the bare summit is just under five miles away. The going can be wet and muddy on the well-worn path as the climbing begins in earnest from the trailhead.

In a little more than one mile you climb over Marble Mountain to deliver an early shot of "we did it." There are looks at the Wilmington Notch here but soon you are working across a long, rocky ridge and views will not kick in again until reaching the rocky glacial deposits near the summit.

The 360-degree views atop Whiteface Mountain are stunning with a look straight down at Lake Placid to the southwest. **The only downer for this all-star canine hike is sharing the summit with the many others who have driven up the Whiteface Mountain Memorial Highway. But Seaman can puff out his chest knowing that he summited the right way.**

BEAR MOUNTAIN/ HARRIMAN STATE PARK

Timp-Torne/Ramapo-Dunderberg Trails

BEAR MOUNTAIN, NEW YORK
Hiking Time: 4-6 hours

S △

When the State of New York proposed at the beginning of the 20th century to relocate Sing Sing Prison to Bear Mountain - so named for its resemblance to a bear in repose - America's conservation consciousness was awakened. In 1910 Bear Mountain-Harriman State Park was dedicated. Within five years it was hosting more than one million visitors per year and 100 years later more people come here than to Yellowstone National Park. The first segment of the iconic *Appalachian Trail* was carved across Bear Mountain in the 1920s.

The Timp Hike starts directly on Route 9W that runs along the Hudson River. The trailhead is an unpromising break in the weeds but things pick up once your dog negotiates the awkward early stages of the journey. You'll pass remnants of the Dunderberg Spiral Railway that was an incline railroad planned in 1890 but never finished. There are tunnels and an old railbed that serves as part of the trail.

The hike splits into the *Ramapo-Dunderberg Trail* (red blazes) and *Timp-Torne Trail* (blue blazes). Heading up the red trail, you break out to views of the Hudson River and you realize why tons of money were burned trying to build a railway here. **The route rolls up and down mountains through boulder foundations until your dog covers the Timp, a peak overlooking the interior of the Hudson Highlands**. Climb back down the Timp and return on the blue trail to complete a tail-wagging 9-mile loop.

 **CATOCTIN MOUNTAIN PARK**

Blue Blazes Whiskey Trail

THURMONT, MARYLAND

Hiking Time: 1 hour

E △

"Any man who does not like dogs and want them about does not deserve to be in the White House."
                    -President Calvin Coolidge

Coolidge himself had at least 12 dogs. **How would you like to hike with your dog where Presidents hike with their dogs**? Everyone has heard of Camp David but where exactly is it? Surprisingly it is located deep inside a national park called Catoctin Mountain Park.

When you take your dog here you will never see Camp David or any evidence that the presidential compound is hidden among the trees. But the trails to hike with Seaman are of Presidential quality nonetheless. Just don't expect to see any First Dogs.

The star trails on Catoctin Mountain climb to overlooks in the eastern side of the park. Unfortunately these are pet-free. So you can fill your day of canine hiking instead with many easy self-guiding interpretive trails.

The rugged Catoctin Mountains provided ideal cover for a moonshining still, made illegal by the onset of Prohibition in 1919. On a steaming July day in 1929 Federal agents raided the Blue Blazes Whiskey Still and confiscated more than 25,000 gallons of mash. Today the airy, wooded *Blue Blazes Whiskey Trail* along Distillery Run leads to a recreated working still and interprets the history of whiskey making in the backwoods of Appalachia. The journey up and down Blue Blaze Creek clocks in at under one mile.

 **CATSKILL FOREST PRESERVE**

Devil's Path / Hunter Trail / Spruceton Trail

HUNTER, NEW YORK

Hiking Time: 4-5 hours

S △ ⌇

Hunter Mountain is the second highest peak in the Catskill Mountains and has seen energetic development over the years. Seaman will pass remnants of old logging roads, tram railways, and ski lifts on his ascent to the 4,040-foot summit. The last tree here was harvested in 1917 and for the past hundred years New York's Forest Preserve has worked to renew one of the Empire State's most popular mountains.

Four trails make the journey to the top of Hunter Mountain where New York's highest fire tower awaits. The purchase is an elevation gain of over 2,000 feet in just over two miles with scarcely a downhill step on the way. There are rock ledges but nothing technically difficult for your dog.

The red-blazed *Devil's Path* is the steepest route up so most canine hikers set off on the old road following the blue blazes of the *Spruceton Trail*. Hunter Brook keeps your dog company for a spell before reaching the Hunter Mountain ski area that was the first resort in the world to employ complete snow-making coverage of a mountain.

No views atop Hunter Mountain but the 60-foot high steel fire tower solves that dilemma. **Dogs can negotiate the wide, open steps and even if the cab is closed the upper stairs are high enough above the treetops for panoramas in every direction**. Seaman's reward at the end of the sturdy 7.5-mile loop is the easily accessible swimming waters of Notch Lake.

CATSKILL FOREST PRESERVE

Wittenberg Cornell Slide Trail

PHOENICIA, NEW YORK
Hiking Time: 7-8 hours

S ⋀

John Burroughs, the "Father of the American Nature Essay," made Slide Mountain one of the most famous mountains in America. In his "The Heart of the Southern Catskills" he described his feelings upon completing the ascent of the highest peak in the Catskills, "The works of man dwindle..."

The *Wittenberg Cornell Slide Trail* is the most popular tough canine day hike in the Catskills. In just over seven miles your dog will gain over 4,000 feet and conquer three mountain peaks across the Burroughs Range before standing on the summit of 4,180-foot Slide Mountain. **Plus there are rock scrambles, mini-cliffs, and ladders along the way. This one is for experienced trail dogs only**.

Wittenberg Mountain is tagged first after four miles and serves up the best views on the hike from a large open rock shelf; the rewards are such that many turn around here. Cornell Mountain is less than one mile ahead with a tricky V-cut to negotiate. If your dog has problems here there is no reason to try for the more difficult ascent of Slide Mountain with a 30-foot rock wall and ladders.

Luckily the views before reaching the roof of the Catskills are every bit as good as the top. If you tag the summit you will find a small plaque memorializing John Burroughs, who was often photographed with his hounds and spent many nights camped up here. The trees weren't as thick 150 years ago so it was easier for him to wax poetic in those days.

DELAWARE STATE FOREST

Bruce Lake Natural Area

SWIFTWATER, PENNSYLVANIA
Hiking Time: 3-4 hours

M ⋀ ⌁

This 80,000-acre chunk of the Pocono Mountains that drains into the Delaware River has been carved up into special trail systems and designated natural areas. Hundreds of miles of canine hiking opportunities await in the managed forest here.

The spring-fed Bruce Lake is one of six bodies of water in the state forest birthed by glaciers. An eight-mile loop circles the ancient relic as well as the man-made Egypt Meadow Lake. After the conifer forests around the lake were completely cut down fires swept the area to expose rock formations along the trails. This route combines wide, paw-pleasing logging roads and the usual rocky Pocono paths as it rolls along.

Additional trotting is open through the Buckhorn Natural Area where the headwaters of Bushkill Creek are preserved in addition to a high mountain swamp and gnarly rock ledges. Those rocks supported more than 1,000 bluestone quarries over the years that built much of northeastern Pennsylvania.

A collection of interconnecting paths includes 26 miles of the Pocono Plateau of the *Thunder Swamp Trail System* that can be cobbled into short loop trails for day use or longer loops for overnight treks. Highlights are the rocky Pennel Natural Area to where the trails reach an elevated part of the forest and the low-lying swamps of the Stillwater Natural Area, a hideout for army deserters during the Civil War.

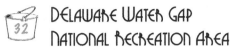

Delaware Water Gap National Recreation Area

Red Dot/Blue Blazes/Appalachian Trails

WARRINGTON, NEW JERSEY

Hiking Time: 3-4 hour

S △ 🏊

Seaman probably won't appreciate it as he is switchbacking up 1,527-foot Mt. Tammany but millions of years ago this area was a level plain. Since then the Delaware River, the largest un-dammed and free-flowing river east of the Mississippi, has ground out the Delaware Water Gap where the water twists in a tight "S" curve. The famous views here spawned great resort destinations in 19th century America that have all faded away.

The sentinels of the Gap are Mt. Tammany in New Jersey and 1,463-foot Mt. Minsi on the Pennsylvania side of the river. An old fire road conquers Minsi that can be combined with the *Appalachian Trail* to form a four-mile hiking loop. The twisting *Red Dot Trail* up Tammany is the more popular of the two summit hikes. It requires 1.5 miles of climbing on the rocky slopes to ascend the 1,200 feet to the top of the Gap.

The route continues on the *Blue Blaze Trail* through thickets of mountain laurel to meet the *Appalachian Trail* skipping along the Kittatinny Ridge. A detour north passes Sunfish Pond, one of New Jersey's "7 Natural Wonders," where the water in the glacial lake is so clear and deep for a long time it was considered to be bottomless. **The loop closes to the south under towering hemlocks and includes a visit for your lucky dog to the tumbling waters and cool swimming holes of Dunnfield Creek.**

Fillmore Glen State Park

Gorge Trail/North Rim Trail

MORAVIA, NEW YORK

Hiking Time: 2-3 hours

M △ 🏊 $

Millard Fillmore was the first president born when George Washington was no longer alive and the last president who was neither a Democrat nor a Republican (he was a Whig). He was also born in a log cabin about five miles from this trailhead.

The main canine hiking experience at Fillmore Glen is on the *Gorge Trail* that crosses Dry Creek on nine bridges and visits five major waterfalls. Much of the sublime stonework along the trail was constructed by Civilian Conservation Corps stonemasons during the Great Depression.

This is an easy trot for Seaman for two miles into the glen, starting flat and becoming increasingly steep as you reach the end of the gorge. **Opportunities for doggie dips abound but none so picturesque as the natural swimming pool beyond the Cowsheds, a magazine cover-worthy waterfall that drops into a semi-circular amphitheater**.

Unlike many canine gorge hikes your dog is not trapped in Fillmore Glen at the end. There is not one, but two options to create a loop back to the parking lot. The south rim route is the more benign of the two as it connects several picnic pavilions. The heartier canine hike is through the towering hemlocks on the higher side of the gorge, the north side which creates a canine loop hike of just over three miles. The most scenic side water plunges from this side, if Seaman hasn't had his fill of water shows already.

GETTYSBURG NATIONAL MILITARY PARK

Big Round Top Trail

GETTYSBURG, PENNSYLVANIA

Hiking Time: 1-2 hours

M

It took Abraham Lincoln only 272 words to capture the importance of the Battle of Gettysburg during the Civil War. It will also not take you long to understand the critical role Big Round Top played during the fighting on this hike with your dog. In fact, by the time President Lincoln delivered the Gettysburg Address less than five months after the battle in 1863 efforts were already underway to preserve this ground.

The trail is historic in its own right. It was originally a steep footpath that led to a 60-foot observation tower erected in 1895. The path was rerouted and covered in macadam in the 1930s and today's canine hike can use either or a combination of both. **The tower was removed in 1968 with the explanation that visitors were too tired to climb it after the hike to tag the 785-foot summit. Your trail dog would not have had that problem!**

The highest point on the Gettysburg Battlefield did not witness intense fighting because it was never cleared of trees like the surrounding farm fields. Colonel Joshua Chamberlain did win the Congressional Medal of Honor for his heroism on Big Round Top and the progress of his 20th Maine Infantry can be traced by monuments along the hike. Informal trails lead to more than 1,400 statues and memorials in the park that constitute the greatest exhibit of outdoor art in America.

HIGBEE BEACH WILDLIFE MANAGEMENT AREA

Dune Trail

CAPE MAY, NEW JERSEY

Hiking Time: 1-2 hours

E 🏊

It's not easy to find a secluded beach in America's most densely populated state but it wasn't so long ago that Higbee Beach was remote enough to be an official nude beach. **It's not anymore but pretty much anything still goes here, including allowing your dog to romp in the sand all year round.** One regular at the beach with his dog was Thomas Higbee, whose family owned a hotel here in the 1800s. Dressed in a long coat and accompanied by a large black dog, Thomas's ghost is often reported to be roaming the dunes.

The two miles of nature trails, much of it in deep sand, include passage through the last remaining dune forest on the Delaware Bay. Wide sand and easy wave action will lure any level of canine swimmer into the water.

The beach next door to Higbee is the similarly dog-friendly Sunset Beach, famous for its Cape May Diamonds. The "diamonds" are actually pieces of quartz that have been eroded from the Upper Delaware River and been polished by a 200-mile journey of churning and jostling that can last a millennium or two.

The stones, that can be cut and faceted to do a passable imitation of a diamond, are found in abundance here because the tidal flow bounces off a unique concrete ship that rests offshore. The *Atlantus* was built to transport soldiers during steel-short World War I and as she was being towed to Cape May to serve as a ferry slip an accident dumped her on a sand bar where she remains today.

HITHER HILLS STATE PARK

Serpents Back Trail

MONTAUK, NEW YORK
Hiking Time: 2-3 hours

M 🏊 **$**

It took an acrimonious three-year battle for New York planner Robert Moses to gain permission for his visionary necklace of public parks along the Montauk shores in the 1920s. The enduring jewel of his struggle is Hither Hills that stretches from ocean to bay and is the largest state park in the tony east end of Long Island.

Hither Hills is a mile of pristine, dune-backed Atlantic Ocean beach and top-rated campground. With such delights, the 1,755-acre park's interior that stretches to Napeague Bay is often overlooked. All the better for trail dogs, who can't swim in the ocean or sleep in a tent here. Miles of informal sandy trails and jeep roads pick through the pitch pine, scrub oak and beach heather.

The 1.5-mile *Serpent's Back Trail* travels through the spine of the park and can be used to form sporty hiking loops that will delight Seaman for hours. Expect plenty of ups and downs as you twist through the pine barrens, leading to panoramic overlooks and the sandy/cobbly shore of Napeague Bay with easy dog paddling in the sheltered water.

Hither Hills is home to unique walking dunes - 80-foot high piles of sand that are blown more than three feet each year by the strong westerly winds. As the sands shift they completely bury trees and vegetation, eventually leaving phantom forests of dead trees. A 3/4-mile trail at Napeague Harbor loops through the giant bowls for Seaman to explore.

LAKE GEORGE WILD FOREST

Black Mountain Trail

LAKE GEORGE, NEW YORK
Hiking Time: 3-4 hours

E 🏊

Black Mountain is the tallest peak around the shores of Lake George; at 2,646 it is just a few leaps beyond a half-mile high. **The canine hike to the summit is one of those climbs where your dog is enveloped inside the woods the entire time with no views in sight, or even imaginable. But the views at the top of the journey? So, so worth it**.

You have your choice of how to claim these unparalleled views of Lake George from its eastern shore. The steeper route (red badges) summits in 2.5 miles and only challenges your dog in the rocky upper stretches. There is a closed fire tower at the summit but the primo views actually come from ledges just below the summit. Fires have visited most of the bare rock clearing views from the spruce and oak-beech forests.

With islands in the lake and a shoreline stretching northward between low-lying mountains, you can appreciate why Thomas Jefferson wrote, "Lake George is without comparison, the most beautiful water I ever saw."

You can send Seaman back down the way you came or close a loop on the gentler rise to the top of Black Mountain. That previous road (yellow badges) not taken unfolds over 4.2 miles. With time and a hot day this is a chance for some refreshing doggie dips in any one, or all, of three ponds. It is also just a quick drive to Washington County Beach for a swim in those crystal blue waters Seaman has been looking at from high above.

LETCHWORTH STATE PARK

Gorge Trail

CASTILE, NEW YORK
Hiking Time: 2-8 hours

M △ $

William Pryor Letchworth entered business at the age of 15 in 1848, working as a clerk in the saddlery and hardware trade. He soon shifted to the iron products business and was successful enough to retire at the age of 48. He donated his 1,000-acre Glen Iris estate along the Genesee River to become one of the cornerstones of the New York state park system.

Dubbed the "Grand Canyon of the East," the wooded gorge was scraped and shaped by glaciers, leaving some of the country's most dramatic waterfalls in their wake. **The *Gorge Trail* traces the ravine for seven miles but most folks don't explore past the first three major hydrospectaculars so you will have no trouble slipping away into the woods with your dog in relative solitude**. Your biggest decision on this canine hike will be pinpointing the spot - if any - when it is time to count up your wondrous views and turn around.

The *Gorge Trail* matches Mother Nature's eye-popping moments with its own collection of stone bridges and stairways carved into the cliff walls by Civilian Conservation Corps workers during the Great Depression. An active railroad bridge across the gorge is no mean engineering feat itself although it came at the cost of a much-beloved steel trestle that stood for 142 years before being condemned in 2018.

The footpath is wide and easy to maneuver through the gorge but the builders were not overly energetic on guard rails so take note.

MINNEWASKA STATE PARK PRESERVE

Gertrude's Nose Loop

KERHONKSON, NEW YORK
Hiking Time: 4-5 hours

M ≋ $

If your dog could talk you would hear about this hike for a looooong time. The state park on the dramatic Shawangunk Mountain ridge is where feuding brothers Alfred and Albert Smiley opened competing vacation houses in the 1800s. When they made nice again the Smileys built a network of carriage roads between the hotels. These wide, carefully graded roadbeds are where you will be doing most of your hiking with Seaman.

The early steps lead to a swimming beach at cliff-fringed Lake Minnewaska. If this was as far as your dog went it would probably be a four-star hike. The *Millbrook Mountain Carriage Road* then moves through mixed forests onto the open cliffs and Patterson's Pellet, a glacial erratic perched improbably on the edge of a cliff.

The carriage road joins *Gertrude's Nose Trail*, a narrow footpath that will eventually spend much of its 2.7 miles poking along flat, open clifftops. There are so many mind-blowing views around Gertrude's Nose they actually become ho-hum after awhile.

Take heed of the red blazes - when they lead inland they are taking Seaman away from potentially dangerous crevices in the Shawangunk conglomerate. An occasional rock scramble adds interest to your dog's hiking day, regardless. Pine trees in all shapes and size decorate the clifftops.

Multiple options close the 7.5-mile loop; Seaman will vote for the one that leads back to Lake Minnewaska for a well-earned doggie dip.

National Arboretum

Mount Hamilton Trails

WASHINGTON, D.C.
Hiking Time: 2-3 hours

M

Paws down, this is the best place to hike with your dog in the nation's capital. Congress established the National Arboretum as a research and education facility and living museum in 1927 on the banks of the Anacostia River. The park began with 189 acres and now has 446 acres on the grounds less than two miles from the National Mall. This is one of the nation's largest urban living plant museums.

Most of your dog's explorations will be on paw-friendly grass to sniff the specimens in the Holly and Magnolia Collection, the Goteli Dwarf Conifer Collection, the National Boxwood Collection, the National Grove of State Trees, and more. One meadow houses 22 sandstone Corinthian columns from the east portico of the United States Capitol built in 1828. They were rescued from the scrap heap and reinstalled in the Arboretum.

There are also landscaped hiking paths, most notably the major trail system that circles Mount Hamilton, at 240 feet one of the highest points in the nation's capital. On the southern and eastern slopes are over 15,000 hardy azaleas that can still see blooms into November. **The route eventually takes Seaman to the top where he can peek through the trees to the west and see the Capitol building and the Washington Monument**. You can bet that with the millions of folks who visit Washington each year that picture is not on many iPhones.

Pennsylvania State Game Lands #110

Appalachian Trail

HAMBURG, PENNSYLVANIA
Hiking Time: 4-5 hours

M

Thru-hikers on the *Appalachian Trail* like to say that Pennsylvania is where boots go to die. Rocks are certainly a theme on this canine hike from extended boulder hopping to the jumble of rock ledges that deliver the finest panoramas in the Keystone State. The two stars are Pulpit Rock and The Pinnacle. They overlook a river of quartzite boulders 500 feet wide and a half-mile long known as the Blue Rocks, souvenirs of the last ice age.

Some of the best places to hike with your dog in Pennsylvania are on its many state game lands. Here, the *Appalachian Trail* links with a fire road to create a nine-mile loop to the ridges along Blue Mountain. Tackling the loop counter-clockwise offers two routes to the Pinnacle: the very rocky, lung-busting *Valley Rim Trail* and a shortcut on a switch-backing access road to a mountaintop observatory (it is not a major time-saving shortcut).

The mountain climbing ends at Pulpit Rock but not the treacherous footing for Seaman as the trail to the much-anticipated Pinnacle is particularly rock-studded here. **A giant rock cairn signals the turnoff to the many rock ledge overlooks at the Pinnacle for your dog to gaze at the cultivated fields of the Cumberland Valley stretching to the horizon below**.

The return trip pitches the rocks for a wide, level fire road: perfectly flat at first and then dropping alongside the fast and fun Furnace Creek. It is almost like Seaman gets two hikes for the price of one on the day.

Pyramid Mountain Natural Historic Area

Blue/Yellow/White/Red Trails
BOONTON, NEW JERSEY
Hiking Time: 2-3 hours

M ⚊

Pyramid Mountain is not what Seaman would expect from a hike in heavily suburbanized northern New Jersey. The mountain is best known for its glacial erratics - boulders that were sprinkled across the landscape by retreating ice sheets long ago. The most celebrated is Tripod Rock, a boulder variously estimated at between 150 and 200 tons in weight, that is suspended heroically off the ground by three smaller stones. Two massive stone monoliths: Whale Head Rock and Bear Rock stand close by. It was the desire to save these treasured rocks that led to the development of the Natural Historic Area that protects more than 1,500 acres of sporty trails, fields, forests and wetlands.

A five-mile loop cobbled together from the Visitors Center takes in all three natural phenomena. As a bonus the route tops out at 924 feet on Pyramid Mountain with views of the New York City skyline. **There are wet paws along the way and enough short, steep, and rocky climbs to remind Seaman he is on a mountain and not in suburban New Jersey**. Switchbacks help lessen the strain of 300-foot elevation gains.

If you are used to hiking with your dog in some of the wilder areas of the metropolitan New York area, Pyramid Mountain may seem like you have signed up for a parade on sunny weekends. Maybe someone will invite you and Seaman to drop in for a backyard barbecue at the end.

Ricketts Glen State Park

Falls Trail
BENTON, PENNSYLVANIA
Hiking Time: 3-4 hours

M △ ⚊

A good waterfall trail might yield three, maybe four waterfalls. How about a trail that goes past 23 named waterfalls? That's what Seaman find on the magical *Falls Trail*, a Y-shaped exploration along two branches of Kitchen Creek. One of the most uniquely scenic areas in the Northeast, Ricketts Glen was slated to become a national park in the 1930s but World War II shelved plans for this development. Instead, 13,000 acres of Civil War hero and timber baron R. Bruce Ricketts became a state park.

Colonel Ricketts hired a crew to build a trail along and across the plunging waters and the project took 28 years. Today the *Falls Trail* remains a maintenance challenge and its steep grades can be muddy and slippery so your dog's four-wheel traction will be most welcome.

Kitchen Creek slices through the Ganoga Glen to the left (the tallest water display, 94-foot Ganoga Falls is here) and Glen Leigh to the right before uniting at Waters Meet. The two prongs of the trail connect at the top of the twin falls via the 1.2-mile *Highland Trail*. The complete falls experience encompasses almost seven miles.

The stem of the trail flows through the Glens Natural Area, among towering hemlocks and oaks, before tumbling over three cascades at Adams Falls on the opposite side of the trailhead. These may be the prettiest falls of them all and they aren't even on the official trail in this National Natural Landmark.

31

SARATOGA NATIONAL HISTORIC PARK

Wilkinson National Recreation Trail

STILLWATER, NEW YORK
Hiking Time: 2-3 hours

E

Saratoga is one of the most famous and influential battlefields in world history. In two battles, three weeks apart in the fall of 1777, American general Horatio Gates pounded British commander John Burgoyne who was awaiting reinforcements that never arrived. The surrender of 6,000 British regulars guaranteed the Colonies would not be split along the Hudson River and went a long way towards gaining American independence. The National Park Service maintains this ground much as it looked more than 240 years ago.

On the *Wilkinson National Recreation Trail* Seaman with follow a 4.2-mile balloon loop that travels on roads used by the British during the two battles. He passes sites of British and German fortifications and enters fields that witnessed intense fighting. Behind the Breymann Redoubt he will see the unique Boot Monument. The footwear in question belonged to American battle hero Benedict Arnold who rode through a cross-fire in front of the defensive position to secure victory, receiving a piercing wound in his leg. The marble boot monument does not mention the eventual traitor's name.

Saratoga isn't just walking in the footsteps of Revolutionary War soldiers - it's a darn good canine hike. Easy trotting crosses rolling grasslands with islands of airy deciduous hardwoods. The Great Ravine, which helped dictate battle strategy, provides a change of pace to the terrain. All in all, a fun outing, even if you learn something along the way.

STOKES STATE FOREST

Appalachian Trail

BRANCHVILLE, NEW JERSEY
Hiking Time: 3-5 hours

S 🏊

Stokes Forest is the chunk of land between the Delaware Water Gap National Recreation Area to the south and High Point State Park to the north giving New Jersey about 30 miles of uninterrupted parkland for the *Appalachian Trail* to travel along the Kittatinny Ridge. **Any type of canine hike is possible here - you could fill up a day just walking on beginner trails that explore attractive streams, visit old mine sites or disappear with your dog in a remote patch of beguiling woods land.** Before you start, stop in the office and pick up the best trail guide in New Jersey.

Most canine hikers aim for 1,653-foot Sunrise Mountain, the second-highest spot in New Jersey but with the best views in the Garden State. From the recreation area at Stoney Lake four heavily wooded trails run up to the *Appalachian Trail* atop the ridge enabling you to create hiking loops of between four and ten miles, depending on how long Seaman wants to walk on the ridge soaking in the views. This is absolutely a workout for your dog and the terrain can be rocky - take care especially coming down across large slabs of stone. The welcome waters of Stoney Lake await your return.

To cap off Seaman's day at Stokes Forest head to Tillman Ravine for easy trotting through a dark, shady evergreen forest of Eastern hemlock. The Tillman Brook that carves this moist ravine is one of the prettiest in the state.

TIADAGHTON STATE FOREST

Golden Eagle Trail
SLATE RUN, PENNSYLVANIA
Hiking Time: 4-5 hours

S 🐾

If your trail dog spends any time in Pennsylvania he is likely to hear tell of the *Golden Eagle Trail* being the ultimate day hike in the Keystone State. Seaman may find this curious as the hike is in an obscure state forest neither in the Pocono nor Allegheny mountains.

The statistics paint a crystalline portrait of what lies ahead: nine-mile loop, over 4,000 feet in total elevation gained, two ascents of 800 and 1,000 feet, and four vistas. Looping counterclockwise gets the steepest climb out of the way early and deposits you on the much celebrated Raven's Horn vista with 270-degree views of the Pine Creek Valley early rather than late. Timber rattlesnakes make their home in the rocks so keep Seaman from being too curious here.

The rocky slopes give way to a long draw up Wolf Run with many opportunities to get paws wet. White pines and old growth hemlocks keep things cool amidst the huffing and puffing on the trail. The abundance of flat rocks bears evidence to an old flagstone quarry. Three more vistas emerge, climaxing at the highpoint of the trail, the Beulahland Vista, elevation 2,180 feet. The view is of a long ago futile attempt to coax crops out of these mountains. **The loop finishes with a descent down Bonnell Run with more tail-wagging stream crossings and tiny waterfalls**. With the tough going behind you assessments can be made on the Golden Eagle's place in the Pennsylvania canine hiking pantheon.

WHARTON STATE FOREST

Batona Trail
TABERNACLE, NEW JERSEY
Hiking Time: 3-4 hours

M ▲

The New Jersey Pine Barrens are a tapestry of impenetrable scrub forest, cedar swamps, and peat bogs. The land is so mysterious it is the home of the legendary winged creature with the head of a horse supported by a four-foot serpentine body known as the "Jersey Devil." One million acres of undeveloped land reside in America's most densely populated state here, including the bulk of Philadelphia financier Joseph Wharton's former 100,000-acre estate.

The *Batona Trail* slices 50.2 miles through this unworldly wilderness, marked by its distinctive pink blazes. This is easy walking on paw-friendly sand for most of its length. **Despite the over-whelming flatness of the surrounding countryside, there are undulating elevation changes on the trail itself that make this a fun romp for any dog**.

An outstanding sample of the *Batona Trail* for Seaman is a four-mike hike to Apple Pie Hill, soaring all of 209 feet above sea level but with a fire tower that delivers views across all of New Jersey from the Delaware River to the Atlantic Ocean. The steps may be too open for most dogs to get those views.

Mostly the views are of millions of pine trees while gobbling wild blueberries and huckleberries along the trail. The starting point for this canine hike is a memorial to Emilio Carranza Rodriguez, the founder of the Mexican Air Force, who perished in a plane crash in the Pine Barrens in 1928 at the age of 22.

WORLD'S END STATE PARK

High Rock Trail

FORKSVILLE, PENNSYLVANIA
Hiking Time: 1-2 hours

S 🏊

Early maps called this place Worlds End, possibly due to the staggering views and difficulties in reaching the area. The unusual name may also be a reference to the swirling S-curve in Loyalsock Creek that blocked lumbered logs from flowing downstream, called "Whirls End." In 1929, the former Department of Forests and Waters began purchasing the logged-out land to establish a state forest park. In 1932, $50 was allotted to create the park facilities, which bought little more than four picnic tables. A few years later four Civilian Conservation Corps (CCC) were established and hundreds of out- of-work campers built many of today's facilities, like the swimming area and dam, cabins, hiking trails and roads.

The 20 miles of hiking trails of Worlds End State Park are mostly rocky with steep sections that climb the surrounding mountains. **For experienced canine hikers this is some of the best, toughest hiking around**. The rewards of the *High Rock Trail* include dramatic views earned on the rugged climb up the mountainside, the park earning its name with each step. In the eastern half of the park the *Canyon Vista Trail* is highlighted by a spectacular view of the Loyalsock Creek gorge at an elevation of 1,750 feet.

You can also use the park as a jumping on point for the famed *Loyalsock Trail* that flows for 60 miles through the park on footpaths, old logging roads and abandoned railroad grades.

South Atlantic Coast

Assateague Island National Seashore

South Ocean Beach
BERLIN, MARYLAND
Hiking Time: 2-3 hours

E A ⮞ $

Assateague Island - the sands were connected to the mainland until 1933 when an August hurricane tore open an inlet to the Sinepuxent Bay - is best known for its free-roaming Chincoteague ponies. Legend has it that the original herd escaped a shipwrecked Spanish galleon and swam ashore. The ponies rule the island and Seaman can see them on the roads or even meet them in the surf.

A lighthouse was erected in 1833 but ships still ran aground, including the *Dispatch*, the official yacht of five American presidents. The cruiser was ruined beyond repair when it reached the shore unscheduled on October 10, 1891.

Dogs are not allowed on the three short channel-side nature trails and can not go on lifeguarded beaches but **once you and your dog start hiking at South Ocean Beach there are miles of undeveloped beach** until the Virginia border is reached and dogs are not allowed further. That is the better part of a dozen miles so Seaman can get a full day of beach hiking at Assateauge on the undeveloped, windswept beach sands.

Dogs are welcome any time of the year but even in summer you may well have most of this beach to yourself and your dog - especially in the off-season. Your best trail companion is also welcome in the National Seashore campground. Pack your own sticks for fetching in the surf; not much driftwood stays on the beach.

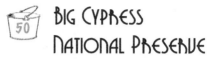

Big Cypress National Preserve

Florida National Scenic Trail
I-75: MM 63, FLORIDA
Hiking Time: 3-6 hours

E

You will **never find a better hike with your dog at a highway rest stop** than this stretch of the *Florida National Scenic Trail* that crosses I-75, better known as Alligator Alley. On the north side of the ribbon of highway volunteers of the Florida Trail Association have used a segment of the 1,300-mile foot trail as the backbone for hiking loops of six, eight, and fifteen miles. Pushing out from the parking lot, trail maps are kindly provided to assuage any trepidation about the ornery wilds lurking ahead.

The *Florida Trail* here is a wide, flat jeep road that traces a canal where Seaman can observe plenty of alligators from a comfortable distance. The cross trails (red and yellow) and the full loop (blue) are single track that traipse through open forests of dwarf cypress and slash pine.

Several pack-in campsites are scattered through the loops, including a cabin that is a souvenir from President Franklin Roosevelt's Civilian Conservation Corps (CCC) during the Great Depression of the 1930s. "Roosevelt's tree army" set up in rural areas building roads, working on flood control and starting beautification projects. Nationally, the CCC was responsible for 3,470 fire towers, 126,000 miles of roads and trails, 89,000 miles of telephone lines and over two billion trees planted.

Shade is at a premium throughout this quintessential Florida hike so have drinking water at the ready.

CAPE HATTERAS
NATIONAL SEASHORE

Nature Trails

OUTER BANKS, NORTH CAROLINA
Hiking Time: less than 1 hour for each

E △ 🏊 ·

There is no better place for *loooong* hikes with your dog on dune-backed beaches than the 70 sandy miles of the Cape Hatteras National Seashore spread across three barrier islands. **There are also a trio of short nature trails - one on each island - to try with your dog.**

The best of the lot is in Buxton Woods on Hatteras Island, near the Visitor Center and lighthouse. This trail bounds across pine and oak-covered dunes with marshy wetlands tossed into the mix. The gnarled trees and shrub thickets provide a shady respite from a day on the beach with Seaman.

Another leafy canine hike is on the *Hammock Hills Nature Trail* on Ocracoke Island which traipses through a maritime forest on the edge of Pamlico Sound for a bit less than a mile. For an easy hike with your dog in the sunshine and salt air stop at Bodie Island Lighthouse. Here Seaman can explore freshwater ponds and marshes that were artificially created by building dams and dikes and artificial dunes to block the intrusion of ocean salt spray.

The Bodie Island Light is just one of five your dog can visit on the Outer Banks built to help mariners navigate the "Graveyard of the Atlantic" - more than 600 ships wrecked off Cape Hatteras. Included in the quintet is America's tallest and most famous, the 208-foot black-and-white swirled Cape Hatteras Lighthouse. Seaman will have to wait outside while you hike the 268 steps to the top.

 CAPE HENLOPEN
STATE PARK

Dune Overlook Trail

LEWES, DELAWARE
Hiking Time: 2-3 hours

M △ 🏊 · $

Cape Henlopen has the distinction of being one of the first parks in America: in 1682 Quaker overlord William Penn decreed that the lands would be for "the usage of the citizens of Lewes and Sussex County." Today the park boasts more than 5,000 acres, including four miles of pristine beach where the Delaware Bay mingles water with the Atlantic Ocean. This is Delaware's largest state park.

The primary destination for dog owners at Cape Henlopen is the 3.1-mile *Dune Overlook Trail*, located south of the pet-friendly campground. The loop is part natural surface, part paved road through pitch-pine corridors and past old fortifications built to bolster America's coastal defenses during World War II.

Do not let Seaman skip the two short spur trails! One leads into the spartina marshes typical of the Delaware Bay estuary and the other is a romp for your dog onto the 80-foot Great Dune, the highest sand pile on the Atlantic shore between Cape Cod and Cape Hatteras.

A good way to explore the undeveloped sands is on the 1.8- mile *Beach Loop Trail* that begins opposite the parking lot in the southernmost section of the park and leads to overlooks of Gordon's Pond Wildlife Area, a unique saltwater impoundment. The soft sand can make for heavy going so don't hesitate to plop down on a dune for a rest. And there is always a chance to play in the lively Atlantic Ocean waves.

CAROLINA BEACH STATE PARK

Sugarloaf Trail
CAROLINA BEACH, N CAROLINA
Hiking Time: 2 hours

E △

The stretch of land along the Cape Fear River just before it spills into the Atlantic Ocean is such a unique environment that it moved the state of North Carolina in 1969 to spend its first money for a park since 1916. **For canine hikers Carolina Beach boasts one of the most extensive trail systems on the Carolina coasts**.

The feature canine hike is the *Sugarloaf Trail* that leads to a 55-foot high pile of sand on the bank of the Cape Fear River. Sugarloaf Dune appeared on navigational charts as early as 1738 and was an important landmark for river pilots. The Confederate States of America also made use of the dune during the Civil War, stationing 5,000 troops near here as part of the defense of the port of Wilmington.

The *Sugarloaf Trail* winds for three delightful miles through a typical Southern forest of pines and live oaks and eventually leads to a triad of ponds, each with its own personality. All told there are six miles of well-marked sandy, paw-friendly trails here. There is no access to Atlantic Ocean beaches at "Carolina Beach" but there is good swimming for your dog in the Cape Fear River.

The *Fly Trap Trail* unveils a shrub bog where the lack of nutrients in the soil have led some plants to turn insectivorous. Venus' Fly Trap grows wild only in these parts of the Carolinas. When an insect twice touches the tiny hairs inside its hinged leaves, the "trap" snaps shut, digesting the victim in lethal juices.

CONGAREE NATIONAL PARK

Boardwalk Loop Trail
HOPKINS, SOUTH CAROLINA
Hiking Time: 2-4 hours

E △ ≈•

One of America's smallest national parks, Congaree nonetheless serves up big adventure for your dog a short drive inland from the Atlantic Ocean. **Not only are dogs afforded a rare chance to enjoy National Park trails but they are also are permitted in the Wilderness Area** and that is virtually unheard of.

Congaree protects the largest contiguous area of old growth bottomland hardwood forest remaining in the United States. More than 52 million acres of floodplain forests have been decimated in the Southeast in the past century so these 2,000 acres of virgin pine, tupelo and bald cypress are special indeed. The park's forests harbor 20 state or national champion trees.

The 150-foot high canopy is one of the highest deciduous roofs in the world. The marquee trail is a 2.4-mile *Boardwalk Loop* that lifts hikers above the flooding of the Congaree River that occurs an average of ten times a year. Everywhere, cypress knees protrude above the water line, mysterious swamp trademarks whose purpose is not entirely known.

Another 20 miles of trail await in the Wilderness Area beyond the boardwalk. The old growth forest is much the same but Seaman's journey is now on sandy loam and dirt rather than pressure-treated wood. You are never far from the tannin-stained waterways that lubricate the park on these primordial passageways.

EDISTO BEACH STATE PARK

Spanish Mount Trail
EDISTO BEACH, SOUTH CAROLINA
Hiking Time: 1 hour

E Δ ⚊ $

Edisto Island was once world famous for its Sea Island Cotton but life has never had a sense of permanence here - the entire town of Edingsville was washed away in a hurricane in 1893 and never rebuilt. The Edisto Company gave 1,255 acres for the park after the cotton trade disappeared.

The *Spanish Mount Trail* features **one of the most unique destinations of any trail on the South Atlantic coasts** - a 12-foot high pile of oyster shells. Known as a shell midden, the oyster pile is typical of American Indian rings found throughout the coastal islands. The Spanish Mount is estimated to be 4,000 years old, the second oldest known in South Carolina. These piles of bleached shells might have been built for ceremonies or possibly they are just ancient trash heaps.

The wooded trail is 1.7 miles one way and moves along a wide, hard-packed dirt road. You can avoid completely retracing your pawprints on the return trip by using the *Forest Loop Trail* or the *Scott Creek Trail*. All the canine hiking here is on natural surfaces and easy going for every dog.

After Seaman gets an extended taste of the maritime forest and tidal creeks - and you'll find some of South Carolina's tallest palmetto trees here - head next for the Atlantic Ocean and the park's 1.5 miles of beachfront. The sand continues into adjoining Edisto Beach, which has remained a low-key residential beach. Save for the busy summer season, dogs can roam off leash on the beach.

FIRST LANDING STATE PARK

Bald Cypress Trail
VIRGINIA BEACH, VIRGINIA
Hiking Time: 2-3 hours

E Δ ⚊ $

It has been almost 400 years since the first English settlers came ashore here at the bottom of the Chesapeake Bay. In addition to the history, First Landing State Park is a National Natural Landmark as the northernmost location on the East Coast where subtropical and temperate plants grow and thrive together.

The trail system features 19 miles of dog-friendly hiking. The marquee walk is the *Bald Cypress Trail* that circles a cypress swamp for 1.5 miles, much of the way on elevated boardwalks. Airborne Spanish moss drapes many of the ancient giants. Looping off that path is the 3.1-mile blue-blazed *Osmanthus Trail*, named for the American olive tree that grows abundantly on the fringes of the dark lagoon. Another worthwhile detour is the quarter-mile *High Dune Trail* that uses wooden sleeper-steps to ascend a tree-stabilized dune.

First Landing hiking is easy going for Seaman on these packed sand and soft dirt trails that are further cushioned to the paw by pine straw from towering loblolly pines. Gentle undulations spice up the visit.

The park stretches to the edge of the Chesapeake Bay where dogs can swim on unguarded sandy beaches. **Dogs are allowed on this beach year-round, the only such Virginia state park allowing dogs in the beach/swimming areas**. Just offshore are naked eye views of the Chesapeake Bay Bridge-Tunnel, one of the seven modern engineering marvels of the world.

Fort Fisher State Recreation Area

Basin Trail
KURE BEACH, NORTH CAROLINA
Hiking Time: 2-3 hours

E 🏊

The largest earthwork fort in the Confederacy was constructed here to keep Wilmington's port open to blockade runners during the Civil War. The Union did not feel confident enough to assault Fort Fisher until December 24, 1864. For two days the sand and earth fortifications absorbed gunboat shells until Northern forces withdrew. On January 12 a bombardment by land and sea finally produced a white flag after six hours of fierce fighting. It was considered the greatest land-sea battle of the Civil War and helped seal the ultimate fate of the Confederacy. Earthworks still remain at the historic site that is now a recreation area.

The *Basin Trail* slips almost unnoticed from the south end of the parking lot into what appears to be a maritime forest. Seaman will twist through a maze of wax myrtles for only a few steps, however, before bursting into the open with nothing ahead but **a stretch of seven miles of tail-friendly, dune-backed sand beaches**.

Along the way you'll pass an old World War II-era hovel where Robert Harrill, the "Fort Fisher Hermit," lived for 17 years. Harrill was far from alone, however. He welcomed all visitors and more than 100,000 made the pilgrimage over the years to listen to his philosophies of simple life. In 1969 the state of North Carolina called him the Tarheel State's second largest tourist attraction behind the battleship *North Carolina*. Not that Robert Harrill ever lived truly alone - he often had a dog by his side.

Great Dismal Swamp National Wildlife Refuge

Washington Ditch Trail
SUFFOLK, VIRGINIA
Hiking Time: 3-4 hours

E 🏊 🚙

At the age of 21 George Washington could be found down on the Virginia-North Carolina border organizing the Dismal Swamp Land Company. His plan was to drain the swamp - so named by the English because there was no need for settlers to force Indian tribes off the land as they had already left - and set up logging operations. Over the next 200 years all of the cypress and Atlantic white cedar forests growing here would be logged at least once.

If you are looking for a place to disappear with your dog on a hike for hours, this is it. During its logging years, over 140 miles of roads were constructed through the Dismal Swamp. Seaman will be hiking on firm sand/dirt roads, level and easy everywhere. Shade is at a premium on hot days so pack plenty of water for your outing.

The refuge has developed an interpretive trail at the site of Washington's former camp, Dismal Town. An extensive boardwalk, nearly a mile long with a couple of spurs, snakes through the heart of the swamp. For a full day's adventure, take Seaman on a 4.5-mile hike along the Washington Ditch which leads to Lake Drummond, one of only two natural lakes in the Commonwealth of Virginia.

You may think a long, straight hike is dull until you see Seaman sniffing and exploring the whole way. Especially when there is a gorgeous private doggie swimming pool waiting at the end.

HICKORY BLUFF PRESERVE

River Trail
OSTEEN, FLORIDA
Hiking Time: 1 hour

E

Hickory Bluff comes by its name honestly - **yes, a natural rise on the Florida peninsula where the average elevation is 12 feet**. These "highlands" spread out over a scenic bank of the St. Johns River as the *River Trail* picks its way through the byzantine system of lakes and marshes that permeate this part of Florida.

This is the Florida coast writ on a Terrier scale rather than the Great Dane scale of some of the park's neighbors. Instead of thousands of acres there are only 150 acres here but your dog can still experience oak hammocks, pine flatwoods, cypress domes and floodplain swamps on two scenic trails, each a loop of about one mile. Wave after wave of saw palmetto are punctuated by a catalog collection of Florida pines - sand, longleaf, slash, and pond. Individual sabal palms make dramatic statements in the mid-story as well. Clumps of prickly pear cactus issue a colorful statement in the desert-like scrub here. The showy reddish-purple berries may reach a length of several inches and can be eaten after the prickly pear spines have been removed - best accomplished by singeing with fire.

These are paw-friendly sand-based paths that become increasing pine-straw covered as Seaman moves onto the red-blazed loop. The St. Johns River seldom looks as attractive as it does from Hickory Bluff along the blue-blazed *River Trail*.

HUNTING ISLAND STATE PARK

Maritime Forest Trail
HUNTING ISLAND, SOUTH CAROLINA
Hiking Time: 2 hours

E △ ⚊ $

So you say you want to shoot the Vietnam jungle scenes for *Forrest Gump* - where do you go? The South Carolina coast, of course. The canopy of cabbage palmettos at Hunting Island, the longest undeveloped beach in South Carolina, frame the sun-bleached sands here. The 5,000-acre island was once a hunting preserve, hence its name. Before that it was a stopover for sailors and pirates.

Hunting Island State Park is **one of the best places you can bring your dog. Dogs are allowed on the park trails and almost all of the four miles of ocean beach**. The dog-friendly campground is only steps from the beach. The island has been rudely treated by Hurricanes Matthew and Irma that have played havoc with some of the beachside trails so some improvisation may be required when you come.

The *Maritime Forest Trail* that travels two miles through the heart of the park running parallel to the ocean serves up Southeast canine hiking at its best. There are just enough rises in the rootless, paw-friendly trail to present a constantly shifting woodland environment. As a side trip, a boardwalk has been constructed through a salt water marsh overlooking Johnson Creek. Beyond is a wide open beachscape, studded by a striking forest of blanched ghost trees from recent storms. This sidetrip will be the main event for any ocean-swimming dog.

41

Huntington Beach State Park

Sandpiper Pond Trail

MURRELLS INLET, SOUTH CAROLINA
Hiking Time: 1 hour

E ⛺ 🏊 $

Archer Huntington used some of the millions his stepfather, Collis P. Huntington, made helping build the Transcontinental Railroad to transform an old rice plantation into a seaside arts center. Huntington created the 10,000-acre Brookgreen Gardens to showcase the works of his wife, sculptor Anna Hyatt. When it was opened in 1932, Brookgreen was the country's first public sculpture garden.

Pared down to 2,500 acres of mostly marshland, Huntington State Park was founded in 1960. The centerpiece is the Moorish castle known as Atalaya that Huntington designed from memory after studying the architecture of the Spanish Mediterranean Coast. Dogs are allowed on the park trails, on the beach and in the campground.

The *Sandpiper Pond Trail* is a rollicking sandy romp past an interdune pond. The Atlantic Ocean beach can be used to close a two-mile loop on this out-and-back trail. Viewing platforms are spaced along the route that serve as ideal resting spots for Seaman after trotting through thick sand.

For many dogs **the best part of Huntington State Park will be the three miles of undeveloped beach**. To leave the sunbathers behind park at the boardwalk and head north on the beach. You will reach a jetty in 1.2 miles and dune-backed sand awaits to loll about and catch the sea breezes on the Grand Strand.

Jekyll Island State Park

Driftwood Beach

JEKYLL ISLAND, GEORGIA
Hiking Time: 1-2 hours

E ⛺ 🏊 $

Jekyll Island is billed as "Georgia's jewel." First developed in the late 1800s as a hunting club for America's richest families (enough titans of industry wintered here that it was once estimated that one-sixth of all the world's wealth was represented on Jekyll Island), today the entire island, including 11 miles of Atlantic Ocean beach, is a state park.

The beaches around Jekyll Point at the south end are undeveloped and Seaman can hike for hours beside natural wind-sculpted dunes. There is ocean swimming and bay swimming - your dog's choice.

The northern nob of the island juts into Saint Simons Sound and the sands are harder and the surf gentler; **Driftwood Beach here is one of the best beach hikes you can take with your dog**. The maritime forests spread right down to the sand and the skeletons of many of those trees decorate the beach. Heading south, you will eventually hit civilization. When you reverse course you can use an inland path to complete a hiking loop. The dog-friendly Jekyll Island campground is an easy stroll away.

Paved bike paths penetrate Jekyll Island's maritime forest and you can also walk Seaman on carriage roads winding through the opulent turn-of-the-20th century "cottages" built by the Vanderbilts, Morgans, Rockefellers, Goodyears, Pulitzers and preserved in the 240-acre historic district. A dog can dream.

JOCKEY'S RIDGE STATE PARK

Tracks in the Sand/Soundside Overlook Trails

NAGS HEAD, NORTH CAROLINA
Hiking Time: 2 hours

M ⌇

Jockey's Ridge, with heights varying from 80 to 100 feet, is the tallest natural sand dune system on the Atlantic seacoast. Once discovered, the naked hilltops served as an important navigational landmark for European explorers. Its name is thought to survive from wild pony races staged in the flats at the base of the dunes. In 1974 Jockey's Ridge was designated a National Natural Landmark and the state park soon followed with 420 protected acres - nearly all of it sand.

This is **the closest thing you will find to mountain-climbing for your dog on the Carolina coasts. Seaman is welcome to play anywhere throughout this vast sand box**. The soft sands, steep dunes and stiff winds can make for invigorating canine hiking at Jockey's Ridge.

For dogs who like their walking more structured there are two interpretive nature trails marked by posts across the dunes. The 1.5-mile *Tracks in the Sand Trail* departs from the Visitor's Center and highlights the signs in the sand left by small mammals, reptiles, birds, insects and even plants that have adapted to this desert environment.

The trail leads to the sandy edge of the Roanoke Sound estuary where the gentle waters make an ideal canine swimming pool - or a cool walkway through the shallows. Across the street from Jockey's Ridge Seaman can jump in the Atlantic Ocean waves of Nags Head Beach, open to dogs year-round.

JONATHAN DICKINSON STATE PARK

Green Loop Trail

HOBE SOUND, FLORIDA
Hiking Time: 3 hours

M △ ⌇ $

Jonathan Dickinson was a long-forgotten Quaker merchant whose sloop shipwrecked off the Florida coast nearby over 300 years ago. The land is better known for hosting Camp Murphy, a top-secret radar training school during World War II. After operations ceased the 10,500 acres quickly became a state park.

Jonathan Dickinson is a magnet for Southeast Florida backpackers and there are certainly enough trails here to fill a dog's weekend. Canine day hikers will be more than fulfilled by the *Green Loop Trail* that rambles up and down ancient sand pine scrub-covered dunes, visits a quiet pond, and explores the remnants of Camp Murphy. A short detour leads to an observation tower atop Hobe Mountain, at 84 feet **the highest natural point in Florida south of Lake Okeechobee**. Views go across to the Atlantic Ocean. The tour length, minus the Hobe Mountain excursion, is 4.9 miles.

In just 1.3 miles on its way to a cypress-studded creek, the *Kitching Creek Nature Trail* packs in over two dozen interpretive stops covering centuries of human and natural life in the area. Take note of the dead cypress snags throughout the park that are an indication of salt water intrusion due to development since skipper Dickinson crashed his ship on Jupiter Island.

After visiting the park take a short drive to the Atlantic Ocean at Hobe Sound, one of the rare chances for Seaman to enjoy the waves on South Florida beaches.

KEY WEST BOTANICAL GARDEN

Trail of Champion Trees
KEY WEST, FLORIDA
Hiking Time: 1 hour

E $

The Key West Botanical Garden began life as a 1930s Depression-era public works project, creating a 55-acre experimental garden with flagstone walkways, lime rock walls, an aviary, and plants from all over the world to learn which would survive in this tropical environment.

The early botanical garden was a popular tourist showplace but it declined during World War II as bits and pieces of the property were appropriated by various government agencies. By 1961 only seven and a half acres and no buildings remained. It was decades before the Key West Botanical Garden Society organized to operate the garden as a family-friendly facility.

Today the Key West Botanical Garden is **the only frost-free botanical garden in the United States**. Seaman can trot along four self-guided nature trails under the lush leaves of tropical flora. Chief among them are the collection of palms, including saw palmetto and the Florida state tree, the Sabal Palm. Two freshwater ponds in the forest, reached by red arrows, are among the last in the Florida Keys.

Yellow arrows lead your dog along the *Trail of Champion Trees*. The Key West Tropical Forest and Botanical Garden is home to two state champion trees and two national champions: the Wild Dilly and the Locustberry. These trees ordinarily are found in low, shrub-like growth but here they have blossomed as full-blown trees.

KIPTOPEKE STATE PARK

Baywoods Trail
CAPE CHARLES, VIRGINIA
Hiking Time: 1 hour

E ▲ ⚊ $

This is an old commercial site, purchased by the Virginia Ferry Corporation for the northern terminus of the Virginia Beach to Eastern Shore Ferry. In 1949, when the terminus was moved to Cape Charles, the abandoned area was named Kiptopeke Beach in honor of the younger brother of a king of the Accawmack Indians who had befriended early settlers. Kiptopeke means "Big Water."

That big water **provides the best swimming hole for your dog on the eastern shore of the Chesapeake Bay**. Nine World War II-era concrete ships weighing almost 5,000 tons each were placed offshore in 1948 as breakwaters, providing less adventurous dogs a chance to play in gentle waves. The southern beach (no dogs allowed Memorial Day to Labor Day) is also ideal for a lazy canine stroll.

More than four miles of fun trail for Seaman traverse this 545-acre bayside park. Kiptopeke's nature paths wind over sand dunes through groves of loblolly pines, sassafras and wild cherry trees. The *Baywoods Trail* slips through an uplands hardwood forest on wide, old field roads and connects with expansive, sandy beaches via an extensive network of wooden boardwalks through the dunes.

Kiptopeke is a center for raptor research and activity is especially brisk from September through November. Kiptopeke's hawk observatory is among the top 15 busiest nationwide.

LITTLE BIG ECON STATE FOREST

Kolokee Trail Loop

OVIEDO, FLORIDA

Hiking Time: 3 hours

E ≈. $

The odd name comes from a mashing of the Little Econlockhatchee River and the larger Econlockhatchee River, a north-flowing, 54-mile-long blackwater tributary of the St. Johns River. That river is the star of the canine hiking in the state forest and this is the **best streamside hike your dog can take on the Central Florida coast**.

Henry Flager used the money he made with John D. Rockefeller's Standard Oil Company to build the visionary Florida East Coast Railway in 1912. The old railbed is now pivotal in canine hiking adventures here, a ramrod-straight multi-use recreational path through the Little Big Econ State Forest.

The most popular way to experience the Econlockhatchee is launching from the Barr Street Trailhead using the *Florida National Scenic Trail* to complete the state forest *Kolokee Trail Loop*, a journey of 4.8 miles. The footpath snakes along the heavily vegetated riverbanks on sandy bluffs. A variety of conveyances are available to move Seaman across low spots and channel cuts.

The turn-around point is that *Flagler Trail*. As you loop back towards the trailhead you enter the flatwoods and longleaf pine restoration areas. If you opt to extend your dog's hiking day in the Little Big Econ, try some of the grassy horse trails where the wide passages will make it seem as if you are trundling down dog-leg par fours with Seaman at the local golf club.

MAGNOLIA PLANTATION AND GARDENS

Estate Gardens

CHARLESTON, SOUTH CAROLINA

Hiking Time: 1 hour

E $

You wouldn't expect to find a formal garden in a guidebook of places to hike with your dog. But how dog-friendly is Magnolia Plantation? **Not only are dogs allowed to walk the grounds but they can ride the tour trams and even go in the plantation house** (if you carry the dog).

And it is quite a treat - you are not likely to have a canine hike like this anywhere else. The prescribed path through the maze of walking paths stops at two dozen points of interest, crosses graceful bridges, looks in on 250 varieties of azaleas, skips through quiet stands of towering bamboo and wanders by 900 types of camellias. More hiking with Seaman is available through the 60-acre blackwater cypress and tupelo swamp. Plus there are nature trails on the property.

Magnolia Plantation has been opened to the public since the 1870s - it was already 200 years old at the time. Thomas Drayton, Jr. and his bride Anne Fox constructed the manor house in 1680 and created America's first estate garden, called Flowerdale.

One of the trees the couple planted was a live oak just off Bridge Square, not too far from the site of the original Plantation House. If Seaman acts strangely at this magnificent Drayton Oak it may be because he senses the presence of J. Drayton Hastie, Sr. When he died in December of 2002, his ashes were spread in the boughs of the spreading giant, perhaps spawning one of Magnolia's many talked-about ghosts.

Merchants Millpond State Park

Lassiter Trail

GATESVILLE, NORTH CAROLINA
Hiking Time: 3-4 hours

M ▲ 🏊

The longest loop of pure canine hiking on the Carolina coasts can be found here - the 6.7-mile *Lassiter Trail*. This is easy going for your dog on soft, pine straw-littered paths. Wooden bridges tame the wilder stretches. Seaman will happily leave the long, flat stretches at the millpond shore for the gentle hillocks under a pleasant mix of pines and hardwoods such as American beech, bounding up eagerly to discover what awaits on the other side.

The star of the park is the 760-acre millpond that harbors ancient bald cy- press and tupelo gum trees. Constructed in 1811, the water supported a sawmill, gristmills and a farm supply store. When development encroached a local outdoorsman, A.B. Coleman, thought the area too beautiful to be altered by bulldozers. He bought and donated the land for the park.

Much of the character of the eerie "enchanted forest" of the Lassiter Swamp comes from the mistletoe that has twisted and gnarled the branches of tupelo gum trees into fantastic shapes. The mistletoe's mooching won't kill the tupelo gum - if the host dies, it dies. Mistletoe will also not kill your dog if the clusters of white berries are accidentally consumed. Though toxic, the effects of the poison are not as severe as once believed.

Do not be as cavalier allowing Seaman to swim in the cypress swamps, however - alligators live here.

 # Skidaway Island State Park

Big Ferry Nature Trail

SAVANNAH, GEORGIA
Hiking Time: 2 hours

E ▲ 🏊 $

Don't let the Savannah address fool you. Instead of townhouse mansions, historic squares, and cobblestone streets think saltwater sloughs, alligator ponds, and fiddler crabs. You'll still get plenty of live oaks and Spanish moss, though.

Skidaway Island has a history that reaches all the way back to Georgia founder James Oglethorpe and includes the Revolutionary War, Civil War, and ties to the Roebling family of Brooklyn Bridge-building fame. Most of the development occurred via paper companies in the days before a bridge to the mainland was built in 1971. Shortly after that the 533-acre state park opened on land donated by the Union Bag and Paper Corporation.

There is no better canine hiking on the Georgia coast than at Skidaway. The *Big Ferry Nature Trail* takes your dog out past Confederate earthworks and even older shell middens before reaching an observation tower over the salt flats. Seaman can even sniff an old bootlegger's liquor still - one of 31 such sites on the property. A full exploration will cover three miles.

A connector trail of about one mile links to Skidaway's popular *Avian Loop* and *Sandpiper Trail Loop* trails, each about one mile in length. The paths are wide and easy on the paw and use boardwalks to traverse the marshes with countless land crabs exposed at low tide. Stately pines and red cedars thriving in the lime-rich soils built from decaying shells dominate the maritime forest.

TUCKAHOE STATE PARK

Tuckahoe Valley Trail

QUEEN ANNE, MARYLAND
Hiking Time: 2-3 hours

E Λ ⤳

The 3,800 acres of state-owned land flanking the easy-moving waters of the Tuckahoe Creek harbor the **best canine hiking on Maryland's Eastern Shore**. The star of the park's hiking routes is the *Tuckahoe Valley Trail* that travels 4.5 easy miles through a climax deciduous forest thick with maple, oak, and beech. Cedar stands remain in the marshlands that were liberally harvested beginning in the 1700s. The route is well-hydrated with tiny streams as Seaman moves along paths of dirt, sand and pine straw.

The level terrain of the Atlantic Coastal Plain makes for pleasurable canine trotting but for more varied hiking fare try the *CreekSide Cliff Trail* that explores the high banks cut by the Tuckahoe. The *Little Florida Trail* visits the remains of an old sand-and-gravel operation; the scarred depressions in the sandy soil from the quarrying provide excellent habitat for frogs and other amphibians.

Four hundred acres have been carved out of the center of the park for the Adkins Arboretum. Dogs aren't often welcome in these living tree museums and this one is a real treat. The well-groomed trails work the upland forests around three creeks and after wandering under towering tulip poplars and loblolly pines Seaman can luxuriate in the grassy footpaths of two meadows.

Blue Ridge Mountains

AMICALOLA FALLS STATE PARK

West Ridge Staircase

DAWSONVILLE, GEORGIA
Hiking Time: 1-2 hours

M 🏊 **$**

The Cherokee named this 729-foot high cascade Amicalola which translates to "tumbling waters." **The falls are the centerpiece of one of Georgia's most popular parks - and the park service has given your dog a cornucopia of ways to experience the plunging water**. The easiest is to start at the Reflection Pool and climb up the paved approach trail to the Lower Observation Platform. A sportier chase would be to hike the *Creek Trail* a half-mile to the Reflection Pool. This dirt footpath begins at the picturesque Little Amicalola Creek before climbing away from its banks.

Once at the Lower Observation Platform the way up is via 175 open-grate steps. If Seaman doesn't do open-grate steps, your exploration is over. Otherwise, 425 more steps lead to the top of the falls, crossing in front of the main drop. You know the way back down from here. For more traditional canine hiking opt to lead Seaman down via the *West Ridge Falls Access Trail*, *Spring Trail* and *Mt. Laurel Loop*.

The *Appalachian Trail* originally started in the park but the southern terminus was switched to Springer Mountain in 1958. Today an 8.5-mile approach trail links the base of the falls to the *Appalachian Trail* terminus and many thru-hikers kick off their hike-of-a-lifetime adventure here, being the closest paved road access to Springer Mountain.

BILTMORE HOUSE & GARDENS

Woodlands Trail

ASHEVILLE, NORTH CAROLINA
Hiking Time: 2-3 hours

E 🏊 **$**

You can hike all day with your dog at Biltmore and never realize you are in the backyard of America's largest house. Biltmore is the handiwork of George William Vanderbilt, a French Renaissance chateau of 250 rooms that required 11,000,000 bricks to construct - more than the Empire State Building.

Outside the exuberant castle is an 8,000-acre estate that includes a forest, a farm, a winery and gardens designed by Frederick Law Olmsted, the co-creator of New York's Central Park and the most influential landscape architect of the 19th century. Seaman is permitted to explore just about everywhere that isn't a building. The paths wind gently down a sloping mountainside from the mansion to the Boat House and Bass Pond, passing through 75 acres of formal gardens, a naturalistic woodland, and meadow plantings. More than three million specimens were sunk into the grounds when the house was built in the 1890s. Covering these serpentine trails is likely to whet any dog's hiking appetite but if not Seaman can take off on a paved bike path or bridle trail that winds around the grounds. You have your choice of 22 miles of trail.

Sheepdogs and Russian Wolfhounds had the run of Biltmore but Cedric, a St. Bernard and the first Vanderbilt pet brought to the estate from Maine, was the family favorite. The pub in Antler Hill Village on the grounds is named for Cedric and is, naturally, dog-friendly.

BLUE RIDGE PARKWAY

Craggy Pinnacle Trail

BLUE RIDGE PARKWAY: MM 364.1
Hiking Time: 1-2 hours

M A ≈ $

There are many, many incredible views along the Blue Ridge Parkway but it will hard to convince Seaman that the 360-degree panorama at Craggy Pinnacle is not the best. And the views aren't even the main reason Craggy Gardens is one of the must-stop pull-offs on America's favorite scenic roadway.

There are no tall trees on top of this 5,892-foot mountain. Instead, the slopes are blanketed with blueberry, mountain laurel, and gnarly Catawba rhododendron bushes. **The sweet birch trees that try and grow here are often twisted into grotesque shapes that make great photo-ops with your dog**. This "garden" explodes in beautiful purple blooms in June and July.

The *Craggy Pinnacle Trail* winds its way up 252 feet over 0.7-mile from the parking lot through tunnels of rhododendron (you'll understand why one mountain off the Parkway is known as Dog Loser Knob after this hike). As you near the summit there are forks and side trails - feel free to let Seaman explore in the grassy open meadows with unobstructed views. The canine hike ends at the low stone walls.

Ambitious trail dogs can also pick up the *Douglas Falls Trail* just south of the Visitor Center which leads 4.2 strenuous miles through hemlock groves and across racing cascades (that is without bridges) to the 70-foot high freefall Douglas Creek finally makes over a wide rock face.

BLUE RIDGE PARKWAY

Linville Falls Trails

BLUE RIDGE PARKWAY: MM 316.4
Hiking Time: 1-2 hours

M A ≈

Linville Falls are so spectacular that trails go to five overlooks to get as many viewing angles as possible. These are the best and easiest water displays on the Blue Ridge Parkway. But don't expect to jump out of your vehicle, spy the falls, and get right back on the road as these trails will test your trail dog.

Erwin's View Trail takes in four of those viewpoints, in a twisting, climbing canine hike of nearly one mile through a virgin hemlock forest to its apex. From high above the Linville Gorge you can grasp the challenges necessary for the determined river to navigate its way through the sheer rock walls.

It is back down to the trailhead at the Visitor Center to find that fifth overlook. This one is along the west side of the Linville River on the *Plunge Basin Trail*. Before you start, however, point Seaman in the opposite direction for a short hike to a lively side waterfall on Duggers Creek.

The descent to the Linville River travels through thickets of rhododendron and mountain laurel with the sound of pounding water as a constant companion. A half-mile down the gorge the trail splits to an overlook just above the thundering falls. Back on the main path Seaman continues another quarter-mile against the towering cliff walls to the gorge floor and the plunge basin. **Climbing back out you have now seen all Linville Falls has to give - and given your dog a workout in the bargain.**

BLUE RIDGE PARKWAY

Moses Cone Park Trail

BLUE RIDGE PARKWAY: MM 294
Hiking Time: 2-3 hours

M ⤳

Your trail dog is used to barreling through narrow ribbons of thick woods and scampering over rocks - and no doubt loves it. But sometimes Seaman wants to just kick back and feel like top dog of the manor while out trotting on a hike. That's what awaits at the ancestral summer home of Moses and Bertha Cone, built with Southern textile mill money in the 19th century.

Most people find the Blue Ridge Mountains sufficient in natural beauty but Cone, known as the "Denim King," planted 32,000 apple trees on his estate and imported sugar maples from Vermont. Gifford Pinchot, first Chief of the U.S. Forestry Service, provided advice on planting hemlocks and pines. **He also constructed 25 miles of finely crushed gravel carriage roads that make this Parkway stop doggie heaven for canine hikers**.

The wide, level trotting paths drop down from the gleaming white manor house through open hillsides to tranquil Bass Lake where the farm fields give way to forest. The Maze makes so many gentle switchbacks that Seaman will likely not even realize he has gained a few hundred feet in elevation.

These lovely trails could well tempt you to turn right instead of left at the Apple Barn and add another three miles to your dog's hiking day at Cone Manor. Or you can cross the Parkway and climb to Flat Top Tower. The steel tower is always open and dogs can handle the six flights of open stairs to the 360-degree views from the top.

BLUE RIDGE PARKWAY

Sharp Top Trail

BLUE RIDGE PARKWAY: MM 86
Hiking Time: 2-3 hours

S △ ⤳

Thomas Jefferson once wrote, "The mountains of the Blue Ridge, and of these the Peaks of Otter, are thought to be of a greater height, measured from their base, than any others in our country." The country was young then and the man on the nickel still hadn't even purchased Louisiana yet. But as Seaman picks his way up the *Sharp Top Trail*, gaining over 1,500 feet in one-and-a-half miles he could very well concur with Mr. Jefferson.

The first inn opened in the Peaks of Otter in 1834 and so many folks have beaten a path to the top of 3,875-foot Sharp Top that they don't even bother to blaze the trail. A good part of that path is comprised of steps cut into the rock, especially around the summit. That mountain top is expansive with views to every cardinal point on the compass amidst the smattering of boulders. The stone shelter has been on the Sharp Top summit since 1858 when it was constructed as an overnight bivouac for inn guests. On the way back down (or up) take advantage of the short detour to Buzzard's Roost that is fairly level with some rock hopping amidst large rock formations at the end.

And the other Peaks of Otter you ask? That would be Harkening Hill (3,364 feet) and Flat Top (4,004 feet). Both have hikes to their summits as well, longer and not as popular. **Whichever peaks Seaman tags here be certain to stop at Abbott Lake before leaving. An easy mile trail laps the rare lake along the Blue Ridge Parkway**.

CARL SANDBURG HOME NATIONAL HISTORIC SITE

Memminger Path

FLAT ROCK, NORTH CAROLINA
Hiking Time: 1-2 hours

When Carl Sandburg packed up his belongings, including 16,000 books, and moved to the Blue Ridge Mountains in 1945 at the age of 65 it could be expected he was ready to relax. Not so. "The Poet of the People" would produce more than a third of his life work in his remaining 22 years and win a third Pulitzer Prize, this time for poetry.

The Greek Revival house preserved here was constructed by Christopher Memminger, one-time Secretary of the Treasury for the Confederate States of America. He did much of the work in creating the five-mile trail system that your dog will enjoy on the property today.

It all starts from the parking lot beside the picturesque Front Lake that finds it way to many a Western North Carolina magazine cover. **The most spirited canine hiking here is the 623-foot climb in 1.5 miles to unobstructed views atop the Big Glassy Mountain rockface**. Halfway up the mountain, exactly when a panting Seaman will welcome a breather, is a dammed creek reservoir that forms an ideal canine bathtub.

The trip back down meanders past Mrs. Paula Sandburg's goat barn that brought international renown to Connemara Farms for the quality of its milk. Dairy goat Jennifer II was the world's top producing Toggenburg in the world in 1960. Paula was as famous in hircine circles as Carl was in literary circles.

CHATTAHOOCHEE NATIONAL FOREST

Bartram Trail

CLAYTON, GEORGIA
Hiking Time: 2-3 hours

Rabun Bald tops out at 4,696 feet to place as runner-up for Georgia's highpoint, less than 100 feet shorter than Brasstown Bald to the west. Seaman can ride to the Brasstown crown but must hoof it 1.6 miles to the Rabun summit. The parking lot at Brasstown is built to accommodate lines of tour buses; the parking lot at Rabun can handle only a handful of vehicles. Guess which one he will choose.

The footpath to the top of Rabun Bald is along the 37-mile *Bartram Trail* that remembers the work of 18th century botanist William Bartram. A Philadelphian, Bartram embarked on an epic journey in 1775 from the the foothills of the Appalachian mountains to Florida, and all the way to the Mississippi River, collecting specimens and sketching plants, establishing himself as America's first naturalist.

Rabun's summit is not truly "bald" but covered with weather-beaten dwarf scarlet oak and evergreen rhododendron. This is an honest pull for Seaman up Rabun Bald with nary a downhill step on the climb to the summit but never so severe as to bring even the least seasoned canine hiker to his knees. The final ascent utilizes lengthy switchbacks through tunnels of rhododendron, bent over by the weather on the exposed mountaintop.

At the end **Seaman can scramble up two short flights of wooden steps on a stone-based observation tower to enjoy the best views in Georgia**. The 360-degree, tri-state panoramas can stretch for 100 miles on a clear day.

CHEROKEE
NATIONAL FOREST

Appalachian Trail

ROAN MOUNTAIN, TENNESSEE
Hiking Time: 6-7 hours

M

Roan Mountain is the kind of place you can imagine having a booming Kodak concession in the parking lot in the days before digital photography. That parking lot is in Culver Gap at the center of the five peaks that make up Roan Mountain.

Hiking north, after a very short stay in a spruce-fir forest Seaman will enjoy stunning unobstructed 360-degree views for seven miles across the summits of three grassy balds - the longest such stretch in the Appalachian Mountains. Save for some short stretches of rock stepping the million dollar views are obtained with little purchase on Round Bald, Jane Bald, and at 6,189 feet, Grassy Ridge Bald. Roan Mountain is the only time the *Appalachian Trail* rises above 6,000 feet. A full day of splendid canine hiking can be carved out here but save time for the south side.

Heading south, the trail turns shady, lush, and mossy. Real views don't come for two miles upon reaching Roan High Knob and the highest back-country shelter on the entire 2,174-mile trail. In Tollhouse Gap, on paths created for a long-razed mountaintop hotel, is the true showstopper in the Roan Highlands. The Rhododendron Garden growing here is the largest of its kind in the world and the June blooms are one of America's finest coming out parties. It lends credence to Native American lore that a great battle between the Cherokees and Catawbas left the rhododendron stained crimson and the mountain treeless.

CHIMNEY ROCK
STATE PARK

Exclamation Point Trail

CHIMNEY ROCK, NORTH CAROLINA
Hiking Time: 2-3 hours

M   ≈ $

The Chimney Rock brochure proclaims "We Love Dogs" - take them at their word. **Seaman is encouraged to experience the same wonders as the wide-eyed tourists that have beat a path to Chimney Rock, a 315-foot monolith guarding Hickory Rock Gorge, since Rome Freeman built a stairway to the top in 1885.**

After Seaman climbs those 500 or so steps and soaks in the 75-mile views from the 2,280-foot promontory it is time to start hiking again. The *Exclamation Point Trail* rises another 200 feet over one-half mile on the bare rock. There are oddities along the way such as the Devil's Head, a piece of rock that was sliding down the mountainside and defied physics by stopping on a narrow ledge, and the Opera Box that is a small room created by a rock overhang.

Exclamation Point is the roof of the park and there is plenty of room to enjoy safe views of the gorge for Seaman from here. Director Michael Mann staged his climactic scene from *The Last of the Mohicans* in 1992 above 404-foot Hickory Nut Falls at this point. Seaman can splash at the bottom of the falls from an easy trail down below.

For a better doggie dip take the short trip down to Lake Lure, the body of water your dog has been admiring from the top of Chimney Rock. The lake doubled as a 1950s Catskills resort for Jennifer Gray and Patrick Swayze in *Dirty Dancing*. You can be sure Seaman will have the time of his life swimming here.

CLOUDLAND CANYON STATE PARK

West Rim Loop Trail

TRENTON, GEORGIA

Hiking Time: 3-4 hours

M △ ⚶ $

To geologists, the impressive gash in the limestone at the western end of Lookout Mountain was Trenton Gulch. Locals knew the 1,000-foot deep gorge as Sitton Gulch. After the Civilian Conservation Corps arrived in the 1930s to carve the first access roads into the area the newly designated state park was bestowed with the more beguiling name of Cloudland Canyon for its opening in 1939.

Cloudland Canyon serves up **some of the most dramatic hiking in North Georgia and your dog can experience every step of it**. The best walk is the *West Rim Loop Trail* that covers about three miles and follows up visits to canyon overlooks with views of the town of Trenton down the western slope. For the full flavor of this scenic trail begin the journey on the East Rim and use the connector trail across Daniel Creek. Don't let the scenery distract Seaman here - the undulating route hugs unprotected ledges as it rolls along.

One thing Seaman won't see on the *West Rim Trail* are the park's stunning water displays, 60-foot Cherokee Falls and 90-foot Hemlock Falls. To get face-to-face with these hydrospectaculars requires conquering 600 steps into the canyon (the Washington Monument has 897 steps, for reference). These steps are of the open-grate variety which will abort the trip for some dogs. If you make it to the canyon floor Seaman can test *Sitton's Gulch Loop Trail* that runs five miles out the north end of the gorge.

DUPONT STATE FOREST

Triple Falls Trail

CEDAR MOUNTAIN, N CAROLINA

Hiking Time: 1-2 hours

M ⚶

The E.I. du Pont de Nemours Company began life on a pristine stream in northern Delaware in 1802 to grind explosive black powder. It was beside another crystalline stream in Western North Carolina that the company landed in the 1950s when searching for pure water and crisp air to manufacture sensitive medical X-ray film. The chemical giant eventually sold over 10,000 acres of pristine forest to the state for conservation. DuPont Forest has since taken several star turns in Hollywood productions, including *The Last of the Mohicans* and *The Hunger Games*.

There are more than 90 - yes, 90 - named trails in DuPont State Forest, all of which are open to your dog. Some are pretty footpaths like the *Jim Branch Trail* and the *Pitch Pine Trail* and others are wide, easy-trotting roads like Joanna and Tarklin. The must-do canine hike for first-timers is the *Triple Falls Trail* that traces the Little River for one mile as it makes several picturesque plunges, each unique in its own way. The falls do not offer much in the way of a doggie dip but continue past the north end of the trail to Dense Lake, a tranquil woodland pond with a dock for diving dogs.

There are more waterfalls to hunt for in DuPont, lakes to swim in and the opportunity to tag Stone Mountain, at 3,620 feet the highest point in the forest, after an elevation gain of over 1,000 feet. Seaman's purchase on these slabs of granite are views across this entire canine hiking paradise.

GORGES STATE PARK

Rainbow Falls Trail

SAPPHIRE, NORTH CAROLINA
Hiking Time: 1-2 hours

Transylvania County bills itself as "The Land of Waterfalls" with 250 hydrospectaulars on display. Rainbow Falls, with the Horsepasture River roaring down a vertical cliff for almost 140 feet, is as impressive as any. Tucked into a pocket of the Blue Ridge Mountains that receives 80 inches of rain a year and is classified as a "temperate rain forest" guarantees a show any time of year.

The moist woodlands abound in mosses and ferns and wildflowers that dominate the 1.5-mile hike to the falls. The trail is gravel-surfaced in its early stages as Seaman bounds gently along. The gravel disappears as the trail transitions into the Nantahala National Forest and a steady ascent on a natural surface to Rainbow Falls begins. A jumble of jagged boulders at the base of the falls release a steady mist rising from the river floor. When the sun is shining the namesake rainbows sparkle in the wide open forest setting.

The trail continues another quarter-mile upstream to Turtleback Falls and 500 yards more to Drift Falls. Under no circumstances allow Seaman in the Horsepasture River above Rainbow Falls as the current is strong and the drop over the cliff only seconds downstream. **The Horsepasture River abounds with superb doggie swimming holes** on the hike back to the parking lot, however. Below the falls.

GRANDFATHER MOUNTAIN STATE PARK

Daniel Boone Scout Trail

BLUE RIDGE PARKWAY: MM 299.1
Hiking Time: 3-4 hours+

S

French botanist Andre Michaux excitedly scrawled in his journal in 1794, "Reached the summit of the highest mountain in all of North America!" Andre was wrong, of course, but he could be excused his joy as Grandfather Mountain, actually a collection of several peaks, rises so abruptly above its North Carolina surroundings.

Many consider the canine hike to the crest of Grandfather Mountain to be the "granddaddy of all hikes on the Blue Ridge Parkway." For its abundance of rare and endangered plant species, Grandfather Mountain has been designated one of the world's few International Biosphere Reserves. **There are 16 distinct ecosystems here and Seaman will be hiking through most of them**.

The *Daniel Boone Scout Trail* gets rolling after a half-mile introduction from the Parkway on the *Nuwati Trail*. Three miles away is Calloway Peak, at 5,946 feet the highest spot on the Grandfather Mountain massif. To get there a steadily rising switchback trail conquers 2,000 feet of elevation gain.

After marveling at the views this is a common turnaround for canine day hikers. The *Grandfather Trail* does, however, lead another 2.4 vista-stuffed miles across the rocky spine of the mountain. The route is studded with ladders and cables that are not impossible for trail dogs but could spell the end of the line if too unnerving. The climax is the famous Mile High Swinging Bridge in the private tourist concession of Grandfather Mountain.

MONTREAT TRAILS

Graybeard Trail

BLACK MOUNTAIN, N CAROLINA
Hiking Time: 5-6 hours

The Reverend John C. Collins led a congregation of clergy and lay leaders into the North Carolina mountains in 1897 and purchased 4,500 pristine high-country acres for a Christian settlement called Montreat, a mashing of "mountain retreat."

There are enough peaks and canine hikes - 20+ miles - at Montreat that **you could take your dog out every day for a week and not set a paw on the same stretch of trail**. Sooner or later every canine adventurer who frequents these trails, however, will make the classic summit climb to Graybeard Mountain, the highest elevation on the property at 5,408 feet. The quickest way is on the 4.75-mile *Graybeard Trail* that can roughly be divided into three hour-long chunks.

The first leg climbs steadily up Flat Creek with easy stream crossings and numerous chances for Seaman to step off the trail into an enticing pool under a small waterfall. Expect as many pawfalls on rock as on dirt during this opening thrust. Once at Pot Cove Gap the trail boards the Old Trestle Road for almost flat trotting on to Graybeard Falls, a sheet of water flowing down a rockface - and more splashing.

The final push for the summit with its west- and east-facing views reverts to a steady footpath climb. Take a five-minute detour at the trail shelter just past the falls to scramble up to the craggy overlook at Walker's Knob where the entire Montreat Valley will spread beneath Seaman's paws.

MOUNT MITCHELL STATE PARK

Deep Gap Trail

BLUE RIDGE PARKWAY: MM 355.4
Hiking Time: 6-7 hours

Until Thomas Jefferson made the Louisiana Purchase in 1803 this was the tallest mountain in America, although no one knew it. Everyone assumed Grandfather Mountain was the regional highpoint but after an excursion to the Black Mountains in 1835 a professor at the University of North Carolina began making claims to the contrary. Elisha Mitchell was correct but he unfortunately fell to his death trying to verify his measurements in 1857.

There are several ways for Seaman to tag the Mount Mitchell summit, including the 280-yard walk to the observation deck from the parking lot atop the mountain. **For canine hikers Mount Mitchell is not the prize but the jumping off point for grander adventures**. Although it has 16 peaks over 6,000 feet in height and six of the ten highest in the eastern United States, the hook-shaped Black Mountain range is only 15 miles long. Setting off on the *Deep Gap Trail* from the summit parking lot Seaman can tag four of them before reaching Deep Gap 4.3 miles away - much of it through the most extensive stand of Canadian-like Fraser Fir remaining in the United States.

If that is too ambitious a canine day hike to Mt. Craig, named for Governor Locke Craig who spearheaded the creation on the park, is only a two-mile round trip out and back. At 6,647 feet it is the eastern United States' second-highest peak with loads of exposed rock that make it more view-friendly than its slightly loftier neighbor.

MOUNT ROGERS NATIONAL RECREATION AREA

Appalachian Trail
VOLNEY, VIRGINIA
Hiking Time: 4-5 hours

M ⛰ $

This is one summit canine hike that gets it all backwards. Seaman starts in wide open spaces with sweeping countryside vistas and ends up in a lush spruce forest where he can't see anything but tree trunks.

Mount Rogers is the roof of the Commonwealth of Virginia and at 5,729 feet the loftiest state highpoint east of South Dakota that lacks a road to the summit. So getting there is one of the best hikes with your dog in Southwest Virginia on any of three routes. The most popular assault launches from Massie Gap; Mount Rogers is 4.5 miles away.

An old farm road leads this trek on the early steps through open pastures. Mount Rogers is clearly visible and the stand-out peak to the west is 5,520-foot Whitetop Mountain. The unobstructed views are courtesy of free-ranging feral ponies that were introduced to help prevent reforestation. **The friendly horses could well tag along with Seaman on the way through the meadows adding a dash of equine charm to this hike**.

After joining the *Appalachian Trail* the stony dirt footpath climbs easily through low rock outcroppings. Stop to allow Seaman to clamber atop a prominent pinnacle rock at the trail junction before using a short spur to reach the top of Mount Rogers. This spur is the only time he will be trotting through forest. There may be no views amidst the fir trees but there is a small rock pile Seaman can jump onto to celebrate tagging the official summit.

NANTAHALA NATIONAL FOREST

Joyce Kilmer Memorial Trail
ROBBINSVILLE, NORTH CAROLINA
Hiking Time: 1 hour

E ⛰

In 1936, at the height of the Great Depression, the Forest Service paid $28 an acre for these woodlands at a time when land was selling for $3 an acre. Why? **These tracts comprised one of the very last stands of virgin hardwoods in all of the Appalachian Mountains**. Depressed lumber prices during the economic crash had sent the local sawmills to the sidelines. Some of the trees in Poplar Cove are estimated to be over 450 years old. Many soar 100 feet high and reach 20 feet around.

The Veterans of Foreign Wars were looking for an appropriate grove to name for Alfred Joyce Kilmer, a young poet who was killed on a scouting mission in the Second Battle of the Marne during World War I. Kilmer was only 31 but had gained fame for the publication of his short verse, *Trees*, in 1913. The government could not have picked a more spectacular cove of hardwood forest to honor the fallen poet.

The two-mile trail meanders in a figure-eight configuration through the arboreal oldsters. Seaman will be trotting effortlessly through a forestland carpet of wildflowers and ferns. The carcasses of fallen monarchs along the way make for visual interest and fun canine climbing. The Little Santeetlah Creek rushes through the landscape to offer spirited dog paddling as refreshment just as the hike winds to a conclusion.

ΠΑΝΤΑΗΑΙΑ ΠΑΤΙΟΠΑΙ FOREST

Panthertown Valley/Little Green/Mac's Gap/
Great Wall/Big Green/Greenland Creek Trails

LAKE TOXAWAY, NORTH CAROLINA
Hiking Time: 4-5 hours

Welcome to the most unique valley in the Blue Ridge Mountains. Even the Forest Service left this backcountry alone, only recently creating an "official" trail system blazed by volunteers enamored by the Panthertown Valley.

There are eight significant waterfalls in the valley and this grand tour takes in five in a roughly nine-mile loop. The canine hike quickly switchbacks into a flat-bottomed valley - a rarity among the typical V-shaped Appalachian gorges. The bottomlands are lubricated by clear bronze streams with many opportunities for dog paddling. **The first big chance comes at Schooltown Falls where it will take some considerable coaxing to get your water-loving dog away from the plunge pool and large fluffy sand beach to continue the hike**.

This Panthertown tour spends long level stretches on sandy dirt that is easy on the paw. A particularly delightful patch is along the *Great Wall Trail* through light woods paralleling a 300-foot high granite rock dome that has caused some to call this - unironically - the "Yosemite of the East." The hiking becomes more challenging at this point and a side trip to the top of the 4,206-foot Big Green Mountain is possible for views across Panthertown.

The hardest work is over but before climbing out of the valley there is a major paws-wet creek crossing and more waterfalls. Oh, the big cats are gone from Panthertown but this is a protected sanctuary for American black bears.

PISGAΗ ΠΑΤΙΟΠΑΙ FOREST - BLACK BALSAM KNOB

Art Loeb Trail

BLUE RIDGE PARKWAY: MM 420.2
Hiking Time: 3-4 hours

"Balds" - where trees fail to grow - are found primarily in the Southern Appalachians, where the climate is too warm to support an alpine zone. Why some summits are bald and some are not is a mystery to scientists. There are two types of balds - heath balds with blankets of evergreen shrubs and grassy balds covered with dense swards of native grasses. Black Balsam Knob, at 6,214 feet, is the highest grassy bald in the Blue Ridge Mountain.

How good is the canine hiking here? There are some who will tell you the three miles of unobstructed views on the *Art Loeb Trail* across Black Balsam Knob and neighboring Tennant Mountain comprise **the best hike they have ever taken with their dog**. A short and scenic fifteen-minute climb brings you to the ridgeline and wide open high country is on the canine hiking menu for the next hour. Parkway poster child Looking Glass Rock is in near-constant view from the trail.

Dropping off the ridgeline the loop closes with the *Investor Gap Trail*, an old logging road with springs pouring across it for refreshment; backpackers can continue on to the Art Loeb terminus at Cold Mountain of literary and Hollywood fame that is admired in the distance to the north.

Matching canine hiking on Black Balsam Knob stride for stride in "wow" moments is the moderate climb to the Sam Knob summit, a heath bald found on the opposite side of the trailhead.

PISGAH NATIONAL FOREST - HARMON DEN AREA

Appalachian Trail

HOT SPRINGS, NORTH CAROLINA
Hiking Time: 2 hours

M △ ⛟

Harmon's "den" was, according to local lore, a rocky outcropping a woodsman named Harmon called home. Today the unrivaled star here is Max Patch Mountain, named for a farmer who cleared the mountain in the 1800s for cattle grazing. Max Patch is the southernmost bald on the *Appalachian Trail* and often referred to as one of the "crown jewels" of the 2,100+-mile walk. But it is not a natural bald - the Forest Service keeps the peak grassy with tractors.

From the often too-small parking lot, **Seaman can be on the summit of Max Patch before he shakes the dust out of his ears from the journey up the mountain on one of the several gravel approach roads**. A grassy path and easy five-minute walk lead straight to the bare mountaintop. On display are the Black Mountains to the northeast, the Newfound Mountains across the parking lot and the Great Smoky Mountains across Tennessee to the west, if you need to put some names to the endless protrusions surrounding you. If you have dropped in on one of the many art galleries in the Blue Ridge you have no doubt seen interpretations of the mountains from Max Patch.

Most canine hikers will delay the summit experience by angling left to set out on the loop trails that send Seaman through a light forest before depositing him in countryside fields below Max Patch. At the junction with the *Appalachian Trail* you can extend your canine hiking day in either direction.

PISGAH NATIONAL FOREST - PINK BEDS

Pink Beds Loop

PISGAH FOREST, NORTH CAROLINA
Hiking Time: 2-3 hours

E △ ⫩

When George W. Vanderbilt purchased 125,000 acres for his Biltmore Estate much of the land was severely over-farmed and in drastic need of re-forestation. Vanderbilt turned the task over to Gifford Pinchot and America got its first scientifically managed forestlands. When his friend Theodore Roosevelt became President in 1900, Pinchot was named the first head of the United States Forest Service. His replacement, Carl Schenck, founded the continent's first school of forestry in the Pink Beds, so named for the profusion of rhododendrons and azaleas that transform the hemmed-in mountain valley each spring.

Pisgah is America's second most-visited national forest and there is **no more delightful romp for Seaman in its half-million acres** than the well-lubricated five-mile *Pink Beds Loop*. This is easy trotting throughout as the trail winds lazily through the cove forest and around a rare mountain bog. The forest service has rebuilt sturdy boardwalks across the beginnings of the South Fork of the Mills River that provides continual refreshment breaks for your dog.

Glimpses of the Blue Ridge Parkway appear through the trees and trail branches lead up into the mountains for extended canine exploring. Next door, the Cradle of Forestry National Historic Site offers two paved interpretive trails about a mile in length that explain the workings of scientifically managed forestry that began right here.

Sky Meadows State Park

North Ridge-South Ridge Circuit

DELAPLANE, VIRGINIA
Hiking Time: 2 hours

M

It was 1731 when James Ball picked up 7.883 acres on the eastern slopes of the Blue Ridge Mountains from Lord Fairfax. Over the years through inheritance the land was divided and divided and divided. In 1966 a housing development was planned that called for further division into 50-acre lots. At this point philanthropist Paul Mellon stepped in and donated 1,132 acres that became Sky Meadows State Park in 1983.

Sky Meadows is **the best place to hike with your dog in Northern Virginia** and those namesake meadows are the star. There simply aren't many open-air hikes like these available in the Appalachians. Save for the *Snowden Trail* nature loop you will be hiking up a mountain at Sky Meadows.

The trail system covers about ten miles of marked paths that can be molded into canine hiking loops, the most popular being the North Ridge-South Ridge circuit. The *South Ridge Trail* utilizes an old farm road while the *North Ridge Trail* picks its way up the mountain like a traditional hiking trail. Seaman is probably best served by going up the South Ridge since it is not as steep and views are longer coming down the North side.

For those looking for a full day of hiking with your dog the *Appalachian Trail* is 1.7 miles away and there are loop options up there as well. If Seaman just wants to enjoy the meadows, confine explorations to the *Piedmont Overlook Trail* on the North Ridge.

Table Rock State Park

Table Rock National Recreation Trail

PICKENS, SOUTH CAROLINA
Hiking Time: 3-4 hours

S Δ 🐾 $

South Carolina does not spring to mind when compiling lists of best mountain hikes but this climb with Seaman to the top of Table Rock will demonstrate how abruptly the Blue Ridge Mountains slam to a halt in the Palmetto State. Whitewater Falls with two 400-foot drops, the tallest waterfall east of the Rocky Mountains, is right down the road and Raven Cliff Falls, another 400-footer, is an "Upcountry" neighbor.

The *Table Rock Trail* begins beside a delightful stretch of the Carrick Creek. Don't let Seaman get too attached, however. After a half-mile the path turns away from the creek and the hike begins in earnest. The top of Table Rock Mountain, a massive open-faced landmark, lies 2,000 feet above. The hard-packed trail snakes its way upward through an open forest sprinkled with large boulders.

After much panting from all involved the 3,124-foot summit is tagged but there is plenty of hiking to still be had across the granite dome. **The views from Table Rock - surprise - are the best South Carolina has to offer**. When Seaman looks down on the blue waters of Table Rock Lake the trail ends after 3.6 miles. After spending some quality time sitting at the very edge of the Blue Ridge Mountains looking at the Piedmont that will flatten as it heads to the Atlantic Ocean, it is time to head back down.

Heart of Appalachia

Alabama

Kentucky

Maryland

Ohio

Pennsylvania

Tennessee

Virginia

West Virginia

Big South Fork National River & Recreation Area

Twin Arches Loop Trail

ONEIDA, TENNESSEE
Hiking Time: 2-3 hours

Breaks Interstate Park

Tower Tunnel-Prospectors-Geological-Overlook Loop

BREAKS, VIRGINIA
Hiking Time: 2 hours

The big "fork" in question is from the Cumberland River that flows north from Tennessee into Kentucky, slicing and dicing the Cumberland Plateau into gorges and rock shelters along the way. The easiest and most popular canine hiking at Big South Fork is around the Bandy Creek Visitor Center but you will want to point your adventurous dog to a more remote section of the park.

The Twin Arches form the largest sandstone arch complex in the East. **The hollows are so thick with second-growth timber that Seaman will not even notice when he is trotting across the top of one of the massive natural bridges**. Don't fret; there will be plenty of chance to appreciate these impressive arches from down below. Wooden steps help tame the steep descent into the rock houses.

There are two loops to explore here; a 1.2-mile expedition to the arches and a full six-mile reconnaissance of the dark hollow. No doubt Seaman will be opting for the whole tour.

It will come as no surprise that massive rock shelters like these deep in the woods were once popular harbors for moonshine stills; old still equipment is on display in the park. There isn't much to sniff at Jake's Place, an old home site along Station Camp Creek, but a log cabin built in 1817 by Jonathan Blevins has been incorporated into the rustic Charit Creek Lodge. Here you'll find restrooms, accommodations and maybe even refreshments - but no electricity.

The Russell Fork River has been working on this stretch of Pine Mountain for 180 million years. The gorge is now carved 1,650 feet deep and known as the "Grand Canyon of the South." Daniel Boone named it the Breaks in 1767 because this was the only way he could find through the wall of wilderness in his travels westward.

The gorge is so thickly blanketed in oaks and hickories that it is difficult to appreciate how big it is - until you and Seaman start hiking into it. The *River Trail* drops all the way down to Russell Fork, switchbacking slowly on a vigorous canine hike suited for athletic dogs.

The *Tower Tunnel-Prospectors-Geological-Overlook Loop* cobbles together trails that descend only 350 feet into the gorge during a 4.5-mile circle. This is canine hiking in close quarters as the rosebay rhododendron and mountain laurel obscure the spectacular rock formations until you are actually picking your way through the passages. **Seaman will enter natural rock tunnels and mini-canyons, pass under cliff overhangs, and investigate small caves on this rambling adventure**. The fractured rock sculptures come fast and furious on the stretch of the *Geological Trail* known as the Notches.

The undulating *Overlook Trail* closes the loop and hugs the cliff edges closely enough for almost continuous views of the canyon. Don't let Seaman get overly curious as the trail travels across unfenced open rock face.

C&O Canal National Historical Park

Paw Paw Tunnel Trail

OLDTOWN, MARYLAND

Hiking Time: 2 hours

E △ ≈

The biggest obstacle to the completion of the Chesapeake and Ohio Canal was five miles of crooked Potomac River water known as the Paw Paw Bends. It was decided to by-pass the curves with a tunnel, destined to be the largest man-made structure on the 184-mile canal.

Rosy-eyed planners began work on the tunnel in 1836 with a goal of 7-8 feet gained a day. Instead, the pace was more like 12 feet a week. Fourteen years later - with a cost overrun of 500% - the 26-foot high tunnel was opened. Encased in the six million bricks used to build the Paw Paw Tunnel at Mile 155 on the canal are tales of unpaid wages, immigrant worker abuse, labor unrest, and even murder.

One of the most unique hikes you can take with your dog starts in a national park service campground and travels a short distance on the well-maintained towpath of the canal until you reach the Paw Paw Tunnel. Hopefully you have remembered to bring a flashlight because the 3,118-foot tunnel (more than a half-mile long) will plunge Seaman into complete darkness. A return trip can revisit the inky towpath or travel across the top of the tunnel that takes it name from the preponderance of Pawpaw trees, also known as a prairie banana or Ozark banana, in the area. This small tree with large leaves bears the largest edible fruit native to North America.

Chickamauga and Chattanooga National Military Park

Big Daddy Loop

LOOKOUT MOUNTAIN, TENNESSEE

Hiking Time: 4-5 hours

M

Lookout Mountain is an 85-mile long ridge that narrows to a point as it reaches the Tennessee River, 1,800 feet above Chattanooga across the water. This was just a sleepy railroad crossroads in the fall of 1863 when Union armies broke through Confederate defenses to clear the way into Atlanta and the heart of the Southern defenses.

Today the western slopes are laced with hiking trails, seven of which can be stitched into a 10-mile loop known locally as "Big Daddy." Several shorter loops are possible but all should include the 1.5-mile stretch from the historic Cravens House, a popular starting point for Lookout Mountain canine hikes, to Sunset Rock on the *Bluff Trail*.

This route is the highest of many across the flank of the mountain and earns it name as it picks it way along towering sandstone cliffs. The drop-offs can be precipitous and unprotected, especially on Sunset Rock itself. Civil War generals surveyed troop movements in the valley below from here but the formal trail was not constructed until the 1930s; **it required hundreds of men and 18 months to carve the full 2.55-mile footpath that stays mostly level as it passes small caves and crosses natural bridges**. Several open vistas emerge and, of course, continuous winter views of the valley. Stone steps and switchbacks help Seaman conquer the spurs to the Instagram-famous rock formations and overlooks of the meandering Tennessee River.

 COOK fORESt
STATE PARK

Longfellow Trail

COOKSBURG, PENNSYLVANIA
Hiking Time: 3-4 hours

M △ ≈

John Cook was the first permanent American settler on the Clarion River. He arrived in 1826 to scout a canal route but instead bought 765 acres of land, built a cabin and started operating a water-driven sawmill. The Cook family lumber empire prospered but the stately hemlock and white pines thriving just outside their back door were so impressive the trees were never cut. The temptation was great - just four of the arboreal monarchs would yield enough lumber to build a six-room house.

This is the natural treasure where you will hike with Seaman. Six tranquil miles meander under the 300-year old trees starring in the Forest Cathedral. The marquee walk is the easy-going 1.2-mile *Longfellow Trail* that visits the heart of the tallest eastern white pinelands in the Northeastern United States; one tops out at 183 feet, although it is not marked.

Canine hiking loops can be crafted with the rolling *Rhododendron Trail* and the flat *Toms Run Trail* that skirts a picturesque stream. **If your cautious dog balks at crossing the swinging bridge connecting the trails, it is an easy scamper through the water**.

Energetic dogs should find the *Seneca Trail* at the Clarion River and begin a one-mile uphill climb to the Seneca Point Fire Tower, passing through a patch of old growth forest ripped asunder by a 1976 tornado. At the top, Seaman can climb the open steps of the 80-foot fire tower and scan this land of giants.

 CUMBERLAND fALLS
STATE RESORT PARK

Trail 9-Eagle Falls Trail

CORBIN, KENTUCKY
Hiking Time: 2 hours

M △ ≈

The largest falls on the Cumberland River - 65 feet high and 125 feet wide - likes to bill itself as the "Niagara of the South." The hydrospectacular is a far sight short of that but Cumberland has something Niagara, or any falls in the Western Hemisphere, does not have: a moonbow.

Most visitors will observe the full moon phenomenon from the viewing platforms built at the Cumberland Falls State Resort Park Visitor Center. But adventurous dog owners will want to sneak off to the other side of the river where *Trail 9* offers some of the best peeks of Cumberland Falls. At 1.5 miles, this natural surface trail seems benign enough but if you complete all of *Trail 9* Seaman will know he's had a workout.

About a half-mile from the trailhead a view of the Cumberland Gorge below the falls awaits. Next comes a spur that drops all the way to the river level and picks its way over rocks to Eagle Falls, a worthy water spout in its own right. **Seaman will be able to play in the plunge pool here so there won't be any hurry to start back up**.

The upper part of the trail traces Eagle Creek upstream to a ridge as the hike becomes very rugged in a breathtaking forest. The loop closes before reaching Cumberland Falls so Seaman can sneak one last look before a well-earned return to the car. An even better treat will be stopping at the Kentucky Fried Chicken in town, where Harlan Sanders opened his first chicken shack in 1930.

Cumberland Gap National Historic Park

Tri-State Peak Trail

CUMBERLAND GAP, TENNESSEE
Hiking Time: 1-2 hours+

M

The gentle, rounded mountains of the Cumberlands might not appear very intimidating but if you were on foot guiding a mule or driving a buckboard wagon in the 18th century you would be mighty appreciative of finding this gap that kept American settlers bottled up on the East Coast until Daniel Boone blazed the Wilderness Road through in 1775. It was rugged enough, however, that no wagons rolled through the pass for another 20 years. Eventually 250,000 grateful folks went through this gap to the promises of the West.

Paved roads used the Cumberland Gap as well. The National Park Service rerouted auto traffic through a tunnel at the end of the 20th century and began tearing up pavement so that Seaman can once again hike on the original contours of the Wilderness Trail.

The canine hike to Tri-State Peak begins in Virginia, hard by an iron furnace from 1819, before moving onto the *Wilderness Road Trail* that leads into Tennessee. The *Tri-State Peak Trail* is a spur leading steadily uphill to the 1,990 foot summit, passing the site of a Civil War fortification manned by the Union Army. **In a little more than half-a-mile Seaman will cap off the climb of 700 feet by standing with a paw in three states**. A pavilion stands where Virginia, Tennessee, and Kentucky all meet up. There is more canine hiking to be had along the *Cumberland Trail* across the ridge with intermittent views before heading back down.

Daniel Boone National Forest

Auxier Ridge Trail/Double Arch Trail

SLADE, KENTUCKY
Hiking Time: 3-4 hours

M A 🚙

There are more than 500 miles of trails in the 700,000-acre Daniel Boone National forest and save for a few designated swimming areas your dog is welcome everywhere. The first destination for many canine hikers is the Red River Gorge Geological Area where 300-foot sandstone cliffs and overhangs are decorated with gnarly rock formations. The more than 100 natural stone arches in the gorge represent the greatest collection east of the Mississippi River.

Unlike most arches in the American West, Red River's natural bridges are tucked among a vibrant deciduous forest and are best viewed up close, often via a short trail from the scenic driving road. Double Arch, with one opening on top of another, takes longer to reach than most, maximing Seaman's adventure in the rock formations.

Start this loop on the *Auxier Ridge Trail*, a narrow clifftop that delivers splendid views of the Red River Valley from multiple vantage points, including the landmark Courthouse Rock, a massive tree-covered monadnock where the two-mile route ends. **Seaman can scramble up the sides of the massive boulder for a ways and a staircase gets you closer as well**. The *Auxier Branch Trail* trips under towering cliffs through a wooded canyon to provide access to the Double Arch with its own postcard views and climbing steps to the top. The *Double Arch Trail* uses an old forest road to close out this fascinating six-mile canine hike.

DeSoto State Park

Blue-Orange Loop Trail

FORT PAYNE, ALABAMA
Hiking Time: 2 hours

M ⛺ 🏊 $

Little River is one of America's longest rivers that spends its entire life atop a mountain. The water begins flowing at 1,900 feet above sea level on Lookout Mountain before rushing off the Cumberland Plateau into Weiss Lake at 650 feet high. Along the way Little River has carved a 12-mile long canyon as deep as 700 feet in places. DeSoto State Park, on the West Fork of the Little River, is the gateway to one of the most impressive canyon landscapes in the Southeast.

The park is populated by some of the Civilian Conservation Corps' best rustic architecture from the the 1930s, including a magnificent stone bridge that was unfinished due to the outbreak of World War II.

Equally impressive is nature's handiwork atop Lookout Mountain, including the powerful 107-foot plunge of DeSoto Falls, north of the main park. **The *Blue Trail* visits a variety of seasonal water features tucked among the rock ridges, including Lost Falls with its fur-shaking plunge pool for dog paddling**.

The parallel *Orange Trail* that twists through the deciduous forest features its own water delights, Laurel Falls for one. The loop is closed by a tree-shrouded boardwalk trail that highlights the Azalea Cascades. The four-mile loop is challenging enough in stretches that Seaman will welcome the chance to cool off in DeSoto's well-lubricated forest.

Forbes State Forest

Quebec Road

HOPWOOD, PENNSYLVANIA
Hiking Time: 3-4 hours

M ⛺ 🏊 🚙

Quebec Run, covering 7,441 wooded acres, is one of 16 state forest areas designated as a "wild area" - no amenities, no developments, including access roads. Two centuries before being so recognized Charles Mason of surveying fame called these woods "a wild of wildes." "There is a remarkable quantity of the large tall spruce trees," he wrote. "Laurel swamps, dark vales of pine through which I believe the sun's rays never penetrated."

That forest has been logged twice since then but the third growth wilderness is still impressive, especially in the thick understory of mountain laurel and rhododendron. *Quebec Road*, open only to foot and paw travel, bisects the wilderness area for 3.7 miles and leads to a honeycomb of canine hiking loops. Loops upon loops. There are more than 20 well-marked trails in Quebec Run that visit sandstone outcroppings, crystal-clear quickstepping streams, and shady hollows.

The spa-like waters of Quebec Run beckon to Seaman along *Rankin Trail* while the water pools deep enough for dog paddling off the *Mill Run Trail*. There are ruins of an ancient grist mill on *Grist Mill Trail* and, if the stories are true, buried stolen Confederate gold along the *Hess Trail*. You get the idea of the options; whichever you choose budget at least two hours.

Expect this to be a solitary hike with your dog. When the rhododendrons are afire in late spring you could possibly see another trail user every half hour or so on the weekends.

HARPERS FERRY NATIONAL HISTORIC PARK

Stone Fort Trail

HARPERS FERRY, WEST VIRGINIA
Hiking Time: 3-4 hours

S ~ $

No place in America packs as much scenic wonder and historical importance into such a small area as Harpers Ferry National Historic Park where the Shenandoah and Potomac rivers join forces. George Washington surveyed here as a young man. Thomas Jefferson hailed the confluence as "one of the most stupendous scenes in Nature" and declared it worth a trip across the Atlantic Ocean just to see. U.S. Marine Colonel Robert E. Lee captured abolitionist John Brown here. Stonewall Jackson scored one of his greatest military victories here during the Civil War. Even Meriwether Lewis and Seaman showed up in Harpers Ferry to get arms for the Corps of Discovery.

The Maryland Heights is where you can see it all, rising ruggedly from the canal towpath to 1,448 feet above the rivers. Wayside exhibits on the *Stone Fort Trail* give an appreciation of the effort involved in dragging guns, mortar, and cannon up the mountainside. Just one 9-inch Dahlgren gun capable of lobbing 100-pound shells weighed 9,700 pounds. The wooded trail leads to the remnants of the Stone Fort which straddles the crest of Maryland Heights at its highest elevation. **Even without pulling heavy ordnance on the steep and rocky trail your Seaman will appreciate the stops at scenic overlooks**.

Back on the towpath, a footbridge across the Potomac River leads to Lower Town in Harpers Ferry - accessible otherwise only by dog-unfriendly shuttle bus.

HOCKING HILLS STATE PARK

Old Man's Cave Trail

LOGAN, OHIO
Hiking Time: 1 hour

E △ ~

The tribes of the Wyandot, Delaware and Shawnee knew this valley as "Hockhocking" for its bottle shape, created when glacial ice plugged the Hocking River. When the first settlers sought shelter in these recesses more than 7,000 years ago they found vegetation deep in the gorges that still harkened back to the last ice age - stately eastern hemlocks and Canadian yew and birches thriving in the moist, cool environment.

Hocking Hills State Park is a superb destination for any dog, but is especially delightful for the canine hiker who is a few hikes beyond those days of the 10-mile treks. There are six destination areas in the park - five for canine exploring: no dogs are permitted in the Conkles Hollow state nature preserve. Each has its own distinct pleasures accessed by short trails.

But if you can do only one - unlucky Seaman - make it the hike to Old Man's Cave tucked into a heavily wooded, twisting ravine. The Old Man was Richard Rowe who moved to Hocking Hills some time around 1796 and lived out his life in the massive rockhouse here, traveling with his two dogs in search of game. Rowe is buried beneath the ledge of the main recess cave. No word about the dogs.

An easy, one-mile trail works its way into and around the ancient gorge; wooden steps and bridges smooth the way. Seaman will marvel at the Devil's Bathtub and enjoy a dip in Old Man's Creek, especially in the pool beneath the Upper Falls.

JEFFERSON
NATIONAL FOREST

Devil's Fork Loop Trail

FORT BLACKMORE, VIRGINIA
Hiking Time: 2-3 hours

Old-timers like to say that the hike to the Devil's Bathtub really used to be beautiful in the days before social media. So many people have posted videos of the magical wanderings in Jefferson National Forest that the trail has become too crowded. Indeed, with only 14 or so parking spots and aggressive towing on surrounding private land, an early weekday start is practically mandatory now that the secret is out.

The main spine of the *Devil's Fork Loop Trail* is actually an old rail trail, although it is hard to imagine how narrow gauge trains hauled coal and timber out of this hemlock forest. Sharp eyes may spot an old rail car by the side of the trail spouting vegetation.

The full loop covers seven miles but this is one canine hike that plays better as an out-and-back. The star attraction is the Devil's Bathtub 1.6 miles from the trailhead. Getting there will take Seaman into the cold Devil's Fork waters 12 times - and that won't even be his favorite part of the hike.

Eventually you will reach one of the most gorgeous blue-green swimming holes your dog is likely to jump into. Many people mistake this crystal pool for the "bathtub" but that phenomenon is actually 500 feet away, up and behind the rocks. You will recognize the distinctive Devil's Bathtub; swimming is actually more problematic here as it is encased by steep sandstone sides. If that is not enough water time there are those dozen stream crossings on the way back.

MAMMOTH CAVE
NATIONAL PARK

Green River Bluffs Trail

MAMMOTH CAVE, KENTUCKY
Hiking Time: 1-2 hours

Not named for extinct wooly elephants, Mammoth Cave earns its name as the world's longest known cave system with more than 400 miles of passages mapped, so many that the guides like to point out that you could put the second and third longest cave systems inside the limestone labyrinth and have more than 100 miles left over. Seaman will not go underground to see the flashlights of the tour guides illuminate such fancifully named formations as Grand Avenue, Frozen Niagara, and Fat Man's Misery.

Dogs are, however, welcome to hike above ground in the dark hollows and hardwood forests that blanket Mammoth Cave. There are over 80 miles of trails that have been left in a natural state. But Seaman need not go exploring for a fine adventure here, he can start right at the Visitor Center.

The *Green River Bluffs Trail* snakes through open woodlands to promontories above the Green River. The singletrack path dips down and switchbacks enough times to provide Seaman a sporty transverse of what may have seemed like only a picnic ground at first blush.

There are plenty of short trails to close this loop that can extend your canine hike to over four miles. Two standout options are the *River Styx Spring Trail* where the underground stream emerges and the *Historic Entrance Trail* where Seaman can look down into Mammoth Cave and catch a blast of cold subterranean air.

McConnells Mill State Park

Kildoo Trail/North Country National Scenic Trail
PORTERSVILLE, PENNSYLVANIA
Hiking Time: 2-5 hours

The ancient 400-foot deep Slippery Rock Gorge was carved so rapidly by glacial meltwater that it left rocky outcrops and massive boulders scattered in the swift waters across the canyon floor that remain to this day. The rocks were once "slippery" because of the oil seeps in the area that triggered America's first rush for black gold. In 1974 the 930-acre Slippery Rock Gorge was designated a National Natural Landmark.

All of your dog's hiking day at McConnells Mill will be spent in the six-mile Slippery Rock Gorge. Luckily for those without a car shuttle or a hankering for retracing pawprints, there are two bridges, one open to traffic and one not, that allow a hiking loop on both sides of the turbulent waters. This two-mile loop begins at the namesake 19th century mill and welds the *Kildoo Trail* on the east bank to the *North Country National Scenic Trail* on the west. **There is plenty of rock-hopping in store for Seaman - more on the east side - and yes, those stone surfaces can still be slippery**. But with the heart-stopping scenery in the gorge no one will be in any hurry to be moving at an unsafe speed.

Seaman is seldom more than a few bounds from Slippery Rock Creek that does calm down enough in places for safe dog-paddling - those life preservers provided along the trail are not for show. Pockets of inviting sandy beach usually indicate it is time to allow your dog into the water.

New River Gorge National River

Kaymoor Miners Trail
FAYETTEVILLE, WEST VIRGINIA
Hiking Time: 2 hours

When your dog hears "821 steps" do his ears perk up or do those ears cover his eyes? If it is the former the *Kaymoor Miners Trail* is calling your name.

Like Greenland, the New River as a geographic name is an oxymoron. This may be the oldest river in North America, flowing in its present course for at least 65 million years. The sandstone it flows through is very hard and so the wide, wooded gorge the New River has cut in that time is only 1/3 as deep as the Grand Canyon.

It is deep nonetheless and you can get a feel for what you are in for by starting at the New River Gorge Bridge, the longest steel span in the Western hemisphere and the second highest in the United States. Now head for the Kaymoor parking lot upstream.

This canine hike begins like many others - on a rough woods path descending towards the river. In short order, you reach the overgrown remnants of an abandoned coal mine opened in 1899. The coal and coke were transported for processing at the river's edge 1,000 feet down the slope by incline railroad.

That is the destination down those wooden steps. The structures of the mining community burned to the ground in 1960 but Seaman can still sniff around mining machinery and coke ovens. The New River is renowned for its world-class rapids but the waters here are fine for a refreshing doggie dip in preparation for the climb back up the daunting 821 steps.

71

OHIOPYLE STATE PARK

Fernwood Trail

OHIOPYLE, PENNSYLVANIA

Hiking Time: 1-2 hours

E △ ☜

Your trail dog can find just about anything on his wish list at Ohiopyle State Park featuring its star attraction, the energetic Youghiogheny River. Waterfalls. Swimming holes. Overlooks. Easy hikes. Vigorous workouts. Check, check, check, check, and check.

The mandatory canine hike is luckily the easiest and most centrally located - the three miles of trails that sweep around and across the Ferncliff Peninsula, where the "Yough" doubles back on itself. In 1973 the Ferncliff Peninsula was declared a National Natural Landmark in recognition of its rare and intriguing plants, many being Southern species at the northern reach of their growing range. Hugging the water for most of its 1.7 miles, the hemlock-draped *Fernwood Trail* leads Seaman to detours through mature hardwoods, carpets of ferns, and past resort hotel ruins.

The famous Lower Yough begins after the Ohiopyle Falls and flows seven miles downstream to the Bruner Run Take-Out. This is the busiest section of whitewater east of the Mississippi River, studded with Class III and Class IV rapids. A half-dozen alone can be viewed from the *Ferncliff Trail*.

Elsewhere, The *Youghiogheny River Trail* is a hike/bike trail so fine that it was tabbed by *Travel & Leisure* magazine as one of the "The World's Best Walks." Seaman won't have to do all 27 miles through the park to agree. That would be a highlight of most parks; here it is scarcely a footnote.

PICKETT STATE PARK AND FOREST

Hidden Passage Trail

JAMESTOWN, TENNESSEE

Hiking Time: 4-5 hours

M △ ☜

Situated in a remote section of the upper Cumberland Mountains, the 17,000 acres of Pickett State Park and Forest, once owned by the massive Stearns Coal & Lumber Company, became one of Tennessee's earliest state parks in the 1930s. **Here are botanical and geological wonders Seaman will find nowhere else in Tennessee**. The Civilian Conservation Corps set up shop in the dark forest during the Great Depression and crafted enough buildings of locally quarried sandstone that the park is listed on the National Register of Historic Places.

With 58 miles of hiking trails you could hunker down with Seaman for a week in these hollows but the attraction of Pickett for most canine adventurers is that most of the more accessible trails are short, ranging from a quarter-mile to three miles so you can sample many of them with your dog in a short visit.

The *Hidden Passage Trail* launches just across the street from the park office but it doesn't take long to feel as if civilization has been left far behind. The big loop ducks in and out of rock houses and slides past waterfalls in its nearly ten miles. Expect to linger with Seaman at the stunning Thompson Overlook.

Pickett is a wild place and trail maintenance may be spottier than the groomed pathways prized in some parks; also make sure you secure a good map to help with the abundance of spur trails. Don't count on Seaman to always find the way.

ROCK ISLAND STATE PARK

Downstream/Upstream Trail

ROCK ISLAND, TENNESSEE
Hiking Time: 2-3 hours

M △ ≈•

There are ten waterfalls in the Caney Fork River Gorge that hog most of the attention at Rock Island State Park. Unlike many waterfalls in the Volunteer State these provide year-round displays thanks to the power-generating Great Falls Dam. The most impressive show, put on by the 80-foot plunges at Twin Falls, aren't entirely natural as the water pouring down the gorge walls is overflow from the nearby Collins River being diverted to the powerplant.

Twin Falls is the demarcation point for the *Downstream* and *Upstream* trails across the gorge. **While the wide curtain-style falls win admiration from waterfall hunters Seaman is likely to prefer Little Falls where he can play in the long cascade that crosses the Downstream Trail**. The side trail up the falls (or in the falls) leads to natural caves for Seaman to explore.

The *Downstream Trail* is a balloon loop that covers 1.55 miles through a leaf-littered hardwood forest. You are never far from the rushing river, including the popular kayak plunge into a rock-ringed section of the gorge known as the Blue Hole.

The *Upstream Trail* is a different hiking beast altogether. It is much shorter and works its way under and around the rock bluffs. As you work your way through with Seaman and onto rocks that have clearly spent time underwater keep in mind that dam releases take place on an irregular schedule and if you hear a siren it is time to skedaddle back to higher ground pronto.

SPRUCE KNOB-SENECA ROCKS RECREATION AREA

Seneca Rocks Trail

SENECA ROCKS, WEST VIRGINIA
Hiking Time: 2 hours

M △

Legend has it that the spectacular crags of white/gray quartzite that soar 900 feet above the flat valley of the North Fork of the Potomac River were the childhood playground of Snowbird, beautiful daughter of Seneca Indian chief Bald Eagle. To determine the warrior who would win her hand in marriage she staged a contest to see who could scale the magnificent cliff.

The first documented roped ascent of the Seneca Rocks, however, took place in 1935. Today there are nearly 400 mapped climbing routes on the rocks. In 1969 the federal government purchased the West Virginia landmark and pieced together the national recreation area with Spruce Knob (the nearby roof of West Virginia) within the Monongahela National Forest.

Seaman can forego the spring-loaded cams, nuts, and quickdraws to get to the top of the Seneca Rocks unaided on foot. A 1.3-mile hard-packed trail ascends the north edge of the rock formation to reach a wooden viewing platform. **There are enough switchbacks and steps to enable any dog to conquer the Mountain State's most recognizable landmark**.

Sure-footed dogs can climb a bit further up bare rock to notches at the very top of the formation for views of the Allegheny Mountains to the west. One view you will most certainly have is of your vehicle down below in the parking lot.

SWALLOW FALLS STATE PARK

Falls Trail

OAKLAND, MARYLAND
Hiking Time: 1 hour

E A 🏊

By 1900, out of every five trees that stood east of the Mississippi River in Colonial days, only one survived. It was highly unusual to see any big tree in Maryland that had escaped a logger's saw, unless it was too costly to reach.

That was the case with the grove of white pines and hemlocks at Swallow Falls. The giants are the oldest in Maryland - some trees are estimated to be 375 years old. Philanthropist Henry Krug refused to allow the trees to be harvested in the gorge and when a World War I plan to dam the Youghiogheny River fell through their survival was assured.

The *Falls Trail* navigates through this natural arboreal museum on its way to Muddy Creek Falls, Maryland's highest single water plunge at 53 feet. Although your best trail companion won't get overheated under the cool, dark hemlocks **there are many enticing doggie swimming holes on the one-mile loop along the Youghiogheny River and Muddy Creek that will set tails to wagging**.

If Seaman is hankering for more trail time there is a 5.5-mile out-and-back trail to Herrington Manor State Park (no dogs allowed once you get there). You'll get more water views and more giant hemlocks - be advised that this canine hike involves a stream crossing that may not be doable in times of high water.

WILLIAM B. BANKHEAD NATIONAL FOREST

Trail 209: Sipsey River Trail

MT. HOPE, ALABAMA
Hiking Time: 2-3 hours

M A 🏊 🚙

With nearly 25,000 acres under protection, this is the third largest wilderness area in the country east of the Mississippi River. Wild-flowing creeks in northwestern Alabama converge to become the Sipsey River, 61 miles of which has been designated Wild and Scenic. Enough water tumbles over cracks in limestone foundations that Sipsey, a part of the Bankhead National Forest, has been hailed as the "Land of 1,000 Waterfalls."

The Sipsey Wilderness is a popular backpacking destination for planting yourself in a camp and exploring the region with your dog on foot. Many of the waterfalls can't be reached by trail regardless - when you hear falling water start bushwhacking through the forest to find the source, often drips over wide, moss-covered rock ledges.

Canine day hikers favor *Trail 209* that links several of the established dirt passages through the unmarked wilderness. Fall Creek Falls, a 90-foot waterspout near the convergence of the Sipsey River and Fall Creek splashes onto a jumble of boulders directly on the trail.

Traveling south from the Borden Creek Bridge trailhead the journey is less than three miles; **this is as lovely a hike as you can take with your dog to a waterfall but involves a water crossing on a sandy creek bed and a memorable 100-foot passage for Seaman through a narrow rock cave** (remember, this is a wilderness).

Gulf Coast

Apalachicola National Forest

Sinkhole Trail
TALLAHASSEE, FLORIDA
Hiking Time: 1-2 hours

E Δ

Leon Sinks is in the heart of the Woodville Karst Plain, a vast area of porous limestone bedrock that stretches for 450 square miles from Tallahassee south to the Gulf of Mexico. The terrain is shaped by rain and groundwater that dissolve the limestone to form sinkholes, swales and underground caverns. A mapping project in 1988 confirmed that the Leon Sinks underwater cave system is the largest known in the United States - over 41,000 feet of passages.

The *Sinkhole Trail* connects more than a dozen sinkholes, some dry and some filled with water. Boardwalk observation decks provide close-up views. The deepest is the Big Dismal Sink at 130 feet. Keep a close hold on Seaman around these sinks - they have steep walls and dogs - and people - have drowned at Leon Sinks.

This is one of the best hikes you can take with your trail dog in Northwest Florida. From the tupelo gum swamps to the sandy ridges it is difficult to experience a more diverse plant world along the trail. At Big Dismal Sink alone more than 75 different plants cascade down the sink's conical walls.

None of the underground limestone penetrates the ground so the trails are paw-friendly sand and a joy for your dog. That includes the connecting *Gunswamp Trail* - sinkholes are formed by the underwater aquifer, swamps are created by surface water.

Avery Island Jungle Gardens

Interpretive Trail
AVERY ISLAND, LOUISIANA
Hiking Time: 1-2 hours

E $ 🚙

Edmund McIlhenny came to his wife's ancestral home on Avery Island in the Louisiana bayou as refuge during the Civil War. The family island yielded rock salt - the nation's first salt mine is there - and it wasn't long until Union troops arrived seeking salt to preserve meat to feed the troops. McIlhenny set out for Texas.

When he returned the family plantation was in tatters. The only thing still growing was a patch of hearty Capsicum peppers. From these humble plants would sprout an empire. McIlhenny chopped the peppers and blended them with vinegar and Avery Island salt. While the fiery potion aged in wooden barrels he came up with a name he liked from a river in southern Mexico - "Tabasco." The spicy sauce was an immediate hit and McIlhenny sold millions of tiny bottles until his death in 1890.

His son Ned, an arctic explorer and naturalist, converted a sand mining pit into a "jungle garden" with 400 varieties of camellias and thousands of types of iris. **Most people tour the gardens in vehicles but get out and walk Seaman to truly soak in the sub-tropical atmosphere of the plantings**. Mix the hard-packed road and walking paths into a three-mile circuit under tunnels of gorgeous live oaks and around moody lagoons. Highlights include an 800-year old Buddha statue and Bird City, a bird sanctuary started in 1895 to save the snowy egret that was rapidly being exterminated for its feathers to decorate ladies' hats.

BALD POINT
STATE PARK

Sun Dew Loop
ALLIGATOR POINT, FLORIDA
Hiking Time: 1-2 hours

E 🏊 $

BIG THICKET
NATIONAL PRESERVE

Kirby Nature Trail/Sandhill Loop Trail
KOUNTZE, TEXAS
Hiking Time: 2-3 hours

E 🏊

Seaman is not likely to soon forget this hike on Florida's Forgotten Coast. Not many canine hikers make their way to Alligator Point where Ochlockonee Bay meets Apalachee Bay in the Gulf of Mexico. Even then most visitors overlook the 18 miles of trails that ramble through coastal marshes, oak thickets, and pine flatwoods. Bald Point is so uncrowded even the rarely seen Florida black bear is known to show up on the beach for a swim.

The *Sun Dew Loop* is the ideal introduction to the undeveloped Bald Point where Florida looks like it always has. The 1.7 miles travel exclusively in sparse pine flatwoods and open prairie where shade is just a rumor so come prepared. The saw palmetto understory is desert-like so views will be long, even for short trail dogs. The upland terrain is studded with wildflowers poking out into the salt air and many namesake carnivorous sundew plants that trap insects in their sticky tentacles.

All Seaman's hiking at Bald Point will be on sand-based natural trails. The *Sun Dew Loop* runs into the *Tucker Loop* that visits a large saltwater lake and is the park's most rigorous test at over six miles, including a detour to an abandoned World War II gun range. Old logging roads are more the norm here than footpaths. Near the end of Bald Point don't miss the *Maritime Hammock Loop* where Seaman will bound through the dunes under ancient oaks before touching on the Gulf of Mexico in a one-mile loop.

The Big Thicket spent millions of years under the Gulf of Mexico until the sea settled in its current position. The receding waters and an ice age left behind one of the most biodiverse lands in America. Here southeastern swamps mingle with eastern hardwood forests and midwestern prairie collides with a southwestern desert landscape. So many different animals live here that the Preserve has been called an "American ark." The Big Thicket even hosts four of the six species of insect gobbling carnivorous plants in the United States.

The *Kirby Nature Trail*, with a series of stacked loops, takes Seaman through several of these plant communities. **Well-maintained footpaths make this easy going under paw in woods so dense and tangled they support claims of the Texas Bigfoot**. Wooden boardwalks and bridges take care of low-lying areas like the extensive cypress slough and the riparian environment along Village Creek.

The *Sandhills Loop Trail* branches off across Village Creek. The longleaf pines here were once so abundant that all of East Texas was known as the Piney Woods. Today they occupy only 3% of their historic range; these are third growth. There is enough elevation here for prickly pear, yucca, and other desert plants to thrive in the sandhills. The two loops cover five miles for Seaman and if you've brought a checklist you may have marked off some of the 1,000 species of plants and 60 species of mammals in Big Thicket.

Camp Helen State Park

Oak Canopy Trail

PANAMA CITY BEACH, FLORIDA
Hiking Time: 1 hour

E △ 🏊 $

It is easy to blow past Camp Helen when traveling along US 98 and that would be a loss for your trail-loving dog. **There is only one trail in the park, covering a bit over one mile, but it is sure to be one of Seaman's favorites**.

Camp Helen began life as a family retreat and then operated as a resort for vacationing workers from Avondale Mills in nearby Alabama. Several buildings remain from its mid-20th century origins.

After exploring the opulent log lodge and cottages the trail drops to the shores of Lake Powell, one of Florida's largest examples of a rare coastal dune lake. Moving on, Seaman is soon traversing a salt marsh before bursting onto the wide, sugary sands of the Gulf of Mexico. Although he can't continue all the way to the Inlet Beach proper, this is one of the few places Seaman can trot the sands, see the waves and at least feel like it's a day at the beach.

Before he can get too giddy, however, the trail crosses the dunes into a dense maritime hammock and the shade of moss-draped live oaks and tall pines. The wide, sandy path swings past Duck Pond before finishing back among the camp buildings of the old resort.

Camp Helen is believed to be haunted by tragedies that have occurred here over the centuries, dating back to the visitation of high-seas pirates. So, if Seaman seems restless on the trail for no apparent reason here, pay close attention.

Colt Creek State Park

Orange Trail

LAKELAND, FLORIDA
Hiking Time: 2-3 hours

E $

It was not until the last of the Overstreet beef cattle were driven from the 5,000-acre ranch that Colt Creek became Florida's 160th state park in 2006. For canine hikers, it was worth the wait.

Second only to the Everglades in wildlife abundance in Florida, the headwaters of the Peace River, Withlacoochee River, Ocklawaha River, and Hillsborough River course through the Green Swamp. Colt Creek is one of the many tributaries that create this hydrological treasure.

This is the place on the Florida Suncoast to go for big, solitary hikes with your dog. There are over 12 miles of trails, mostly wide, grassy roads tripping through airy pine flatwoods. The star walk is the multi-hour excursion on the *Orange Trail* loop. **Simply point Seaman down the orange blazes or craft a canine hiking day with blue-blazed side trails and cut-offs**. Most of his time will be spent with the saw palmetto and longleaf pines but the needle-blanketed trails also touch on the expanses of heritage pastureland where Seaman can channel his inner cattle dog.

Lime rock mining was carried on here for decades - the lakes in the park are artifacts of the old mining pits. You can still spot large lime rocks as you hike with your dog on the Colt Creek trails; if you don't see any "wild rocks" in the woods you can see lime rocks used as roadway barriers.

DAUPHIN ISLAND PARK AND BEACH

Dune Edge Trail
DAUPHIN, ALABAMA
Hiking Time: 2-3 hours

E ⛺ 🏊 $

Dauphin Island is your go-to beach destination with Seaman between Florida and Texas. There is more here for your dog than a romp in the sugar sands of the Gulf of Mexico, however.

Three miles of tightly packed trails course through the Audubon Bird Sanctuary where 420 of the 445 avian species documented in Alabama have been spotted. The centerpiece of the trail system is the freshwater Gaillard Lake surrounded by a richly diversified maritime forest. An occasional alligator can be spotted from the elevated boardwalk.

The *Dune Edge Trail* is a half-mile excursion through a beach meadow that spills onto an undeveloped beach at either end. To the west you can walk with Seaman for miles, including to Pelican Island which has become a sandy peninsula within the past twenty years. If Seaman chooses to swim out in the calm waters of the back bay he will likely be joining an armada of windsurfers.

Walking east along the shore will soon enough find low-lying dunes and scruffy gray sands on a half-mile beach canine hike to Fort Gaines at the eastern tip of the island. The brick bulwark of the Confederacy was a focal point of the critical Battle of Mobile Bay when victorious Union admiral David Farragut issued his famous war cry, "Damn the torpedoes! Full speed ahead!" Civil War cannons surround the fort and at the entrance Seaman can pose with the huge anchor and chain from Farragut's flagship, *Hartford*.

FLORIDA CAVERNS STATE PARK

Visitor Center Trail
MARIANNA, FLORIDA
Hiking Time: 1 hour

E ⛺ $

It has only been the blink of an eye, geologically speaking, that Florida has not been under water. During its time undersea, coral, shellfish, and marine skeletons piled up. This created a layer of limestone hundreds of feet thick. When the sea level fell, acidic groundwater gradually dissolved the porous limestone to form cracks and passages. **The result is that in this part of the Florida panhandle the rock has been pushed up and Seaman gets to trot across some sizable hills**.

The delightful *Visitor Center Trail* is the only Florida coastal hike that winds through rocky terrain - a fairy garden of whimsical limestone formations. Towering hardwoods frame the footpath as it visits twenty-foot vertical bluffs above the floodplain and descends down to swampland where tupelo gums are anchored in the soggy soil.

And the caverns? Altogether, there are 10 acres of caves here. Seaman can't take the tour through limestone stalactites, stalagmites, soda straws, flowstones, and draperies but can find his own unique 100-foot underground adventure through Tunnel Cave.

For longer, albeit more traditional Florida hiking fare, head up to the multi-use *Upper Chipola Trails* that explore the basin of the Chipola River. The waterway collects flow from 63 springs, the largest number of any rivershed in Northwest Florida. There are more than six miles of shaded woodland trails across the rolling terrain to entertain Seaman here.

GRAND ISLE STATE PARK

Fiddlers Loop Trail
GRAND ISLE, LOUISIANA
Hiking Time: 1-2 hours

E Δ ⚊ $

Resting on the eastern tip of Louisiana's only inhabited barrier island deep in the Gulf of Mexico, *Fiddlers Loop Trail* takes more punches from nature than just about any other footpath in America. A hurricane arrives, on average, every three years. This century alone Isidore, Lili, Cindy, Katrina, Rita, and Gustav all have visited.

Despite the occasional upheavals and the crush of summer visitors a stick's throw away, this is an exceedingly tranquil canine hike, circling a lagoon for about 2.5 miles. The south side of the loop travels through a tidal marsh and the trail through the grasses can range from slippery under paw to out and out flooded. Those namesake fiddlers crabs are much in evidence as are just about every species of American shorebird.

A long wooden boardwalk - a popular roosting spot for brown pelicans - crosses the lagoon and deposits canine hikers in a long alley of wildflower-bearing bushes. The splashes of year-round color continue all along the northern side of the loop.

Following the *Fiddlers Loop Trail* hike Seaman can climb the six-story park observation tower for views of the gulf and Grand Terre Island to the north where pirate captain Jean Lafitte and his band of salty sea dogs once holed up. He is not allowed on the beach but for fun in the waves head next door to the town and miles of tail-friendly sand on one of Louisiana's rare beaches. Grand Isle tilts just enough to the northeast for splendid beach sunrises.

GULF ISLANDS NATIONAL SEASHORE

Brackenridge Nature Trail
GULF BREEZE, FLORIDA
Hiking Time: 1-2 hours

E ⚊

Live oak trees, prized for their rot-resistant and incredibly dense wood, have long been the lumber of choice for building durable sailing ships. President John Quincy Adams, who considered the United States Navy, to be "our wooden walls," started America's first tree farm here in 1828 for the single purpose of growing live oaks for shipbuilding.

More than seven miles of hiking trails explore these historic forests. The *Brackenridge Nature Trail* is a good place to start on the south side of US 98 where exhibits describe how live oaks were used in shipbuilding. There are always leaves on the footpath under live oaks since the trees lose their leaves at different times, hence, they always appear to be "live." Laid out in a figure-eight, this lush, narrow pathway runs along a bluff above the Santa Rosa Sound. **Seaman can also leave behind the casual strollers and continue down the 1.2-mile *Fishing Trail* through the thin strip of live oak forest**.

Across the highway, Seaman can stretch out on the sandy and wide *Andrew Jackson Trail*, a two-miler that runs the entire length of the Naval Live Oaks property. This time-worn path is a remnant of the Pensacola-St. Augustine Road, the first road connecting East Florida to West Florida. Detours here lead to Brown Pond and while not allowed on the Gulf of Mexico beach there are spots Seaman can slip into the Santa Rosa Sound for a swim.

HILLSBOROUGH RIVER STATE PARK

Seminole Trail

ZEPHYRHILLS, FLORIDA
Hiking Time: 2-3 hours

E △ $

What are those strange things in the water your trail dog may wonder at Hillsborough River? Indeed, those are the only Class II rapids on the Florida peninsula where the average elevation is about six feet. **There are just enough Suwannee limestone outcroppings in the river to inject the sound of rushing water into this canine hike**.

The jungle-like woodlands that envelop the Hillsborough River demand Seaman's notice as well. In addition to the requisite Florida sabal palms there are cypress-filled wetlands and groves of wild citrus trees. Just the tiniest bit of elevation brings stands of hickory and sweetgum. On the bluffs above the river are amazing ancient live oaks. It is little wonder this slice of "wild Florida" was one of the nine original state parks created in the 1930s.

The *Seminole Trail* loop visits them all, spending half of its 3.4 miles hard by the river and half inland. Since the canine hiking is on the north side of the Hillsborough River and the main park is on the south side a swinging wooden suspension bridge gets you started. The beautiful rustic structure was built by the Civilian Conservation Corps when the park opened. Two shorter loops, the *Rapid River Nature Trail* and the *Baynard Trail*, complete Seaman's day along the blackwater river. That day should begin with a moment at the "Prayer of the Woods" sign posted at the trailhead, a bit of wisdom from Portugal to launch your canine hike in the right spirit.

HONEYMOON ISLAND STATE PARK

Osprey Trail/Pelican Trail

DUNEDIN, FLORIDA
Hiking Time: 1-2 hours

E 🏊 $

Honeymoon Island is the best place to hike with your dog along the Gulf of Mexico on the Florida peninsula. The island was cleaved from a larger island by the Hurricane of 1921 and purchased by Tampa entrepreneur Clinton Washburn. The undeveloped island had been used to raise hogs but the new proprietor cooked up a scheme with *Life* magazine in 1940 for a contest to win Florida honeymoons. Thatched bungalows were hurriedly built and 164 enraptured couples enjoyed all-expenses-paid nuptial trips before World War II intervened.

The *Osprey Trail* runs up the spine of a sand spit for over one mile, working through one of Florida's last old growth slash pine forests with trees almost 200 years old. It is all easy trotting for Seaman on a mixture of grass and sand under paw. Inverted osprey nests can be spied in the bare pine snags. Bald eagles have also arrived in recent years. Interpretive stops explain the barrier island's unique ecology.

At the end of the spit the canine hike moves onto the *Pelican Trail* for the return trip along the shoreline, dominated by black and red mangroves. This will be slower going, both because of the luxurious sugar sand on the trail and the time your water-loving dog will be spending in the gentle waters of Pelican Bay.

Oh, and about those honeymooners. In 1991, those celebrating their golden anniversaries were invited back, including Althea Meyer and her husband, Fido.

81

PADRE ISLAND
NATIONAL SEASHORE

Grasslands Nature Trail

CORPUS CHRISTI, TEXAS
Hiking Time: 1 hour+

E △ 🏊 $ 🚙

Everything is bigger in Texas. It just is. That includes the world's longest undeveloped barrier island. Seaman can romp for over 65 miles and see nothing but surf and dunes.

Across the Intracoastal Waterway in the 19th century Richard King was running longhorn cattle and building the largest ranch in Texas. Most ranchers who got squeezed out headed west but Patrick Dunn moved east and bought most of Padre Island for his herds. Save for a scattering of hermits who got by salvaging the wreckage from Gulf ships the cattle were the primary residents of Padre Island.

The *Grasslands Nature Trail* recalls this legacy as the macadam path moves easily through low-covered dunes. Wildflowers proliferate in the sandy spray and the prairies are alive with vibrant wildflowers waving in the breeze year-round (the average wind speed is 11 mph). **The songs of birds fill your dog's ears and sandhill cranes can be spotted nesting in the grasses and ponds early in the year**.

The mile-long nature loop is across from Malaquite Beach, the main vehicle-free area on Padre Island. For less communal hiking with your dog head to South Beach where the first five miles of sand are suitable for all vehicles. Beyond that the primitive beach sand turns soft. Seaman can find quite an array of curiosities on this hike as anything tossed into the Gulf of Mexico, including objects from offshore gas platforms, eventually washes up here.

RAINBOW SPRINGS
STATE PARK

Sandhills Nature Trail

DUNNELLON, FLORIDA
Hiking Time: 1 hour

E △ $

There was a time before Mickey Mouse when families would come to Florida to ride through jungle-like forests on glass-bottomed boats and watch fish swim in the crystalline rivers. Rainbow River, pouring from Florida's fourth largest spring, may have been the most beautiful. Before the tourists, this area was the first in Florida to be mined for phosphate, triggering a major industry in the Sunshine State.

The *Sandhills Nature Trail* illuminates both eras of Rainbow Spring's colorful past. Some of the deep pits around the spring were planted with thousands of flowering azaleas and camellias. Others were turned into man-made waterfalls. From there the wide, sandy footpath leads away from the hustle and bustle of tourist life on the river into a natural oak hammock.

Seaman will soon be bounding up and over more undulating terrain than normally encountered in Florida, courtesy of some very extremely aggressive digging in the limestone. The spoil piles and mine pits are mostly recovered by saw palmetto and slash pines these days. This is how nature reclaims the land and you will be treated to a pine needle-and-leaf covered landscape as far as Seaman's eye can see.

The *Sandhills Nature Trail* has more surprises in store, including overlooks of the Rainbow River, a National Natural Landmark, and time in a romp-worthy old pasture. The loop through the sandhills community comprises nearly three miles.

ST. GEORGE ISLAND STATE PARK

Gap Point Nature Trail

ST. GEORGE ISLAND, FLORIDA
Hiking Time: 2-3 hours

M A ≈ $

You can just about count the number of Florida panhandle Gulf of Mexico beaches that welcome dogs on one paw. St. George Island, a narrow 22-mile strip of land that creates oyster-rich Apalachicola Bay, is one of those places so you can be sure many dog owners will want to make their way across the Bryant G. Patton Bridge to the park where nine miles of beaches and dunes have been spared from development.

As a bonus for canine hikers who want more than a long walk on a sparkling white unspoiled beach the *Gap Point Nature Trail* offers a 2.5-mile ribbon of sand road through slash pine forests and hearty coastal scrub. In days gone by turpentiners made their way to this island four miles offshore to tap the large pines for naval stores. Many "cat-face" scars can still be seen in tree trunks on this canine hike.

Elevation change will be minimal, save for the occasional dune, but the sugar sands will take their toll on weary legs. **As you close in on Gap Point at the end of the peninsula opportunities for Seaman to jump into the friendly waters of Apalachicola Bay will come in a flurry**. The bayside beach is studded with photogenic ghost trees and a few surviving arboreal warriors still waging the good fight at land's end. All provide perches for a variety of seabirds and ample ammunition for a game of fetch in the Gulf of Mexico before retracing the sandy pawprints to the trailhead.

TATE'S HELL STATE FOREST

High Bluff Coastal Hiking Trail

CARRABELLE, FLORIDA
Hiking Time: several hours possible

E A 🚙

Your dog is likely to figure he is closer to heaven than hell when hiking here. Tate's Hell State Forest has only one dedicated hiking trail but it is a beauty. The *High Bluff Coastal Hiking Trail* is a linear 4-mile, natural surface pathway through a coastal scrub habitat. The ancient sand dunes have been colonized by small oaks, saw palmetto, and isolated groups of sand pines that let plenty of sunlight in along the trail. When the route drops off the ridge, the scrub gives way to shady pines.

Under paw Seaman will enjoy a soft sand and pine straw surface along the roomy path. Up above, eagles and osprey soar and a Florida black bear may even stray this far down to the coast.

Among the signature trees in Tate's Hell State Forest are several stands of the distinctive "dwarf cypress." These trees have been growing since the Civil War but are still only 15 feet tall. "Hatrack cypress" are a puzzle to biologists - if seeds from these cypress trees are planted in another location they grow to their normal height.

And why was this Cebe Tate's "hell?" Seems in 1875 Tate was tracking a panther that had killed some of his livestock and wandered into the swamp. After a week he burst into a clearing near Carrabelle, living long enough only to murmur the words, "My name is Cebe Tate, and I just came from Hell!" His hunting dogs survived the ordeal - and probably even enjoyed the outing.

TOPSAIL HILL PRESERVE STATE PARK

Morris Lake Nature Trail

SANTA ROSA BEACH, FLORIDA
Hiking Time: 2 hours

M ▲ $

Topsail Hill is the best place on the Florida coast that you can take your dog for an extended hike along the Gulf of Mexico. The trail of choice is the *Morris Lake Nature Trail*, a 2.5-mile balloon route laid out through ancient coastal dunes. The park takes its name from the landmark 25-foot high dune that resembles a ship's topsail.

The tramping is wide open and exposed to the elements so bring plenty of water for Seaman on a hot day and since every step of the way is across glistening white soft sugar sand, he will get a workout any time of the year. In fact, look for iron tracks laid down during World War II that allowed heavy trucks to travel across the thick sand when these dunes were used as a bombing range.

There are 14 identifiable eco-systems, including freshwater coastal dune lakes, wet prairies, scrub, pine at- woods, marshes, cypress domes, seepage slopes, and 3.2 miles of white sand beaches - the remnants of quartz washed down from the Appalachian Mountains.

Morris Lake is one of three freshwater coastal dune lakes on the property. These rare oases are found only along the Gulf Coast in America and while tempting to visit for your dog, are inhabited by alligators. The trail climbs briefly into a Florida shrub community where Seaman can find some shade among the sand pines and shrubby oaks before finishing along the Gulf of Mexico beach.

 ## TORREYA STATE PARK

Torreya Challenge

ROCK BLUFF, FLORIDA
Hiking Time: 3 hours

M ▲ $

Hardy Bryan Croom, a planter and naturalist of some renown, began amassing land in northern Florida in the 1820s and purchased 640 acres of the Lafayette Land Grant for what would become Goodwood Plantation. While exploring from his cotton plantation, Croom discovered one of the rarest conifers in the world growing along the banks of the Apalachicola River. He named the small evergreen "torreya" after the botanist Dr. John Torrey. It would turn out the torreya was native to only six spots in the world - one in California, four in Japan and China, and on the bluffs of the Apalachicola.

There are two hiking loops at Torreya, each about seven miles around. Along the Apalachicola River the *Rock Bluff Trail* dips and rolls through ravines and the *Torreya Challenge* in the eastern section of the park. **This is the best workout Seaman can get in Northwest Florida, hiking across terrain more familiar in Appalachian foothills**. He will think he has left Florida on this scenic ramble.

Indeed, the mix of hardwoods thriving at the various elevations in the park conspire to whip up Florida's best display of autumn colors - Seaman will find the elusive torreya trees mostly in the ravines cut by the streams forging their way to the Apalachicola River.

Great Lakes

Indiana
145. Indiana Dunes National Lakeshore
146. Indiana Dunes State Park

Michigan
140. Grand Island NRA
141. Hiawatha National Forest
144. Huron-Manistee National Forests
148. Mackinac Island State Park
150. Pictured Rocks National
      Lakeshore
151. Porcupine Mountains Wilderness
      State Park
154. Sleeping Bear Dunes National
      Lakeshore
156. Tahquamenon Falls State Park

Minnesota
139. Gooseberry Falls State Park
155. Split Rock Lighthouse State Park
157. Tettegouche State Park

New York
149. Niagara Falls State Park

Ohio
137. Cuyahoga Valley National Park
142. Hinckley Reservation
143. Holden Arboretum

Pennsylvania
153. Presque Isle State Park

Wisconsin
136. Apostle Islands National Seashore
138. Devil's Lake State Park
147. Iron County Forest
152. Potawatomi State Park
158. Whitefish Dunes State Park

APOSTLE ISLANDS NATIONAL LAKESHORE

Lakeshore Trail

LAKE SUPERIOR, WISCONSIN
Hiking Time: 2-3 hours

M △ ⌁ $

Most of the action at Apostle Islands is offshore on 21 bejeweled Lake Superior islands. Dogs are allowed anywhere in the park but they are not allowed on the boat shuttle to the islands so, save for a private boat, there is no hiking with Seaman out there.

Instead, dog owners will want to head to Meyers Beach and the one hiking path on the mainland. Here the *Lakeshore Trail* rambles 4.5 miles to a primitive campground. Things begins benignly enough on a long boardwalk before taking on some rough terrain. Slopes climb sharply and streams have carved small ravines on their way to Lake Superior. Most canine hikers will turn around after two miles where there are unprotected overlooks of sea caves below.

The west end of Meyers Beach offers a wonderful time for Seaman on a long crescent of unspoiled coarse sand. Driftwood is in abundance for your favorite fetcher. Add hours of beachwalking to your dog's day on the Wisconsin shoreline here.

Everyone gets excited when the winter chill freezes the Lake Superior waters along Meyers Beach. It doesn't happen every year but conditions are eagerly monitored when temperatures drop. When the ice is thick enough you can visit those sea caves you hiked above that are now dressed in icicles and ice crystals. **You may be able to hike over the ice with your dog, ski with your dog, snowshoe with your dog, or take your personal sled dog team to the caves**.

CUYAHOGA VALLEY NATIONAL PARK

Ledges Trail

BRECKSVILLE, OHIO
Hiking Time: 1 hour

E △ ⌁

Raise your hand if you knew that America's first national park of the 21st Century was created in..............Cleveland? To the first people who came here 12,000 years ago the Cuyahoga was the "crooked river." Locals began coming to the orange and yellow rock formations on William Ritchie's land to picnic as early as the 19th century.

As befits its history as a recreation destination, the steep-valleyed Cuyahoga permits dogs on its trails. It doesn't have the feel of the grand American national parks but instead evokes an intimate feel on the trails that are squeezed between highways, farmlands and neighborhoods.

The main path through the park is the nearly 20 miles of the *Towpath Trail* along the route of the historic Ohio & Erie Canal. Ten trailheads make it easy to hike the crushed limestone path in biscuit-size chunks.

The easy-trotting ramble around Ritchie Ledges covers 2.2 miles in a loop that hugs the towering rock formations shrouded in virgin hemlocks and yellow birches. **There are plenty of cracks and crevasses for Seaman to investigate, including Ice Box Cave that disappears 50 feet into the Ledges**. Be on the lookout for profiles of men and a horse carved into the rock face by pioneer farmers.

The west-facing overlook is a popular destination on the *Ledges Trail*, especially at sunset. Many connector trails also tap into the park's larger hiking network, including a refreshing sojourn to Kendall Lake.

Devil's Lake State Park

East Bluff/East Bluff Woods Trails

BARABOO, WISCONSIN
Hiking Time: 2-3 hours

M A ⚊ $

Devil's Lake State Park is one of the highlights of the Wisconsin cross-state *Ice Age Trail* but only a portion of this stunning landscape is attributed to the crunching of glaciers. The quartzite bluffs ringing the lake are remnants of the Baraboo Hills that are much older - 1.6 billion years old, when the mountains were taller than the Rockies.

This is one of Wisconsin's most popular parks but one way to shed the crowds is to tackle the *East Bluff Trail* with Seaman. **The paw-friendly route uses natural dirt and rock steps to ascend 500-foot bluffs leading to calendar-worthy observation points of Devil's Lake**. Short loop trails take in rock formations such as Devil's Doorway and Balanced Rock that you will be certain were sculpted by man, not nature.

The Baraboo Hills are home to one of the largest contiguous deciduous forests in the Midwest and on top of East Bluff is one of the most magical. Here the shagbark hickories and white ash trees struggle with nutrient-deficient soils on the super hard quartzite and have only reached 20 feet tall after 125 years of growth. You could wrap Seaman's collar around the trunks of some of the stunted trees in the pygmy forest.

The *East Bluff Woods Trail* dials down the excitement and returns your dog away from the cliffs through an airy forest highlighted by a tumbling stream to complete a 3.5-mile loop. Or retrace pawprints along the bluff for even more views in the opposite direction.

Gooseberry Falls State Park

Fifth Falls Loop Trail

TWO HARBORS, MINNESOTA
Hiking Time: 1-2 hours

E A ⚊

The westernmost edge of Lake Superior is characterized by craggy headlands blanketed in thick coatings of pine and birch. Along the coast dozens of fast-flowing streams are cascading down small mountains to mingle with the waters of the Great Lakes.

Five of those hard-charging water spouts surge down the Gooseberry River on Minnesota's North Shore. **The Upper, Middle, and Lower Falls hog most of the visitors with easy access on stairways and boardwalks so canine hikers will want to aim inland for Fifth Falls**. It is actually possible to access the Gooseberry River trail system from a wayside right on Highway 61.

The *Fifth Falls Trail* uses a segment of the 300+-mile *Superior Hiking Trail* to create a two-mile loop around the park's smallest water display. A bridge across the top of the falls links the two streamside paths.

Although hilly this ramble is never taxing for Seaman and there are calm spots to host a doggie dip. The hiking path combines boardwalk, gravel and dirt surfaces. Distinctive multi-colored rock structures built by the Civilian Conservation Corps during the 1930s enliven the landscape.

The appeal of this away-from-the-crowds outing will likely spark Seaman's desire for more adventure in the North Woods and a series of short canine hiking loops penetrate both sides of the Gooseberry River from Fifth Falls. Don't be so quick to put that leash away.

GRAND ISLAND NATIONAL RECREATION AREA

Thumb Trail

MUNISING, MICHIGAN
Hiking Time: 2-3 hours

E △ ⤳ $

Grand Island is the largest island in south Lake Superior, about the size of Manhattan. It is only a ten-minute ride across the perpetual 48-degree waters on a small boat that holds about a half-dozen people and dogs. **The ferry makes only a handful of trips a day so you can expect hiking with Seaman along wide dirt and sand roads to be a mostly private affair.**

A full 23-mile circuit of Grand Island (campsites available) uses a multi-use unsurfaced trail that works atop 300-foot bluffs and into deserted sand beaches. But most canine hikers will opt for an exploration of an appendage to Grand Island connected by an ancient sand bar called a tombolo. When Superior waters were higher thousands of years ago this was actually a complex of three islands.

The journey to this "thumb" travels through remnants of settlement: a stone quarry, weathered cabins, an historic cemetery, and an old farm field that has been repatriated by hundreds of thousands of native wildflowers that bloom in summer. An artesian spring at Ferrell Cottage shaded by the tall birch and pines makes an ideal refreshment stop for Seaman.

The trails around The Thumb are hiker-only so you can leave the occasional bike and park tour van behind. The destination for your dog is the shallow, crystalline waters of Trout Bay. The sandy horseshoe beach is framed by wooded sandstone bluffs that create a perfect doggie swimming pool.

HIAWATHA NATIONAL FOREST

Lake Michigan Sand Dunes

POINT AUX CHENES, MICHIGAN
Hiking Time: 1-2 hours

E △ ⤳

Once you have been hiking with your dog for a while you reach the point where you get fatigued reading beach signs with rules and regulations regarding pets. Sometimes you just want to open the door and let your dog run. Maybe more than sometimes. **So when you find a place that has no facilities, no lifeguards, no anything Seaman's ears are certain to pick up. Welcome to the Lake Michigan Sand Dunes.** These are just about the northernmost dunes on Lake Michigan, on the southern shores of the Upper Peninsula. The views are spectacular, the dunesland enchanting, and the waves welcoming.

Lake Michigan Scenic Route 2 runs right through the sand at this point and parking is permitted on the shoulder. Pull off on the water side of the road and three miles of dune-backed, sandy white beach are at your dog's disposal.

For more traditional hiking fare, at Point Aux Chenes is the parking lot for the *Sand Dunes Ski Trailhead* and a connector path to try a stretch of the seven-state *North Country Trail*. A few miles further down the road at the St. Ignace Ranger Station a new (2013) *Gros Cap Trail* system has been carved through that enchanting forest where the fall season brings radiating colors of crimson, yellow, gold, green and brown. The three interlocking loops on hardened and natural paths form a full circle of 1.6 miles while revealing the story of this high natural headlands above Lake Michigan.

HINCKLEY RESERVATION

Worden's Ledges Loop Trail

HINCKLEY, OHIO

Hiking Time: 1-2 hours

M 🐾

Before there were the Great Lakes what would become Ohio was under an ancient sea. When the waters receded mazes of sandstone ledges were left behind. Some of the most fascinating to hike through with Seaman are in Hinckley Reservation. Judge Samuel Hinckley of Massachusetts was the original land owner in the early 1800s.

Hinckley sold land to Robert Whipp who came from England in 1824 to graze cattle. He grew so rich that his second wife, many decades his junior, enlisted the help of her brother and another man to murder old man Whipp. The burly Englishman fought off his attackers. When he died in 1890 - of natural causes - his land was sold to pay debts. Much of it has been reassembled for Hinckley Reservation that spans more than 2,600 acres.

Two separate sets of ledges and cliffs are standout attractions in the park. **A short climb to one of the highest points in Northeast Ohio leads to the base of Whipp's Ledges where Seaman can easily scale the 50-foot high rock cliffs**. Worden's Ledges are beguiling for the handiwork of Frank Worden who carved figures into the stone in the 1940s. You can pick out a schooner that honors his father, a cross and Bible as a nod to his wife, a sphinx, and more. Worden also sculpted the faces of three of his heroes in the ledges: George Washington, Thomas Jefferson, and baseball immortal Ty Cobb. Each trail is only about one mile long but will linger much longer than that in memory.

HOLDEN ARBORETUM

Old Valley Trail

KIRTLAND, OHIO

Hiking Time: 2-3 hours

M 🐾 $

In addition to smelting more silver ore in the 19th century than anyone in the country, Albert Fairchild Holden was an avid botanist. Even though his mother was instrumental in founding the Cleveland School of Art and his father owned the city's major newspaper, *The Plain Dealer*, Holden intended to spread his money around in Boston where he went to school. His sister convinced him otherwise and the Holden Arboretum has since grown into one of America's largest tree museums with 6,000 varieties of plants and trees spread across 600 meticulously cultivated acres and another 3,000 maintained in a natural state.

Most formal arboretums do not welcome dogs so it is a rare treat to be able to visit these trails with your best hiking companion. The park brochure even proclaims, "We Love Dogs." Seaman will want to visit all the dozen or more trails, ranging from garden strolls to meadow romps to mature woodland hikes.

A good start will be on the *Old Valley Trail*, a true woodland hike of nearly three miles that trades the crushed gravel paths for soft dirt. You may be distracted by the beauty of the mixed hardwood forest and not even notice the several hundred feet of elevation changes as you hike but Seaman will be getting quite a workout in Holden Arboretum. Pierson's Creek and a few of Holden's 26 man-made ponds supply the water features on this pleasurable canine hike.

HURON-MANISTEE NATIONAL FORESTS

Nordhouse Dunes Wilderness Trails

MANISTEE, MICHIGAN
Hiking Time: 3-4 hours

M △ 🏊 $

The Nordhouse Dunes is the only federally designated wilderness area in Michigan's lower peninsula. Despite the name, the trail system here is easily accessed from the paved road into the Lake Michigan Recreation Area.

The protected area is a patchwork quilt of windblown dunes (some as high as 140 feet tall), conifer forests of juniper and jack pine, and a slice of the largest area of freshwater interdunal ponds in the world. Nordhouse Dunes is relatively small but like any true wilderness it is minimally signed. There are about ten miles of trails, including logging cuts and jeep roads that are indistinguishable from footpaths so come armed with a trail map.

One tail-wagging route to try with Seaman is to Nordhouse Lake where the shallow waters will tempt even water-averse dogs in for a swim. Regardless of where you choose to explore in the wilderness area you will close your canine hiking loop with a trot down one of the prettiest stretches of pristine beach in the Great Lakes region.

The undeveloped dunesland alternates between low, rolling sand piles covered in grasses and the rare Pitcher's Thistle to large wind-sculpted dunes. The beach trail shifts from narrow to wide as Seaman races along, the blue waters of Lake Michigan to one side and the deep green curtain of the national forest to the other.

INDIANA DUNES NATIONAL LAKESHORE

Dune Ridge Trail

PORTER, INDIANA
Hiking Time: 1-2 hours

M △ 🏊

The Indiana Dunes are not what your dog is expecting. Yes, there are vast stretches of piles of sand; Mount Baldy in the extreme eastern point of the park rises 123 feet above Lake Michigan. But there are also more than 1,400 plant species identified within park boundaries, ranking Indiana Dunes 7th among all national parks in native plant diversity.

That is what the *Dune Ridge Trail* is all about as it loops for 0.7 mile above Kemil Beach. Growing zones clash here so southern dogwood mixes with arctic bearberry and northern conifer forests thrive alongside cacti. Canine hikes begin on an old roadbed before tackling the sandy dunesland and climbing to views of the Great Marsh, the largest wetland complex in the Lake Michigan watershed. When you reach the oak savanna the footpath under paw transitions to packed dirt.

Seaman's best day in the national seashore doesn't end back in the parking lot. Kemil Beach is one of the dog-friendly beaches at Indiana Dunes so there are doggie dips awaiting in Lake Michigan. Heading east on your canine beach hike leads past five refugees from the Homes of Tomorrow exhibit in the 1933 World's Fair in Chicago. The quintet of futuristic houses were barged to the dunes with plans to be the centerpiece of a resort community that never came to market. The most prominent house visible from the sand is the pink-hued Florida Tropical House, fashioned in the Art Deco style.

INDIANA DUNES STATE PARK

Trail 10

CHESTERTON, INDIANA
Hiking Time: 3-4 hours

M A ⚇ $

After visiting Yosemite in 1900 Indiana businessman Richard Lieber became a leading cheerleader for conservation, thrusting the Hoosier State to the forefront of creating state parks. Indiana Dunes was protected in 1925, four decades before the national lakeshore that surrounds it.

Seaman is forced to study a sheet of regulations to figure out where he is allowed in the federal property next door but the only thing to know in Indiana Dunes State Park is not to go on the small swimming beach. Beyond that, the remaining 2,182 acres are all tail-friendly.

The star at the state park is Mount Tom, a 192-foot vegetation-covered sand dune that is the tallest in Indiana. A long wooden staircase (*Trail 4*) leads to the summit and views across Lake Michigan to the Chicago skyline. The descent (*Trail 8*) sends Seaman hurtling down the sand pile.

Trail 10 is a long 5.5-mile horseshoe trail that connects to either end of the route over Mount Tom. Half the canine hike rolls easily through a mixed-pine and hardwood forest and the other half follows the long, deserted beach. Most of the way the trail mixes sand and dirt but there are also stretches of loose sand. Highlights include the Big Blowout where wind has blown away sand from dead stumps after burying the trees alive. The preferred direction for this canine hike is counter-clockwise as this leaves the beach walk for the end; you can avoid the hard climb over Mount Tom if so desired.

IRON COUNTY FOREST

Potato River Falls Trail

GURNEY, WISCONSIN
Hiking Time: 1 hours

E A ⚇

The north woods of Wisconsin are laced with waterfalls and are a worthy destination for any hydrospectacular connoisseur. But dog owners beware - many of the Dairy State's most popular water cataracts are in state parks (Brownstone Falls and Copper Falls in Ashland County, for example) and are reached via designated nature trails. And dogs are not allowed on Wisconsin state park nature trails.

Iron County, south of Lake Superior, has the state's most displays of tumbling water - 15 - and three are among the state's six highest. **Since most of these water displays are off the beaten path Seaman will be welcome if you make the effort to seek them out**. The most beautiful of Iron County's falls are on the Potato River southwest of tiny Gurney at a rustic campground.

Three deeply wooded trails totaling a little over one mile visit a trio of viewing platforms. A 131-step timber stairway leads Seaman to the brink of the powerful Upper Falls as the water maneuvers around old volcanic rock. The impressive Lower Falls can be explored by adventurous canine hikers on steep, informal trails that lead into the river gorge and a ford in the river. Seaman won't mind getting his paws wet but if the Potato River is frothing save this tail-wagging adventure for another time.

Mackinac Island State Park

Tranquil Bluff Trail
EAST BLUFF, MICHIGAN
Hiking Time: 2-3 hours

M ⩲

At first blush, tourist mecca Mackinac Island in Lake Huron would seem to be a horrible place to bring a dog - teeming with crowds and literally thousands of bikes in the narrow streets. But do not despair. No one is coming to Mackinac to hike so once you walk Seaman a half-mile from the landing dock, past the fudge shops and beyond the historic fort, you reach a Mackinac Island that existed long before any settlers arrived. Your trail dog is likely to go for an hour or more and never see anyone.

The *Tranquil Bluff Trail* covers most of the length of the island - about three miles. The canine adventure begins at Arch Rock, an iconic natural limestone bridge looming over the shoreline that made Mackinac a national park for two decades in the 19th century.

These wooded highlands reach heights over 300 feet - enough elevation change to support a lively hike and provide inspired Great Lakes views but not enough to tire a vacationing dog. The pleasing mix of natural footpaths and wide cartpaths were laid down for long-ago Victorian guests.

The island's unique location and elevation changes support an enchanting mix of North Woods conifers and southern hardwoods with a vibrant understory. **There are several rock caves for Seaman to poke his nose into along Tranquil Bluff**. A well-marked trail system offers an array of linking options inland to form a circuit hike, including a stop at the photogenic land stack known as Sugar Loaf.

Niagara Falls State Park

Niagara Gorge Rim Trail
NIAGARA FALLS, NEW YORK
Hiking Time: 2-5 hours

E $

Niagara Falls reigns as one of the world's premier sightseeing destinations and Seaman is welcome to enjoy the spectacle. **Of all the crown jewels in America's natural tiara - Yellowstone, the Grand Canyon, Yosemite - none is as dog-friendly as Niagara Falls**. Save for special guided tours, your dog can walk anywhere you walk to view the world-famous falls. He can stand on Terrapin Point at the brink of Horseshoe Falls and then walk across Goat Island to the edge of the American Falls. He can trot across the roaring Niagara River on the arched pedestrian footbridge and head back to the precipice of America's greatest water display.

The flat, paved *Niagara Gorge Rim Trail* then traces the river, one of the shortest on the planet, as it rumbles another turbulent seven miles before disgorging its contents into Lake Ontario. The rapids are among the fiercest in the world, hustling by at over 20 mph. You can watch from the trail as whirlpool jet boats test such famous hydrospectaculars as the Whirlpool Rapids and Devil's Hole.

Several sets of 300+ steps descend into Niagara Gorge to reach connecting trails along the river's edge for adventurous canine hiking loops. These include the *Great Gorge Railway Trail* that follows the road bed of the historic railroad. The railway operated until 1935 when 5,000 tons of rock slid down the cliffs and buried the tracks - that is why it is advised not to hike below the rim from May to November.

Pictured Rocks National Lakeshore

Miners Beach

MUNISING, MICHIGAN
Hiking Time: 1-2 hours

E △ ≈•

When the federal government decided to begin protecting America's "third seacoast" in the 1960s by designating national lakeshores, the "pictured rocks" on Lake Superior was the obvious choice to start. After all, there is enough water in Lake Superior to easily fill the other Great Lakes combined to overflowing.

The sandstone cliffs here can soar 200 feet above the water. They are painted by groundwater that seeps out of cracks in the rock. The oozing water contains iron (red and orange), manganese (black), limonite (white) and copper (green) that brush the cliff faces with color as they trickle down to the lake.

Dogs are not allowed on the trails at Pictured Rocks but can join in the beach walking at Miners Beach and the short trail to the lakeshore. This is mostly a cobble beach with rocks polished to a shine by the aggressive Lake Superior waves.

Seaman can also hike the trail to three overlooks of Miners Castle, a towering rock turret that is an icon of the Lake Superior first named in 1771. Stairs help navigate the steeper portions of this canine hike that provides one of the best views of the Pictured Rocks from the mainland.

The best beach for dogs is at the western end of the park; Seaman is allowed on Sand Point until the trail begins to climb the cliffs. In addition to the wide sand beach the icy Lake Superior waters are shallower here and better suited for doggie paddling.

Porcupine Mountains Wilderness State Park

Escarpment Trail

ONTONAGON, MICHIGAN
Hiking Time: 3-4 hours

M △ ≈•

The Porcupine Mountains make up Michigan's largest state park and one of the most expansive undisturbed wilderness areas in the Midwest. There are 90 miles of tail-friendly trails here that will take your dog through virgin maple-hemlock forests, to the top of 1,958-foot Summit Peak, and to a large natural spring. The park's premier river, the Presque Isle, makes a final sprint to Lake Superior and Seaman can hike one mile on either side of the energetic waters to experience a series of wide drops over bare rock.

But the canine hike to take in the Porkies is the *Escarpment Trail* that traces a long basalt bedrock formation that parallels Lake Superior. This is an out-and-back affair connecting entrance road M-107 to the popular Lake of the Clouds Overlook. If you have a car shuttle, start at the overlook and work downhill; otherwise begin down below with fresh steps.

Coming up the escarpment, Seaman travels through old growth trees on a rocky surface past the remains of an old copper mine. The views start coming fast, including a glimpse out to Lake Superior. Cuyahoga Peak is the first feather in your trail dog's cap at 1,604 feet and soon he is trotting on an open ridge above the Porkies. Four hundred feet below are the blue waters of the Lake of Clouds and the Carp River snaking from its outlet through a verdant valley. If there is any energy left before heading back the *North Mirror Lake Trail* drops down to a doggie dip in the Lake of Clouds.

POTAWATOMI STATE PARK

Ice Age Trail
STURGEON BAY, WISCONSIN
Hiking Time: 2-3 hours

M ▲ 🏊 $

PRESQUE ISLE STATE PARK

Dead Pond Trail
ERIE, PENNSYLVANIA
Hiking Time: 2-3 hours

E 🏊

If you have hiked with your dog on any part of the *Ice Age Trail* that meanders for over 1,000 miles across Wisconsin you may have encountered trail signs for Potawatomi State Park with insane distances. That is because Potawatomi is the eastern terminus of the foot path that traces the leading edge of glaciation from the last ice age.

The first (or last) pawfalls are placed in the shadow of a 75-foot wooden tower with wide, dog-friendly steps and landings that was built in 1932 and still peeks out over the treetops for Seaman to scout this upcoming Door County adventure. About that time Potawami on the shores of Sturgeon Bay was given consideration as a national park.

The trail slices through cedar, sugar maples, aspen, birch, and pine woodlands and travels among bedrock outcrops that are souvenirs from the Niagara Escarpment that arches from New York to Wisconsin. A welcome set of rock steps carved by the Ice Age Trail Alliance helps tame the ancient cliffs 150 feet above the bay level.

The *Ice Age Trail* stays in Potawatomi for 2.8 miles as it angles toward the Sturgeon Bay shoreline where there are several views through the trees out into the water. Along the way the *Ice Age Trail* ties in to a pair of park loops, the *Hemlock Trail* and *Tower Trail*, so any length of canine hiking loop can be crafted with Seaman to find your way back to the observation tower.

In French, "presque isle" means almost an island. For your dog, however, there is no "almost" about it - this is one place high on his list of places to hike. The main attraction is "Pennsylvania's seacoast," a large chunk of the Keystone State's 57 miles of Lake Erie shoreline. **Seaman can't go on the swimming beaches but there are plenty of other opportunities for canine aquatics on the water playground manifest at Presque Isle.**

Dead Pond Trail, at two miles, is the longest of many short walking paths in the park. The route dives into the the "flying spit" of sand that is the largest in the Great Lakes region. The sandy footpath samples all the ecological zones in the park: the oak-maple woodlands, the pine barrens, and the grassy sand plains that are home to seasonal wildflowers. Seaman even gets a bit of elevation change as the route travels over sand ridges and former dunes.

The canine hiking loop is closed with the paved multi-use trail that circles the sand peninsula, where you are likely to encounter most of the trail users in Pennsylvania's most popular state park.

Dog paddling in Lake Erie is available at either end of the out-and-back *Dead Pond Trail* hike. At the east end, across the parking lot jump onto the half-mile *North Pier Trail* that covers a dog-friendly stretch of beach where Seaman can frolic freely in the frisky Lake Erie waves.

SLEEPING BEAR DUNES NATIONAL LAKESHORE

Cottonwood Trail

EMPIRE, MICHIGAN
Hiking Time: 1-2 hours

M 🏊 **$**

In 2011 the ABC morning program *Good Morning America* anointed Sleeping Bear Dunes the "Most Beautiful Place in America." A park can live off that type of publicity for a long time.

Pierce Stocking knew about the allure of these 400-foot lakeside dunes before Sleeping Bear was declared a national lakeshore in 1970. The lumberman built a 7.4-mile road through the forest and dunes with gentle curves and overlooks of Lake Michigan. Today the Pierce Stocking Scenic Drive is the most popular way to see America's most beautiful spot.

The *Cottonwood Trail* is the place to stop on the scenic drive and get out of your vehicle to hike with your dog. **This is a rollicking rollercoaster of a canine hike and even though it is only 1.4 miles you are working through thick sand all the way**. The loop leads out into dunes speckled with the bleached remains of overwhelmed trees and the hardy survivors adapting to their sandy world. Seaman will appreciate the tenaciousness of these trees to provide occasional shade and resting areas.

Neither the scenic drive nor the *Cottonwood Trail* provide access to Lake Michigan. For a well-earned cooling off a half-mile spur off the *Sleeping Bear Point Trail* through dune grasses and low-lying shrubs will do the trick. This rolling 2.8-mile loop behind blue posts delivers a workout as well and passes the massive blowout known as the Devil's Hole.

SPLIT ROCK LIGHTHOUSE STATE PARK

Split Rock River Loop Trail

TWO HARBORS, MINNESOTA
Hiking Time: 2-3 hours

M ⛺ 🏊 **$**

There are 246 lighthouses, more or less, on the Great Lakes and the light at Split Rock is the most photographed. There were no roads in the area when the squat, octagonal tower was constructed in 1910 so the building materials had to be lifted by crane from the water to the top of the 130-foot volcanic rock cliff. Split Rock was selected as Lake Superior's lighthouse for a series of stamps issued by the United States Postal Service and took a star turn in the 2013 Hollywood version of *The Great Gatsby*. Of course your dog will want to see it.

Short trails in the park to do just that - from up close on top of the promontory, from down below along Ellingsen Beach, and on top at Dry Hill. With your camera sated your trail dog will be ready to head out on the five-mile *Split Rock River Loop*. This is one of the rare chances to sample the long-distance *Superior Hiking Trail* in a circuit. For planning purposes, the west side of the loop will produce more panting than the east side of the river; the elevation gain is about 300 feet. If coming up the east side be sure to look back for stunning views of Lake Superior.

The *Split Rock River Loop* serves up an seemingly continuous parade of waterfalls and pools waiting for Seaman to swim and splash in. And, yes, there is what appears to be a namesake split rock, but the park name actually derives from the frost wedging of the volcanic rhyolite rock that comprises the base of this scintillating canine hiking landscape.

Tahquamenon Falls State Park

Tahquamenon-River Trail
PARADISE, MICHIGAN
Hiking Time: 3-4 hours

E △ ⟋⟍ $

Only two waterfalls east of the Mississippi River send more water over their lip than the Upper Tahquamenon Falls. The Upper is only 50 feet high but a massive 200 feet across, creating a supreme curtain of water. That water is a sparkling golden brown thanks to tree tannins leeched into the river from cedar swamps upstream.

There is also a Lower Falls, a series of five cascades and tumbles around an island in the Tahquamenon River in a wide panorama. A 4.8-mile trail connects the two. Tahquamenon Falls is a popular spot and one of the few places on the Upper Peninsula Seaman may be mingling with a crowd. The *Tahquamenon River Trail* is a sure escape valve from the multitudes.

The dirt path is a narrow and rooty affair with plenty of ups and downs to pique Seaman's interest. The spruce and cedar and hemlock shroud this entire canine hike but views of the close-by river come at regular intervals. Steps and short boardwalk bridges tame some of the rougher patches of this beautiful, but primitive meander. Bogs, marshes, and an impressive beaver dam flesh out a true northern trail experience.

The Lower Falls offer the chance for canine aquatics with broad pools and tamer waters. You can even rent a rowboat and paddle to the island and a half-mile trail there. The Upper Falls is for photography only - and the 94 steps to the viewing platform are open metal that are not paw-friendly.

 # Tettegouche State Park

High Falls Trail
SILVER BAY, MINNESOTA
Hiking Time: 1-2 hours

M △ ⟋⟍ $

The Baptism River has been working on the rugged rhyolite ridges above the Lake Superior shoreline for one billion years. There is still plenty of work to be done as witnessed by the highest waterfall wholly contained in the state of Minnesota (Canada claims half the droplets from the Pigeon River High Falls that helps form the international border).

The *High Falls Trail* is a broad brown brush stroke of dirt through a lush North Woods forest of birch, aspen, and pine. This is a 1.5-mile one-way canine hike to reach the 70-foot High Falls but there are side delights along the way, including multiple viewpoints of the vivacious Baptism River. A ten-minute side trail leads to a wide double drop in the river known as Two Step Falls.

The well-established trail reaches the High Falls at a wooden platform with a dramatic overlook of the plunging water. Seaman is not done yet, however. **The trail continues down a long set of wooden steps to a swinging suspension bridge at water level leading your water-loving dog to the plunge pool**. This will require a crossing on an open grate bridge that may give cautious dogs pause.

There are more falls to hunt on the Baptism River in Tettegouche on the opposite bank, a little less than one mile one way. Back at the visitor center, the half-mile ramble to Shovel Point atop the palisades high above Lake Superior is a quick must-do for your dog.

WHITEFISH DUNES STATE PARK

Red Trail

STURGEON BAY, WISCONSIN
Hiking Time: 2-3 hours

E 🏊 **$** 🚙

Door County, an arm of the Wisconsin shoreline that reaches into Lake Michigan, is sometimes called "the Cape Cod of the Midwest." That is more likely a reference to the number of vacation homes here rather than the resemblance of the coves and harbors. Whatever, your dog's best place to experience Door County and its 300 miles of shoreline is at Whitefish Dunes State Park.

The highest dunes in Wisconsin are here. The trail of choice for canine hikers, among over 14 miles of foot paths, is the *Red Trail*. **Its main attraction is that after a mile from its start at the nature center it leads to one of the best dog beaches on the Great Lakes.** This generous stretch of tail-friendly sand is nearly as large as the off-limits swimming beach. Seaman can join in a friendly scrum in the waves or seek out a more solitary patch of sand.

You can create a canine hiking loop by heading inland and returning on the *Yellow* or *Green* trails. This route leads over 93-foot Old Baldy, completely on boardwalk. Old Baldy is Wisconsin's biggest pile of sand.

If Seaman is not particularly interested in beach swimming, call an audible in the parking lot and head for the 1.5-mile *Brachiopod Interpretive Trail* instead. This exploration of the sporty forested dunes follows the adventures of Byron, a prehistoric one-footed clam-like creature, as you walk your dog out onto a rock shelf to view Wisconsin at its finest.

GREAT RIVER ROAD

CAHOKIA MOUNDS STATE HISTORIC SITE

6.2 Mile Nature/Culture Trail

COLLINSVILLE, ILLINOIS
Hiking Time: 2-3 hours

E

Cahokia was America's first metropolis, a cultural center constructed by the Mississippian Indians between 600 AD and 1200 AD that housed what is believed to have been as many as 20,000 people. These ancient "Mound Builders" dragged an estimated 50 million cubic feet of alluvial soil in baskets to construct over 100 ceremonial and functional mounds. Almost half of that dirt was used in building Monks Mound, the largest prehistoric earthen construction in the Western hemisphere. Cahokia is a United Nations Educational, Scientific and Cultural Organization World Heritage Sites, one of a select few in the United States.

That significance will likely be lost on Seaman while touring "America's pyramids" on easy-to-trot crushed gravel paths in a park-like setting. The *6.2 Mile Nature/Culture Trail* delivers what it promises with woodlands, meadows, and ponds while also visiting all the most important man-made prehistoric treasures at Cahokia. That includes excavated evidence of posts that functioned as circular sun calendars in what has been dubbed Woodhenge.

Also on the trail is the 154-stair climb up the two-tiered Monks Mound, where experts believe a 50-foot high wooden building stood at the center of Mississippian civilization. **Once on top the 100-foot flat-topped mound Seaman will marvel at a sight the Mississippians never enjoyed - an unobstructed view of the St. Louis skyline and the Gateway Arch**.

CLARK CREEK NATURAL AREA

Improved/Primitive Trail

WOODVILLE, MISSISSIPPI
Hiking Time: 3-4 hours

S ⚊ $

Rugged terrain. Waterfalls. Challenging. Not what Seaman was expecting in the land of Mississippi Delta cotton fields.

These are the Tunica Hills, ridges of windblown sand-clay loess that have been sculpted into a maze of ravines and gorges. The locals call the area Tunica Falls, a catch-all for the 50 or so spring-fed waterfalls that percolate through the natural area, some as high as 30 feet.

The *Improved Trail* (really just some pea stones spread on the wide, packed clay footpath in spots) makes a rollercoaster trip of 1.75 miles through the lush hardwood forest. Wooden staircases have been installed as workarounds on the steepest, potentially muddiest slopes. The hardiest climbs are down to overlooks of the falls spilling into secluded grottoes. The steps lead all the way into the streambed for alternate canine hiking and boulder hopping in the water.

The *Improved Trail* links into the *Primitive Trail*, a barely discernible gash in the forest floor for a 2.6-mile loop. There will be more waterfalls to scout but overall only a fraction of Tunica Falls water shows will be on display without bushwhacking.

Waterfalls are just the start of Clark Creek's favors. John James Audubon found many of the subjects for his seminal *Birds of America* in these woods. The trail also rambles past record trees - the Mississippi champion Hophornbeam and the largest Mexican Plum growing anywhere in the world.

CRYSTAL BRIDGES MUSEUM OF AMERICAN ART

Rock Ledge Trail

BENTONVILLE, ARKANSAS
Hiking Time: 1-2 hours

M

Fueled by over $300 million of Walton family money, the Crystal Bridges Museum of American Art opened in the home of Walmart in 2011 to great acclaim as one of the country's finest art museums. **The world class collection is free to the public, as is the tail-friendly 3.5-mile trail system that meanders across the wooded hillsides that frame the stunning Crystal Bridges architecture**. The trails are always open, even when the museum isn't.

Seaman won't see the American masterworks inside the museum but inspiring outdoor sculptures inhabit the *Art Trail*. He can sniff the 560-pound bronze happy hog known as Stella, a visitor favorite. He will also encounter an iconic Usonian house from Frank Lloyd Wright and the *Fly's Eye Dome* from Buckminster Fuller.

The grounds feature ponds, ravines, and natural limestone springs bubbling to the surface. Namesake quartz crystals can be spotted along the walkways. The *Rock Ledge Trail* visits bluffs blasted out of the hills for a long-ago planned railroad that was never built. The crushed gravel path travels through lush forests of white pines and Eastern red cedars that feature patches of wild hydrangea bushes.

The *Rock Ledge Trail* leads away from the crowded hub of Crystal Bridges for a half-mile before linking with the multi-use *North Forest Trail* - the longest on the property - for the return jaunt past more sculptures and hundreds of dogwood trees.

DEVIL'S DEN STATE PARK

Yellow Rock Trail

WEST FORK, ARKANSAS
Hiking Time: 1-2 hours

M △ ⚊ $

The Boston Mountains are the most wildly eroded of the three plateaus that make up the Ozark Mountains. The sandstone here has been cracked into some 60 crevice caves, the largest such concentration in the country. The most dramatic is Devil's Den Cave that reaches 550 feet into the wooded slopes.

There was no easy way to explore this unique landscape until the Civilian Conservation Corps (CCC) was tasked with building a road through the Lee Creek Valley in 1933. The crews stayed to build a stone dam, cabins, and a lodge for the new state park. The rustic-style wood and stone buildings remain as one of the most intact Depression-era work camps in America.

The CCC workers also hacked the first hiking trails out of the lush forests and rock formations. The signature *Devil's Den Trail* covers 1.5 miles with less than a 100-foot elevation gain and leads to Devil's Den Cave, Devil's Ice Box, and trailside crevices. The caves are safe to explore so bring a flashlight to help Seaman poke around.

The best canine hiking at Devil's Den is on the *Yellow Rock Trail* through the park's old-growth woodlands tall enough to hide massive rock houses until your dog is trotting past them. Stone steps and switchbacks help tame the early uphill stretches of the 2.7-mile loop with spurs to breathtaking overlooks of the valley, some from unprotected ledges and one from a handsome CCC trailside shelter.

Effigy Mounds National Monument

Fire Point Trail
MARQUETTE, IOWA
Hiking Time: 1-2 hours

M 🏊

The Upper Mississippi River Valley is characterized by so many overlooking bluffs that no one is sure which is the highest. One of the best public places for your dog to look down on the Great River combines scenic views with some of America's finest prehistoric relics.

Mound building cultures that inhabited the Mississippi region 2,500 years ago constructed mounds for religious, ceremonial, burial, and elite residential purposes. More than 200 mounds have have been documented in the monument, including 31 in the shape of spirit animals, or effigies. Nowhere have more been found.

No vehicles are permitted to mar the sacred site that contains 14 miles of self-guiding trails weaving among the mounds. The *Fire Point Trail* is a two-mile canine hike that passes all four types of mounds: conical, linear, compound, and an effigy (Little Great Bear). **Seaman will find a serious trail here as the dirt path switches to the top the bluffs. Panting tongues will recede after that**.

Today the Effigy Mounds resemble an English woodland park with a grassy understory in the forest. The mounds are identified by higher grass. As the *Fire Point Trail* works its way to overlooks from hundreds of feet above the Mississippi there is no hurry to finish the loop. Atop the bluffs this agreeable canine hiking can continue to more scenic views and more effigies, including the Great Bear Mound Group, one of largest of its ilk.

Fort Snelling State Park

Pike Island Trail
ST. PAUL, MINNESOTA
Hiking Time: 1-2 hours

E 🏊 $

This is the best urban hike you can take with your dog along the Mississippi River. The Dakota Indians considered the spot at the confluence of the Minnesota and Mississippi rivers the center of the world; European visitors recognized its strategic importance for trade and defense.

On his way to lasting fame in the Rocky Mountains, on September 21, 1805 Zebulon Pike picked up 100,000 acres here in exchange for $200 of trinkets, a keg of whiskey and the promise of a trading post. Colonel Josiah Snelling shaped the installation into a military fort when he arrived in 1820 and it operated as such through World War II. Fort Snelling was spared destruction when it was named as the first National Historic Landmark in Minnesota in 1960 and the park - now the state's most visited - opened two years later to conserve open space in the heart of the Twin Cities.

The standout hike among 18 miles of trails at Fort Snelling is the loop around Pike Island. This is easy trotting under the biggest trees in the Twin Cities area with plenty of opportunity for Seaman to play in the water. The wide, crushed gravel paths cover a 3.2-mile circuit with cut-off options for shorter hikes and access to the interior. At the far point of the loop the Minnesota River flows memorably into the Mississippi River for its journey through America's heartland.

Hoosier National Forest

Hemlock Cliffs National Scenic Trail
WEST FORK, INDIANA
Hiking Time: 1-2 hours

Hikers looking to disappear with their dog in the Southern Indiana woods know to head for the 13,000 acres of the Charles C. Deam Wilderness in the Hoosier National Forest, the only recognized wilderness area in the state. But when it came time to designate a "Special Place" in the forest the powers that be looked elsewhere.

Hemlock Cliffs may have been better known 10,000 years ago when the rock shelters and caves in the lush box canyon were occupied on a regular basis. The limestone cliffs no doubt offered excellent defense against intruders. These days the frogs and salamanders see comparatively less human traffic.

The 1.4-mile loop begins innocently enough before dropping abruptly into the cool, damp environment of the semi-circular canyon. The presence of iron ore is responsible for the "honey-combing" in the rock house.

Plants not often seen in Indiana, such as wild geranium and wintergreen, are common here. Hemlocks thrive along and above the trail, which uses stone steps to navigate tricky passages. **When necessary the narrow footpath plunges Seaman right into the rock shelters**.

Hemlock Cliffs Falls and Messmore Cliffs Falls decorate the canine hike seasonally. Spur trails lead to the plunge pools where Seaman can scoot behind the cataracts tippling over the rock lips. Adventures in the shady stream dictate when it is finally time to climb out of this special place back to the trailhead.

Hot Springs National Park

Sunset Trail
HOT SPRINGS, ARKANSAS
Hiking Time: 3-4 hours

The water that bubbles to the ground at 143 degrees Farenheit fell to earth 4,000 years ago, percolating deep into the earth before seeping out of the lower west slope of Hot Springs Mountain. In 1832 the Federal government reserved land around the springs - the first "national park" to protect a natural resource. Private bathhouses sprung up to cater to tourists visiting the "healing" waters. Finally in 1921, Hot Springs became a true national park, a unique blend of a highly developed small city set in low-lying, rounded mountains.

You'll get both on the *Sunset Trail* that skirts the perimeter of the park for about 10 miles. Many of the paths that comprise the route were carved for spa visitors who were encouraged to walk daily. **Although the mountains only top out at little more than 1,000 feet expect to find some climbs that will Seaman panting**. The trail tags Music Mountain, the highpoint in the park at 1,405 feet.

There are not many viewpoints along the way but the beauty of the trail will sustain foot travelers. For those who want the Hot Springs Mountain experience without the full tour the *Sunset Trail* is broken into three segments. Keep a sharp eye out when the route crosses roadways. Back in town, take Seaman on a tour of Bathhouse Row with a half-mile saunter down the Promenade, visiting several of the 47 springs that flow at an average rate of 850,000 gallons a day. No dogs in the bathhouses to soothe tired paws, however.

ITASCA
STATE PARK

Schoolcraft Trail

PARK RAPIDS, MINNESOTA
Hiking Time: 1 hour

E △ ⚊ $

Itasca is Minnesota's oldest state park and one of its most popular. The park spreads across more than 32,000 acres but most first-time visitors head for a 20-foot strip of rocks near the north entrance. These are the headwaters of the Mississippi River.

The most powerful river on the continent kept the secret of its source for centuries. It wasn't until 1832 that geographer Henry Rowe Schoolcraft figured out that the Mississippi begins its 2,552 mile journey to the Gulf of Mexico by flowing north, not south. Out of the North Arm of Lake Itasca.

The most meaty canine hiking in the park is south of the lake. A multitude of trails skirt sparkling waters and the largest white and red pines in the state. But the must-do trail for Seaman is just a few bounds from the Visitor Center to that long-sought source of the Mississippi River. Once there **he can prance across the river without getting his tummy wet as it sneaks out of the channel at the back of the lake**. What was historically a muddy swamp is now lined with grasses and wildflowers with smooth pebbles and boulders in the channel.

After the novelty of stepping across the great river, step away and take Seaman down the North Arm of Lake Itasca on the mile-long *Schoolcraft Trail*. The charming footpath hugs the shoreline for extended doggie dips under the pines before looping back to the trailhead.

MARK TWAIN
NATIONAL FOREST

Blue Spring Trail

WEST PLAINS, MISSOURI
Hiking Time: 1-2 hours

E △ ⚊ $

Plenty of places name natural springs in their streams "blue hole" but few can match the vibrancy of color found in the Mark Twain Forest. There are so many that there aren't enough shades of blue to name them all. This canine hike is to the Blue Spring feeding the North Fork River, not the Blue Spring in the Current River.

This is an easy walk with your dog on a narrow dirt strip through streamside oaks, maples, flowering dogwood, and redbuds. The *Blue Spring Trail* passes by and under ledges of cherty Gasconite dolomite that spice up the canine hike. At this point you are hard by the North Fork River which is muddy and brown and giving up no hints of the wonders it holds up ahead.

In less than one mile the star of the hike emerges, the natural spring nestled in a dramatic rock amphitheater, disgorging seven million gallons of water per day. **If you didn't know better you would think this large grotto with deep blue water was designed specifically as a doggie swimming hole**. Rock blocks line the edges for dogs to plunge into the pool and there is also a level bank for walking easily into the water.

If Seaman is feeling frisky after a dip in the 57-degree water he can tackle the Devil's Backbone Wilderness that surrounds a long ridge through the Missouri Ozarks. There are thirteen miles of maintained trails here and the 300-foot climb to McGarr Ridge just beyond Blue Spring will be the biggest challenge to your dog.

 Natchez Trace Parkway

Boardwalk Trail

E

Nothing barks "Mississippi Delta" like a cypress swamp. Bald cypress and tupelo trees take root when the soils are dry and thrive when the land floods and other tree species die away. Their appearance always inspires wonder for their flared trunks and often elaborate root system that pokes above the surface as "knees." Cypress trees have the knees, tupelos have a smoother base. No one really knows what purpose these protruberances serve but the best guess is that they provide oxygen to the tree during floods.

Cypress swamps are famed for their haunting impenetrability but Seaman can explore this one just by pulling off the Natchez Trace Parkway. A boardwalk bridge immediately deposits canine hikers in the heart of the swamp amidst scores of mature trees. **The doggie leg-stretcher continues onto drier land and passes a tranquil woodland pond before looping back and finishing a relaxing half-mile stroll with your dog**.

The Cypress and Water Tupelo Swamp is a popular spot along the Parkway for bird and nature watching. Some of that wildlife includes alligators so while the dark waters of the swamp look like an easy spot for a doggie dip it is better to keep the beach blanket in the car for another stop.

 Natchez Trace Parkway

Potkopinu Trail

M

So you've floated down the Ohio and Mississippi rivers and delivered your hogsheads of whiskey to the traders in Natchez and sold your boat for lumber. Now it is time for you and the dog to begin the trek back overland to Tennessee or Kentucky on the "path through the wilderness" that travelers have been using for 10,000 years or so. This is the Old Natchez Trace and the *Potkopinu Trail* is the longest remaining original stretch of its 444 miles.

Canine hikers can access this three-mile woodswalk from either end at milepost 17 or 20 from the Natchez Trace Parkway. If you had hosted foot traffic for ten millenia you would start to sag a bit and the ancient sandy trail here is sunken in places by as much as 20 feet. "Potkopinu" is a Natchez Indian word that translates to "little valley" and Seaman will indeed be traveling through leaf-littered sluices above his head here.

The banks are still eroding and it is not unusual to encounter a fallen tree toppled into a gully for Seaman to bound over or under. While the *Potkopinu Trail* is well-marked and maintained the park service does want to capture the feel of what it would have been like to journey on this historic wilderness trail 200 years ago before the age of steam. For that reason Bullen Creek and seasonal streams are not bridged. Whatever temporary hardships Seaman does encounter here at least he doesn't have 400 more miles to go ahead of him.

Natchez Trace Parkway

Rocky Springs Trail

NATCHEZ TRACE PARKWAY: MM 54.8
Hiking Time: 1-2 hours

M ∆ 🚙

Ernest Hemingway famously wrote in *The Sun Also Rises* about bankruptcy happening two ways: gradually and suddenly. Such was the case with the town of Rocky Springs that got its start as a natural watering hole along the Old Natchez Trace. By the middle of the 19th century nearly 5,000 people lived in the area. The Civil War drained part of the population and afterwards Rocky Springs was visited by yellow fever and boll weevils that destroyed cotton crops. A steady degradation of the land drove more people away until the final store shuttered in 1930. About the same time the namesake spring dried up.

Today, the Rocky Springs ghost town has given way to a Natchez Trace campground with a variety of trail experiences for your dog. Paths lead through the old town site where nature has just about totally reclaimed the rocky hillsides. Seaman can sniff around an old steel safe built into a post office stone wall here. The trail winds to the top of the hill and the only remaining structure from Rocky Springs - a handsome brick Methodist church with a truncated wooden steeple. Out back the town cemetery hides in the pines.

From the campground, trails lead to canine hiking along the original Trace for a spell and onto a segment of the *Natchez Trace National Scenic Trail*. The go-to destination here is Owens Creek waterfall but a drop in the water table has left the once reliable water display dependent on the vagaries of rainfall.

Ozark National Forest

White Rock Rim Trail

WOODS GAP, ARKANSAS
Hiking Time: 1 hour

E ∆

When President Franklin Delano Roosevelt created the Civilian Conservation Corps (CCC) during the Great Depression rural Arkansas is the kind of place he had in mind to provide outdoor work to unemployed young men while developing natural resources. On White Rock Mountain Roosevelt's "Tree Army" crafted a trio of one-of-a-kind natural stone cabins and a rustic low-slung lodge.

The work continued out on the 2,309-foot promontory that gets its name from the lichens that grow on the cliffs making them appear white. **Seaman will be traveling atop those sheer bluffs on a path constructed by CCC crews to see those lichens under his nose.** The two-mile loop circles the mountaintop to deliver nearly continuous views of the surrounding Ozark mountains. The stonecutters were also busy adorning the trail with four rock-and-wood beam shelters, most notably the dramatic sunset shelter. The elevation gain is negligible on this scenery-packed canine hike but keep an eye out for the trail edges as one thing not on the CCC project list was guardrails.

If the *White Rock Rim Trail* inspires Seaman for more hiking the recreation area intersects at mile marker 17.4 of the 270-mile *Ozark Highlands Trail*. Sampling the trail in the Boston Mountains will take your dog through the most rugged and scenic parts of the Ozarks.

PEA RIDGE NATIONAL MILITARY PARK

Battlefield Hiking Trail

GARFIELD, ARKANSAS
Hiking Time: 2-3 hours

M $

On March 7, 1862, snow still covered the frozen ground when the Union Army of the Southwest, 10,500 troops under Brigadier General Samuel R. Curtis, clashed with 16,000 Confederates commanded by Major General Earl Van Dorn. The battle raged at two separate sites: Leetown and Elkhorn Tavern.

The Union, most of whom were immigrant German farmers who spoke no English, prevailed at Leetown while the outcome at Elkhorn Tavern was less decisive, although Southerners left the field under heavy Union artillery bombardment. When the Battle of Pea Ridge ended the next day, the State of Missouri was secure for the Union.

Dogs are welcome throughout Pea Ridge, the first battlefield west of the Mississippi River to be declared a national military park. It is also the largest. The seven-mile hiking loop travels through fields and woodlands - a splendid natural canine romp with an overlay of pivotal American history.

The trail visits skirmish sites and rock outcroppings with small caves; building foundations and quiet stream beds; cannons and small sandstone canyons; zigzag split-rail fences and flowering dogwoods. **There is enough challenge to the Pea Ridge battlefield to set Seaman to panting and long stretches where he can bask with sunlight on his neck**. There may even be enough water in the seasonal streams to enjoy a refreshing splash.

PETIT JEAN STATE PARK

Seven Hollows Trail

MORRILTON, ARKANSAS
Hiking Time: 2-3 hours

M △ ⚊

"If you think dogs can't count, try putting three dog biscuits in your pocket and then give him only two of them." – Phil Pastoret

The *Seven Hollows Trail* actually only visits four hollows (the other three are on private land) but this 4.5-mile loop packs so much scenic wonder your dog is likely to lose count. Petit Jean (forget your high school French, it is "petty jean') was an obvious choice to be Arkansas' first state park, a slice of land between the Ozark and Ouachita mountain ranges considered so beautiful it was under consideration to be a national park before being deemed too small.

There are many scenic spots in the eroded bluffs and forested canyons lubricated by Cedar Creek, including 94-foot Cedar Falls where Seaman can enjoy a refreshing swim in the plunge pool. The *Seven Hollows Trail* is on the opposite side of the park.

The route takes Seaman from lush hardwood forests to desert-like terrain where the sandstone is known as Turtle Rocks for their mottled appearance. Each hollow on this sporty canine hike has its own delights, from a hefty natural rock bridge to a secluded grotto in a box canyon beneath a rock overhang. Seaman may even find a waterfall and seasonal swimming hole here, conveniently located about halfway through his hike. Be sure to stop at Stout's Point to learn the story of Petit Jean at her gravesite and soak in the impressive views of the Arkansas River.

ROUTE 66
STATE PARK

Outer Loop Trail

EUREKA, MISSOURI
Hiking Time: 1-2 hours

E 🏊

This is a canine hike unlike any your dog is likely to enjoy. Not so much for the actual trotting, which is flat and easy, but for the ground under paw.

The park is located on the townsite of the one-time resort community of Times Beach, a money-making scheme of the publisher of the bygone St. Louis *Star-Times* in 1925. All went well until the 1970s when a local contractor used contaminated oil to spray on the gravel roads. The potion was so noxious that Times Beach was completely evacuated by 1985 and not only was the town torn down but all the debris and soil incinerated until there was no trace of Times Beach.

When a clean bill of health was finally issued the state created a park. Since a short stretch of the iconic Route 66 slipped through Times Beach it was decided to hook the park to the legacy of the Mother Road.

The *Outer Loop Trail* gives your dog a chance to get some kicks on Route 66 as it uses the old road bed. The trail also incorporates part of the former Times Beach street grid during its 3.25 miles. The paths are wide and flat and move through corridors of trees and open fields. There is also a small pond and a boat ramp into the adjoining Meramec River for doggie aquatics.

Times Beach is silent these days but this walk with Seaman will be accompanied by freight trains and interstate traffic. You can mitigate the ambient noise of modernity by switching to the *Inner Loop Trail*.

STARVED ROCK
STATE PARK

River Trail/Bluff Trail

UTICA, ILLINOIS
Hiking Time: 3-4 hours

M △ 🏊

As legend has it, during a dust-up between local American Indian tribes in the 18th century one of the warring factions made the ill-fated call to hole up on a 125-foot sandstone bluff on the south side of the Illinois River. The other side laid siege until their trapped enemies died of starvation.

Today a wooden staircase takes Seaman to the top of Starved Rock. Boardwalks protect most of the bluffs from the national park-level visitation that the Illini's first and most popular park receives. The stars for canine hikers at Starved Rock are the 18 rock-walled box canyons strung out along the river. The fascinating rock formations were left after glacial meltwater washed away everything but the defiant St. Peter sandstone. Fourteen of the canyons feature waterfalls of varying intensity. If you come in spring when the flows are strongest Virginia bluebells will fill the understory of the forest.

A full tour of Starved Rock's canyons covers 13.4 miles; more targeted itineraries from the Visitor Center will aim for St. Louis Canyon via the *Bluff Trail* 1.5 miles to the west and LaSalle Canyon two miles down the *River Trail* to the east, each of which feature reliable water displays in the park.

Trails were cut through the interior rock canyon floors in spots and expect wet paws, especially when walking behind cataracts of water. **And when you finish up be sure to stop at the Veranda for Seaman to make a well-deserved selection off the Doggie Delights Menu.**

TISHOMINGO STATE PARK

Outcroppings Trail

NATCHEZ TRACE PARKWAY: MM 304.5
Hiking Time: 1 hour

M △ ≈

The French mapped a trail from the Tennessee River to the Mississippi River as early as 1733 that became the heavily traveled Natchez Trace. Ohio Valley traders floated goods down to Natchez, sold their flatboats for lumber and walked the 400+ miles home. Today you don't have to walk the Trace but can experience it on the 444-mile Natchez Trace Parkway from Nashville to Natchez.

The route is studded with short leg-stretchers for your dog on the unhurried trip through the Old South. Tishomingo State Park is the largest recreation area on the Trace with over 12 miles of hardwood forest trails.

You can literally see the Appalachian Mountains breathe their last in the park where Seaman will explore huge rock outcroppings along the ridgeline. These rock formations are unique to the state of Mississippi. *Outcroppings Trail* splits its two miles about evenly amidst the rocks, including the eye-catching Jean's Overhang, and a streamside sally along Bear Creek, which makes for excellent dog paddling when the current is not too swift. An impressive Swinging Bridge erected as a Great Depression-era project in the 1930s is your gateway to this canine adventure.

If you're not in a hurry - and one should never be in a rush on the Trace - test out the *Flat Rock Trail* lubricated by small streams before reaching the campground at Haynes Lake or the *Natchez Trace Trail* that travels under the Parkway.

Great Plains

Black Hills National Forest

Flume Trail #50 - Loop A

ROCKERVILLE, SOUTH DAKOTA
Hiking Time: 1-2 hours

M Λ 🏊

Transporting Seaman back to the bustling mining days of the 1880s is one of the most historic hikes to take with your dog in the Black Hills. A wooden flume was constructed to bring water 20 miles from Spring Creek to placer mines near Rockerville that eventually washed $20 million in gold from the diggings. By 1885 the operation was over.

Eleven miles of the trail follow the original Rockerville Flume, including long stretches in the actual bed. The route passes through a pair of small square-timbered tunnels. Sharp eyes will spot square nails, artifacts, and parts of the flume along the route. This is a National Recreation Trail because of its value to Black Hills heritage.

Canine hikers can jump on the *Flume Trail* in four spots; the Upper Spring Creek Trailhead offers a 2.7-mile loop to sample the entire scenic journey. **This slice includes the tunnel fun for Seaman (there are ways to scramble up and over) and also brings him to the shores of Sheridan Lake for extended water play**. He will also enjoy the feeder streams that flow through prairie meadows and forested canyons.

The Coon Hollow Trailhead at the eastern terminus delivers more sporty hiking fare for Seaman with steeper elevation gains and a spur to the 360° views of the Black Hills and the nearby Badlands atop 5,331-foot Boulder Hill. Damage from the Battle Creek Fire that burned this area in 2002 can still be seen.

Black Hills National Forest

Mount Roosevelt Trail

DEADWOOD, SOUTH DAKOTA
Hiking Time: 1 hour

E 🚙

On February 14, 1884, when Theodore Roosevelt was 25 years old and a New York legislator, his wife and mother died, only hours apart. Devastated, Roosevelt abandoned politics and struck out for the Dakota territories where he had first visited as a lad to help cure his asthma. This time he hoped to rebuild his body and restore his spirit with the hard work of ranching. After a blizzard wiped out his prized herd of cattle in 1885, he returned to eastern society.

In his spare time out West Roosevelt worked as a deputy sheriff hunting outlaws. When bringing in a horse thief one day he met Deadwood sheriff Seth Bullock, beginning a lifetime friendship.

When Roosevelt died in 1919, Bullock lobbied to get a favorite peak, Sheep Mountain, renamed Mount Roosevelt and worked tirelessly, even though he himself was close to death, to construct the nation's first monument to the man who would one day end up on nearby Mount Rushmore. The cylindrical stone "Friendship Tower" was dedicated just before Bullock passed the very same year as his frontier friend.

The *Mount Roosevelt Trail* winds in a slight uphill loop to the summit - an easy romp for your dog even though the entire hike is over one mile high. Spiral stone steps inside the tower rise to views that include Wyoming, North Dakota, and Montana. The high lip inside the tower, will likely confine Seaman's best views to the entrance steps.

 BLACK MESA
NATURE PRESERVE

Summit Trail

KENTON, OKLAHOMA
Hiking Time: 3-4 hours

M △ 🚙

The "black" in the mesa in the far northwest tip of the Oklahoma Panhandle is a layer of lava rock that coated the region about 30 million years ago. The mesa is also the highest point in Oklahoma at 4,973 feet.

The ascent to the roof of the Sooner State covers 4.2 miles and is dead flat the first half of the way before Seaman begins switchbacking up the rear of the mesa. **There is nothing growing high enough to obscure the view of even a dachshund on this canine hike**.

The *Summit Trail* is an easy go for Seaman with a wide, paw-friendly trail save for the slopes of volcanic residue on the mesa. Total elevation gain is 600 feet. As he rises your best trail companion will be scanning a landscape unlike any other in Oklahoma.

Once on top another level 15-minute hike is required to reach the red granite monument marking the actual highpoint. This will not be the summit of Black Mesa, only the highest spot to stand in Oklahoma. Dirt scars across the flat top lead to overlooks of three other states: Texas, New Mexico, and Colorado. There is little shade and no water out here, however, so take the proper precautions.

The Nature Preserve is a lonely 15 miles northwest of the small Black Mesa State Park where you can camp, hike a couple of short nature trails with Seaman and let him enjoy swimming in Lake Etling if water conditions are right.

 CIMARRON NATIONAL
GRASSLAND

Santa Fe Companion Trail

ELKHART, KANSAS
Hiking Time: 1 hour+

E 🚙

The Cimarron National Grassland is the largest swath of public land in Kansas. It also contains the longest publicly owned stretch of the historic Santa Fe Trail remaining with 23 miles of the Great Prairie Highway. **One of the easiest - and most scenic - spots for your dog to access the old trading route is the Point of Rocks Interpretive Site**.

The Point of Rocks, a rough low mesa jutting over the hillside was a much-anticipated sight for 19th century travelers as it marked one of the few reliable water sources on the Santa Fe Trail. The spot is the third highest point in Kansas and looks over the verdant Cimarron River Valley. The riverbed flows under the sand and water is normally evident only in flood times.

To protect the actual Trail remnants an alternate path was carved as a *Companion Trail*. Limestone posts tag the original trail route and well-preserved wagon ruts can be seen. Grasses were mowed and cacti removed to facilitate walking this historic route. There are 19 miles of easily hikable trail through the remote Cimarron National Grassland.

Grass, yucca, and sage brush are Seaman's constant companions on this hike in either direction from Point of Rocks. Except for the passage of 150 years this canine hike could take place in the Santa Fe Trail era. Of course, the *Companion Trail* is a lot less busy now then it was then: this canine hike is for dogs who cherish peace, quiet, and open spaces to roam.

Custer State Park

Trail 9: Black Elk Peak Trail
LOMA, COLORADO
Hiking Time: 3-4 hours

M △ ⩰ $

General George Armstrong Custer headed an expedition into the Black Hills in 1874, then considered one of the last unexplored regions of the United States. Custer and his men discovered gold and the region was a secret no more. Precious metals are just part of the cornucopia of riches found in the Black Hills. Custer State Park, the largest state park in the continental United States, supports its 73,000 acres without government money.

One of the best places to begin exploring this vast outdoor playground with Seaman are the trails around Sylvan Lake, a calendar cover-worthy pool of water flanked by giant granite boulders that formed when Theodore Reder dammed Sunday Gulch in 1921. A pleasant one-mile loop circumnavigates the lake and offers plenty of dog-paddling along the way.

Sylvan Lake is also a popular jumping off point to climb Black Elk Peak, at 7,242 feet the highest point in America east of the Rocky Mountains. The most traveled route to the summit is on *Trail 9*, an 8-mile round trip through Ponderosa pines, spruce, and aspen. **There is some rock scrambling near the top but Seaman can make it all the way and even go up the steps into the abandoned stone fire tower**. Native stone was hauled to the summit for construction during the mid-1930s. Views from the craggy open summit - the mountain has over 2,900 feet of prominence - reach into four states, including the world's largest buffalo herds that graze in the park.

Enchanted Rock Natural Area

Loop Trail
FREDERICKSBURG, TEXAS
Hiking Time: 1-2 hours

M △ ⩰ $

If you have ever tried to dig a large rock out of your backyard with a shovel you know how long it can take before you have excavated enough dirt to leverage the stone to the surface. Imagine how long it would take to uncover a 425-foot high batholith - an underground rock formation exposed by erosion.

That is the Enchanted Rock, the largest isolated pink granite rock in the United States. Pink granite was used to build the landmark Texas State Capitol. Enchanted Rock is the most popular attraction in Texas Hill Country and was even more popular when dogs were allowed on the *Summit Trail* to the top of the rock. That privilege was suspended in 2016 because so many dogs refreshed themselves in vernal pools around the rock that the mini-ecosystems became degraded.

Dogs *are* still welcome to hike the 4-mile *Loop Trail* around the massive modnadnock. It does not take long for this dirt trail to turn serious in a hurry once the crowded paved parking lots are left behind. **This is a true Hill Country hiking experience for your dog with scrubby vegetation, lots of rocks, and plenty of sunshine overhead**.

Moss Lake will have water for dog paddling and Sandy Creek may be flowing as well. The payoff is looks at Enchanted Rock from every angle and even a western-facing overlook with panoramic views of its own. Not top of Enchanted Rock views but...

FORT ROBINSON STATE PARK

Smiley Canyon Loop Trail
CRAWFORD, NEBRASKA
Hiking Time: 3-4 hours

M △ ⫯⫯ $ ⭕⭕

With more than 22,000 acres, Fort Robinson is one of Nebraska's largest recreation areas. There is also plenty of canine history for your dog to honor here. The military post was established in 1874 and evolved into the world's largest facility for training horses and mules for cavalry forces. During World War II the country's K-9 Corps training center was established at Fort Robinson. More than 14,000 dogs were trained for military duty and civilian service here.

Seaman won't recognize Fort Robinson as a military installation - the only fences are strands of barbed wire. He can sniff historic buildings and visit the stone pyramid memorial to Lakota Sioux chief Crazy Horse who was killed in Army custody here.

This is a land or eroded buttes and bluffs and Smiley Canyon provides the ideal scenic entree to the 60+ miles of trails here, mostly on ranch roads and cattle paths. The seven-mile loop (several options shorten it) gets underway by crossing through cottonwoods and willows growing along Buffalo Creek before entering the sandstone badlands. Pine trees decorate the hills in various stands of density.

Seaman will seldom hear a word, discouraging or otherwise, at Fort Robinson. Bison and antelope play and even the occasional bighorn sheep can be spotted in the buttes. The bluffs make ideal doggie resting spots to soak in the vast grasslands and history spreading beneath the *Smiley Canyon Loop Trail*.

GUERNSEY STATE PARK

Oregon Trail - Guernsey Ruts
GUERNSEY, WYOMING
Hiking Time: less than 1 hour

E △

The Oregon Trail is America's most famous foot trail. Between 1840 and 1869 some 500,000 pioneers walked the more than 2,000 miles from western Missouri to the Oregon Territory. Today you can still see faint traces of the epic migration in the soil but nowhere is evidence of the historic Oregon Trail more obvious than in Guernsey State Park. At this point the North Platte River became too marshy to navigate and almost every wagon heading west ascended this short hill to cross a ridge in the exact same place.

Seaman can trot the same route across soft sandstone carved five feet deep by thousands of iron wagon wheels. The landmark ruts are reached by a short paved loop trail. Two miles to the southeast of Deep Rut Hill is Register Cliff, a natural "chalkboard" where emigrants scratched their names into the stone.

A century later the Civilian Conservation Corps (CCC) came to Guernsey during the Great Depression. Their work in the campgrounds and recreation areas around the newly formed Guernsey Reservoir is considered the finest in the Rocky Mountain region. The "Castle" at Brimmer Point is one of the nation's absolute best examples of CCC rustic architecture.

In addition to the explorations on Deep Rut Hill, Guernsey State Park offers a 14-mile trail network established by the Corps during their stay in the 1930s.

Helena-Lewis and Clark National Forest

Sulphur Springs Trail
GREAT FALLS, MONTANA
Hiking Time: 1-2 hours

E 🏊

There were many times that Seaman's expedition of the Corps of Discover led by Meriwether Lewis and William Clark could have come a cropper. One of the most serious occurred when Indian guide Sacagawea took deathly ill during the portage of the Great Falls of the Missouri. Clark tried bleeding her for days to rid her of the disease with no effect. Only when Lewis discovered sulphur springs on the north side of the river here did the crucial wayfinder begin to recover.

The healing springs are still there today and reachable on a fun and easy hike with your dog through the Montana native prairie. The out-and-back crushed gravel trail is 1.8 miles long and leads to overlooks of this historic stretch of river. The area around the parking lot sports evidence of the abandoned Morony Dam town site.

Lewis called the falls the grandest sight he had seen on the journey but 20th century dams have submerged the hydrospectacular. Signs along the *Sulpher Springs Trail* tell the tale and across the river the Lewis and Clark Interpretive Center covers the whole story. There is classic plains hiking there as well, into small bluffs and around one of the largest freshwater springs in the country.

It won't ruin Seaman's fun to reveal that scientific inquiry has determined that the sulphur springs never had any real medicinal qualities and Sacajawea's drinking the waters probably coincided with her infection running its course.

Hill Country Natural Area

Heritage Loop/Medina Loop/Chaquita Falls Trail
BANDERA, TEXAS
Hiking Time: 2-3 hours

M ⛺ 🏊 $ 🚙

When Louise Lindsey Merrick gave her family's Bar-O-Ranch to the the State of Texas it was with the stipulation that it "be kept far removed and untouched by modern civilization." Even the campsites are little more than a place to spread out your dog's bedroll. The 5,000+ acres of the natural area are the ideal introduction to the hardscrabble Texas Hill Country.

The 40 miles of old ranch roads and horse trails roll up and down limestone hills, cross grassy valleys, and visit spring-fed streams. Ashe juniper and Texas live oak decorate the landscape while low-growing claret-cup cactus cling to the trail edges.

This quintessential Hill Country canine hike breaks trail from the command center of the historic ranch, highlighted by the 1892 quarter horse barn with plenty of antique tack around. On the *Heritage Loop* Seaman will be constrained by century-old Kitselman woven wire fence.

You will soon be off on the meaty chunk of this paw-scraping hike as you ascend the *Medina Loop*. **This is scenic beauty with rough edges as Seaman channels his best inner ranch dog trailing the chuckwagon.** The destination after 2.5 miles is Comanche Bluff with its views above the West Verde Creek.

Following that water course will close the loop but expect Seaman to be splashing in the creek while you try to figure out what exactly constitutes Chaquita Falls.

LITTLE MISSOURI NATIONAL GRASSLANDS

Maah Daah Hey Trail/Long X Trail

WATFORD CITY, NORTH DAKOTA
Hiking Time: 4-5 hours

M Δ ⚊ ⚊

Is it possible for one million acres to be a "hidden" gem? If so, that is how to describe the Little Missouri National Grasslands, the largest federally managed grasslands in the country.

For this canine prairie hike disabuse Seaman of any notions of an easy trot through a pasture. The *Maah Daah Hey Trail* - from the Mandan Hidatsa Indian language for "area that has been around for a long time" - courses through an eye-popping variety of terrain in its 144 miles. Yes, your dog will get time bounding through endless flat grasslands but there will also be climbs through some of the baddest of Dakota's badlands.

At the northern terminus of the *MDHT* a sporty counter-clockwise 11-mile loop can be welded with the *Long X Trail*, an historic cattle passage where Texas longhorns once kicked up sod. Seaman will likely still see cattle on the *Long X* today. **The route begins in the bottomlands of the Little Missouri River, perfect for splashing and swimming for your dusty trail companion, before switchbacking on ledges through the clay buttes and coulees to magnificent views of the surrounding moonscape**.

After linking with the *MDHT* the going is brisk along the single track scar across the prairie. For extra mileage, head right at the *Summit Trail* junction and see the largest juniper tree in North Dakota in about one-half mile. By the time you finish this one Seaman should be ready to sign on for a cattle drive.

LOESS HILLS WILDLIFE MANAGEMENT AREA

Sylvan Runkel State Preserve Trail

TURIN, IOWA
Hiking Time: 3-4 hours

M ⚊

Iowa is the most developed state in America. Development is not just houses, skyscrapers and parking lots. It is agriculture as well. And when all the cornfields and soybean cropland are totaled together there is less undeveloped land in Iowa than anywhere in the United States. Fewer than 1% of the tallgrass prairie remains; all but 5% of the state's wetlands have been filled in; and almost all the forests have been converted to cropland.

The Hawkeye State's foremost naturalist, Sylvan Thomas Runkel, dedicated his life to preserving and teaching about what is left. That includes the Loess Hills, an extensive native prairie covering steep hills formed by the namesake windblown silt.

The narrow main trail in the preserve sends Seaman to the top of a prominent grassy ridge, facing west towards the Missouri River and east towards the most productive farmland in the world. The parallel horizontal ridges evident in the Loess Hills are the result of the oft-saturated soil losing its support and "slumping." Traversing these "cat steps" on this rollercoaster canine hike will absolutely give Seaman an unexpected Great Plains workout.

More than 200 plant species have been identified in the Loess Hills, including some found nowhere else in Iowa. Many of those plants are hardwood trees that dominate the northern end of this out-and-back trail before heading back.

OGLALA NATIONAL GRASSLANDS

Toadstool Loop
CRAWFORD, NEBRASKA
Hiking Time: 1-3 hours

M △ **$** 🚙

Seaman may come to these national grasslands expecting to hike through amber waves of grain but the attraction here is the "Little Badlands" of the Nebraska panhandle. America's badlands received their ominous moniker when early settlers found it impossible to safely roll a wagon through the cracked lunar landscape in the Upper Midwest. Our most famous badlands are preserved in Dakota national parks - and off limits to canine hikers.

At Toadstool Geologic Park Seaman will be trotting across stark, eroded rock formations where the tag team of water and wind have been at work for millions of years. The "toadstools" form when underlying soft claystone erodes faster than the hard sandstone that caps it. **Your curious dog can also explore off the path for close-up looks in the gullies at fossil bone fragments that lace the rocks and 30-million year-old footprints preserved in the stone.** A mile-long interpretive loop tells the tale.

For extended hikes with Seaman, Toadstool Park connects to the world-renowned Hudson-Meng Bison Boneyard via a three-mile trail. This archeological site seeks to unravel the mystery of how over 600 bison died nearly 10,000 years ago in an area about the size of a football stadium. Human predation is the leading suspect. As you near the prehistoric kill bed Seaman will experience the head-high grasses on the trail he was looking for from the Oglala Grasslands.

PALO DURO CANYON STATE PARK

Lighthouse Trail
CANYON, TEXAS
Hiking Time: 2-3 hours

M △ **$**

The "Grand Canyon of Texas" is one of the largest in America, yawning for over 120 miles and reaching depths of 800 feet. This is particularly impressive since the gaping chasm is invisible as you drive east from the only access town of Canyon. Early Spanish Explorers are believed to have discovered the area and dubbed the canyon "Palo Duro" which is Spanish for "hard wood" in reference to the abundant mesquite and juniper trees. Palo Duro Canyon State Park opened on July 4, 1934 with over 26,000 acres in the scenic, northern most seven miles of the canyon.

With all that, the classic Palo Duro canine hike has nothing to do with the canyon. Instead, point Seaman towards the park's signature rock formation, a multi-tiered, 300-foot high pier of Trujillo sandstone known as the Lighthouse. **It will be three miles before reaching the base of the tower but Seaman will see it in the distance long before that, sticking out above the prairie grasses, cholla cactus, and mesquite bushes.**

The *Lighthouse Trail* is a joy for Seaman to trot on - smooth, hard-packed dirt and usually wide enough to handle a pack of trail dogs. The route follows dry washes and troughs between small hills as you gain an easy 900 feet in elevation. There are overlooks from the Capitol Mesa and while red dominates the color palette there are bands of yellow, purple, and brown in the buttes as you close in on this designated National Natural Landmark.

ROUGHLOCK FALLS NATURE AREA

Roughlock Falls Trail

LEAD, SOUTH DAKOTA
Hiking Time: 1 hour

E 🏊

Scientists estimate Spearfish Canyon is six times as old as the Grand Canyon. The 400-foot high limestone cliffs lord over some of the greatest botanical diversity in the region. Of the 1,586 identified plant species in South Dakota, 1,260 grow along the Spearfish Creek. Spearfish Canyon is the place to come in the Black Hills for waterfalls and looks at these hydrospectaculars can be purchased at very little cost.

Roughlock Falls is one of the few waterfalls that requires more than stopping at a pull-off on the road. The multi-channeled water display pours down from Little Spearfish Creek just before entering Spearfish Canyon. Much money has been spent to make the one-mile nature trail fully accessible and an easy ramble for dogs and humans; benches appear at regular intervals. Elevation gain in the canyon is about 150 feet.

This canine hike is a jumble of tumbling waters, pools reflecting mossy boulders, and towering Ponderosa pines. The rocky walls play a more prominent role in the Spearfish Canyon saga as a wooden bridge system approaches the falls.

Seaman will be sharing these waters with the rare American Dipper that patrols Roughlock Falls. The dark blue, long-legged birds zip over the surface and plunge in and out of the cascading water in search of food. They use their wings to "fly" underwater and can even be seen walking on the stream bottom pecking for food just as if they were walking on the trail.

SCOTTS BLUFF NATIONAL MONUMENT

Saddle Rock Trail

GERING, NEBRASKA
Hiking Time: 2 hours

M $

Hiram Scott was one of thousands of anonymous fur traders sent into Indian Territory during the early 1800s to bargain for valuable pelts of muskrat, rabbit and, especially, beaver. That he got his name attached to the most significant bluff in American history is by virtue of his premature death here - most likely from disease but with every retelling the circumstances became increasingly more dramatic.

Rising 800 feet above the North Platte Valley, this arid bluff was the "hill that was hard to go around" for emigrants on the Oregon Trail. Seaman can even trot along a stretch of the actual pioneer roadbed, next to a re-created wagon train.

The *Saddle Rock Trail* leads 1.6 miles up into the prairie badlands. **It is paved the entire way but this will be the sportiest hike your dog ever takes on macadam**. You even get a tunnel hacked through the sandstone and no trail dog worth his biscuits doesn't love a mysterious tunnel. The bluff is decorated with little bluestem grass, western wheatgrass, wind-stunted pines, and wildflowers.

When Scotts Bluff National Monument was established in 1919, it was believed to be the highest point in Nebraska (the state high point is actually at a rise in the prairie known as Panorama Point that your dog can visit over in Kimball County near the Colorado state line). It will feel like the highpoint, however, when Seaman tops out on the bluff at the North Overlook.

Smith Falls State Park

Jim McAllister Nature Trail

SPARKS, NEBRASKA
Hiking Time: 1-2 hours

E A ⚊

There is a lot going on here for an easy leg stretcher with your dog. The Niobrara River has spent eons grinding 300 feet out of the chalky white sandstone base of northern Nebraska. Almost 250 waterfalls, most just a couple of feet tall, have been identified in a 35-mile corridor. In these canyons can be found such unexpected Great Plains residents as Ponderosa pine, paper birches, red cedars, and aspens.

Seaman will see all that and more on the *Jim McAllister Nature Trail* passing through the Sandhills prairieland for 1.5 miles. From a secluded side canyon, approached via trail across a grassy field and spilling 63 feet into the Niobrara River is the champion of Nebraska waterfalls, spring-fed Smith Falls. The classic fan-shaped falls hug an exposed cliffface as the waters broaden into an attractive chimney shape. The wooden walkway leads down to the plunge pool but there is nothing more than splashing here for Seaman. No worries - there is plenty of dog paddling in the nearby Niobrara River.

A highlight of the Smith Falls State Park trail system is the Verdigre Bridge, a 160-foot steel truss span that was constructed to bring Model A automobiles into the town of Verdigre. **The bridge was disassembled after being taken out of service and put together here so Seaman doesn't have to swim across the Niobrara River, although he could**.

Tallgrass Prairie National Preserve

Southwind Nature Trail

STRONG CITY, KANSAS
Hiking Time: 1-2 hours

E

Once upon a time 170 million acres of tallgrass prairie covered North America. Today, 96% of that ecosystem is gone. Most of what remains is in the Flint Hills of southeastern Kansas where the limestone and shale deposits repelled even John Deere's best steel plows. The *Southwind Nature Trail* is Seaman's best chance to experience the Great Plains like his ancestors following the Conestoga wagons when pioneers described this landscape as "an ocean of grass."

The Preserve was once Spring Hill Ranch where Texan Stephen Jones began running cattle in the 1870s. **This is an exceedingly pleasant outing for your dog, trotting on dirt ranch roads and finely crushed stone paths**.

There are 70 species of grasses flourishing here, dominated by Big Bluestem. A single blade might have a root system descending over eight feet underground - deep enough so the plant will emerge in the spring even without rainfall. Given more ideal growing conditions these tallgrasses can reach eight feet into the sky creating wide chutes of hiking lanes for your dog. The grasses are high enough to provide shade on a hot summer day.

The 1.75-mile canine hike loops past stone fences and along the bottomlands of Fox Creek. A spur across the stream leads up a small hill to a stone school donated by Jones. It will all leave Seaman nostalgic for the loss of America's most endangered ecosystem.

VALENTINE NATIONAL WILDLIFE REFUGE

Civilian Conservation Corps Fire Tower Trail
VALENTINE, NEBRASKA
Hiking Time: 1 hour+

More than one-quarter of America's 15th largest state is blanketed with grass-stabilized sand dunes that ripple across the landscape. Most of the Nebraska Sandhills have never seen a plow.

Aside from the beautiful rolling hills, 39 spring-fed marshy lakes are the stars at Valentine National Wildlife Refuge, nine of which are fished year-round. Sounds like a place Seaman is going to want to hike.

The Civilian Conservation Corps (CCC) came to the federal game preserve in Valentine in 1933 to work on soil erosion projects. To keep an eye on things the Corpsmen built a fire tower and a three-foot wide sandy trail through the dunes. **The nature trail is less than a mile but delivers a sporty introduction to the Sandhills for your dog with 15% grades to conquer 200 feet of elevation gain**. A set of informational signs interpret the forces that created this special area.

An observation deck has been raised thirty feet in the tower that provides a marvelous look at the surrounding sand hills prairie. The panoramic vantage point can also be used to plot out additional canine hiking as there are no formal trails out by Hackberry Lake. Maintenance roads and the lightly traveled Little Hay Road Wildlife Drive can be cobbled into a hiking route for Seaman along the maze of lakeshores.

 WICHITA MOUNTAINS WILDLIFE REGUGE

Charons Garden
INDIAHOMA, OKLAHOMA
Hiking Time: 2-3 hours

This is one of the oldest (1901) and most significant wildlife refuges in America. When the bison was extinct from the Southern Great Plains for nearly two generations six bulls and nine cows were transported from the Bronx Zoo in 1907 to re-establish the herd here that now numbers over 650.

The granite outcroppings of the Wichita Mountains are some of the planet's oldest rocks - 500 million years in the making. **Much of Seaman's hiking day in the Wichitas will be fun boulder scrambling, especially when the *Charons Garden Wilderness Trail* passes through the Valley of Boulders**. There are other unexpected flatlands delights such as the seasonal Post Oak Falls and a couple of the refuge's 13 lakes.

The trail picks its way through lichen-covered rocks and post oaks and if you come in spring wildflowers will blanket the landscape for as far as Seaman can see. All canine hiking is of the out-and-back variety; one-mile spurs lead to the granite domes Elk Mountain and the aptly named and wonderful to behold Crab Eyes. Unlike other delicately balanced rock formations where glaciers or water erosion do the heavy lifting, the "crab eyes" are credited to the winds.

Peaks in the Wichitas are in the 1800- to 2200-foot range and deliver stunning views of the surrounding landscape, even if the climbing to the summit is too technical for your dog. The elevation gain to Elk Mountain is 590 feet, the most in Charons Garden.

ROCKY MOUNTAINS

ANtelope Island State Park

White Rock Loop

SYRACUSE, UTAH
Hiking Time: 3-4 hours

M △ ⫙ $

Seaman has not seen all the wildly diverse hiking terrain Utah has to offer until he comes to Antelope Island, the largest of the Great Salt Lake's 10 islands. Fifteen miles long and over four miles wide in places, this survivor from ancient Lake Bonneville reaches elevations as high as 6,596 feet.

The *White Rock Loop* is one of the easiest ways for your dog to experience much of what the park has to offer. The balloon trail leaves from the campground by the lakeshore where the waters are so salty only two things can grow - brine shrimp and algae the shrimp feed on. The wide beach and flat water will, nonetheless, suit Seaman just fine.

A series of long ascents and descents push into the hills from the shoreline. Like most of the canine hiking on Antelope Island, the landscape is exposed all the way. The trail is paw-friendly sand and dirt and roomy most of the time. Every dog will want to include a quarter-mile spur to Beacon Knob on the day-hiking agenda. This trail high point serves up panoramas of the Wasatch Front Range across the Great Salt Lake.

The ancestral antelopes for which John Fremont and Kit Carson named the island in 1843 disappeared but were reintroduced to the 28,022-acre park in 1993. The animal stars of the park, however, are the bison, first shipped here in 1893 and now number 600 strong. The regal beasts roam freely so expect to see a shaggy bovine or two on the 6.2-mile loop.

Bannack State Park

Town Walk

BANNACK, MONTANA
Hiking Time: 1-2 hours

E △ $

The town of Bannack once boasted 3,000 citizens and was the first territorial capital of Montana. Gold in Grasshopper Creek was its lifeblood and it did not play out completely until the 1950s. The population dwindled steadily during that time until the town was completely abandoned. Since then the state has maintained 60+ structures in the remote valley in a state of arrested decay.

Your dog can walk through the ghost town streets and even into the empty buildings. Some, like the School House and stately Hotel Meade appear like they could be in operation tomorrow; others feature peeling asbestos floor tile and crumbling ceilings. Go inside any building that is not locked - just remember to close the door on your way out.

There is an opportunity for canine hiking beyond the town site. A trip up Hangman's Gulch leads Seaman to the site of the gallows and the nearby cemetery where the first gold hunters were buried in 1862.

Trotting down the road east of town winds through a broad canyon and to the site of the Hendricks Mill where Bannack gold - 99% pure compared to the typical 95% - was processed. The round-trip for this easy exploration is just short of three miles.

Another hiking loop south of the Bannack follows an old stage road into the hills for views of wildflowers and the old mining community, one of America's best preserved ghost towns.

BRIDGER-TETON NATIONAL FOREST

Highline Trail

PINEDALE, WYOMING

Hiking Time: 3 hours

M A ≈ ᗛ

The Wind River Range doesn't get as much hype as its famous neighbors at Yellowstone and the Tetons but there is more glacial activity here than any place in the Lower 48. That scouring and shaping has created the tallest mountain in the middle Rocky Mountains (Gannett Peak at 13,804 feet) and many spectacular alpine lakes. Sitting at 8,000 feet, the Green River Lakes are considered the headwaters for the Green River that is the primary feeder into the great Colorado River.

The *Highline Trail* begins at the base of the Lower Green Lake and crosses the outlet to the Green River to begin a meadow ramble that will trace the east shore for three miles. **The south shore features a broad pebble beach where your dog can swim beneath the jagged Wind River peaks.** You can complete a trip around the lake at this point by diving into a thick spruce forest on the *Lakeside Trail* if you desire.

More popular is pushing up the *Highline Trail* to Upper Green Lake and ever-closer views of Squaretop Mountain that has dominated Seaman's views since his first steps. The turquoise waters lap up against the White Rock Cliffs and the trail visits more meadows beyond.

Eventually you will need to decide when to turn back as time and energy dictate since the *Highline* continues for 14.5 miles. Don't listen to Seaman's vote to just keep heading deeper into the staggering Wind River Range - which is his natural inclination.

CARSON NATIONAL FOREST

Williams Lake Trail

TAOS SKI VALLEY, NEW MEXICO

Hiking Time: 2-3 hours

M A ≈ ᗛ

At 11,040 feet in elevation Williams Lake is a proud member of the select club of two-mile high American lakes. Once upon a time the lake high in the Sangre de Cristo Mountains belonged to a gold prospector named William Frazer, who staked claims here.

The canine hike to Williams Lake kicks off in the Taos Ski Valley village and covers two miles. Although you gain about 1,000 feet in elevation the ramble through Engelmann spruce doesn't push straight up like many Rocky Mountain trails. Short, steep stretches intermingle with mostly level trail that recharges Seaman's engine. The footpath swings into meadowland and scattered moraine fields from time to time as well.

Williams Lake sits in a gorgeous natural bowl ringed by rocky peaks that are the handiwork of 10,000-year old glaciers. **The shallow waters freeze in the winter so there are no fish in the lake - it is deep enough for dog paddling, however, and Seaman has easy access from any point on the shore**.

One of those mountains looming over Williams Lake is Wheeler Peak, the roof of New Mexico at 13,161 feet. The trail to tag the summit is two more miles and switchbacks steeply through loose scree far above the treeline. You will be envious of Seaman's four-wheel drive across this patch but technical gear is not required. Needless to say, the views from Wheeler Peak are stupendous, including a full view of Williams Lake.

CHAUTAUQUA PARK

Royal Arch Trail
BOULDER, COLORADO
Hiking Time: 2-3 hours

S $

Every town has that one go-to attraction that is the default place to take visitors. In Boulder, that place is Chautauqua Park. This being the outdoor mecca of Boulder, there are over 40 miles of hiking trails available.

Chautauqua was a 19th century movement to bring knowledge and culture to rural areas in a camp setting. Chautauquas (shuh-TAW-kwuh) began in western New York and the Colorado camp, started in 1898, is the oldest continuing member operating west of the Mississippi River.

The lower altitudes of Chautauqua Park spreads out in front of the signature Flatiron Mountains overlooking the city. **The meadows of the *Bluebell-Baird Trail* just about demand that your dog come romp through the golden grasses**. Seaman will be in no hurry to leave here but the wonder of the Royal Arch awaits.

The *Royal Arch Trail* will certainly get Seaman's attention with a 1,400-foot gain in elevation in under two miles. Even so, it may be the most crowded canine hike in Colorado. Rock steps and switchbacks help keep Seaman's spirits high on the steep ascent. The fragrant pines chip in as well.

The real views don't break out until the arch is reached at 6,915 feet. A downhill stretch extends false hope before a final rock staircase leads through the arch and a drop the mic view of Boulder. The way back down should generate a second wind for Seaman to try longer loops back to the trailhead.

CUSTER GALLATIN NATIONAL FOREST

Hyalite Creek Trail
BOZEMAN, MONTANA
Hiking Time: 2-8 hours

M △ ⩰ 🚙

John Bozeman opened the first wagon trail through a break in the mountains that American Indians called "Valley of the Flowers." Revered as a sacred hunting ground, the Sioux killed Bozeman and no one dared try his trail again for nine years. These days nothing can keep canine hikers off the trail to this outdoor paradise that serves as the northern gateway city to Yellowstone National Park.

South of town Custer Gallatin National Forest bursts with 2,000 miles of trails and the canine hike along Hyalite Creek through a U-shaped glaciated canyon encapsulates the beauty of them all. **There are three primo destinations in Hyalite Canyon, depending on your trail dog's hunger for adventure**.

Grotto Falls is the most popular of the many side spurs that lead to waterfalls spilling into the canyon. Inclines are easy and the coniferous forest thick as the trail makes several crossings of Hyalite Creek. In a little over two miles the wide and frothy waters plunge into an inviting doggie swimming hole.

An even better swim for Seaman awaits another three miles up the trail at Hyalite Lake, a glacial tarn framed by stunning craggy gray pinnacles. One of those cliffs is Hyalite Peak and it is two miles more to the 10,298-foot summit. The deep green forests are giving way to wildflower meadows and rocky paths by this time as Seaman gains 1,400 feet in elevation past the lake - about what he covered from the trailhead to Hyalite Lake.

FLAMING GORGE NATIONAL RECREATION AREA

Little Hole National Recreation Trail

MANILA, UTAH
Hiking Time: 2 hours+

E △ ≈.

Trailblazing 19th century scientist and explorer John Wesley Powell named the Flaming Gorge after he saw the sun shining off the red canyon walls on his epic 1869 exploration of the Green and Colorado rivers. Powell would recognize those walls today but the 502-foot high dam built in 1962 has changed the appearance of the Green River forever.

The best way to see the the 1,400-foot deep Red Canyon is on the *Canyon Rim Trail*, a multi-purpose path accessed at the Red Canyon Visitor Center. Seaman, however, will much prefer the *Little Hole National Recreation Trail*, a delightful one-way walk below the Flaming Gorge Dam. **A swim-loving dog is likely to spend as much time in the crystal green waters as on the level, easy-going footpath**. Seaman might even spot a few plump trout in the Green River that are the quarry of anglers floating merrily along - 22-pounders have been pulled from these waters.

The river is constrained by the red shale and sandstone cliffs as the trail gradually ascends to 1,000 feet above the water. Boardwalks conquer tricky areas in the canyon. You can turn back any time on this out-and-back ramble but the further you go the further you will want to go.

The Green River eventually emerges from Red Canyon and spreads out at the Little Hole Recreation Area after six miles. The parking area here makes this a candidate for a vehicle shuttle canine hike as well.

FOSSIL BUTTE NATIONAL MONUMENT

Historic Quarry Trail

KEMMERER, WYOMING
Hiking Time: 2-3 hours

M

Looking around at the sagebrush and bone-dry desert in this 9,000-acre park it takes imagination to picture this as the Great Lakes region of America 50 million years ago. There isn't even anything to eat here - Fossil Butte National Monument is one of a few areas in southwestern Wyoming not grazed by cattle and sheep. But long ago there were three major lakes in what is today Colorado, Utah and Wyoming. This one, Fossil Lake, spread across 1,000 square miles. The animals that lived here enjoyed sub-tropical weather. Their remains piled up in the bottom of the lake and fossilized into a rock layer of laminated limestone and volcanic ash. Few places on earth can match the specimens of Fossil Lake for sheer abundance, crystalline preservation and remarkable variety of fish, mammals, plants, reptiles and birds.

The limestone butte rises above the sagebrush and the *Historic Quarry Trail* loops across the face, gaining 600 feet in elevation over 2.5 miles. This a *big* canine hike with views for miles up and down the valley the entire time.

A steep spur trail leads up to the diggings where Seaman can examine the workings and perhaps spot a brownish fish skeleton. A short distance away is a century-old A-frame cabin David Haddenham used while harvesting fossils from the butte. Keep Seaman on the lookout for wildlife - there are more pronghorn antelope than people in the state of Wyoming and a herd 100 strong roam the lightly trafficked national monument.

GARDEN OF THE GODS

Palmer/Siamese Twins/Scotsman Trails
COLORADO SPRINGS, COLORADO
Hiking Time: 2-3 hours

M

The indigenous Ute Indians referred to this area of protruding, jagged red rocks as "the old red land." The story goes that when the original surveyors of Colorado Springs discovered the sandstone remains of an ancient ocean floor, one referred to it as a great spot for a beer garden. Fellow surveyor Rufus Cable, of a more romantic bent, protested the majestic muted crimson rocks were more suited to be a "garden for the Gods."

Garden of the Gods Park is enormously popular - attracting more than one million visitors every year - so contemplative hikes with your dog can be problematic. A good place to start is on the *Perkins Central Garden Trail* where a paved pathway winds through the heart of most of the most towering rock formations.

Jump off the asphalt onto the natural surface *Scotsman Trail* and head south in relative isolation. Across the park road the *Siamese Twins Trail* leads to a unique formation with a window that looks directly at Pikes Peak. Away from the Central Garden the jagged sandstone peaks are highlighted by lush green pinyon-junipers and become even more photogenic.

The canine hiking in the 15-mile trail system outside the Central Garden travels through five different ecosystems at 6,400 feet above sea level. Most of the time Seaman will be trotting easily in open prairie grasslands and mountain shrub. **There is also an area dogs can run unleashed in the park**.

GOLDEN SPIKE NATIONAL HISTORIC SITE

Big Fill Trail
PROMONTORY SUMMIT, UTAH
Hiking Time: 1-2 hours

E $

Perhaps nothing as important in American history happened in as remote a location as the completion of the first transcontinental railroad in the Promontory Mountains on May 10, 1869. The Promontories don't appear as imposing as their lofty neighbors but this is the toughest grade to pull a train in the entire Rocky Mountains.

The original tracks are long gone; the 17.6-karat golden spike driven by Central Pacific president Leland Stanford had been whisked away for safekeeping immediately after linking the railroads. A section of track has been restored and a polished railroad tie laid at the historic linking spot; two replica locomotives are available to help recreate the ceremony.

Beyond that not much has changed in the desolate grassy prairie in the past 150 years. The *Big Fill Trail* takes Seaman along the original grade where the two competing railroads came together, each with a different idea of how to conquer a ravine 500 feet wide and 70 feet deep. The Central Pacific took two months and 250 dumpcart teams to fill the ravine while the Union Pacific constructed a trestle, the foundations of which remain.

A 1.5-mile loop visits the sites of both efforts. **No need to worry about tiring Seaman on this hike - the grade was mandated by the Pacific Railroad Act of 1862 never to be greater than 1.6 percent**. You can continue hiking with your dog on the grade beyond the Big Fill, soaking in the beauty of the wide open spaces.

GRAND MESA NATIONAL FOREST

Crag Crest National Recreation Trail

DELTA, COLORADO

Hiking Time: 4-5 hours

M △ 🏊

The Grand Mesa in western Colorado may be one of America's least known natural wonders. At 500 square miles it is the largest flat-topped mountain in the world. The Grand Mesa is speckled with pristine alpine lakes, wildflower-filled meadows, and deep green Englemann spruce forests. The *Crag Crest Trail* delivers all in abundance.

The canine hike is a 10.3 loop with trailheads at the eastern and western ends - starting at the eastern end by Eggleston Lake affords the chance to get the climbing out of the way early in a counter-clockwise direction. Starting from the western end the pull to the top is more gradual. The lake sits at two miles in elevation and gains 1,000 feet to the top of 11,189-foot Crags Crest.

At either end the journey begins in broad meadows that afford views of the craggy ridge ahead. Once the rocky shoulder is conquered the crest rolls gently for miles above the treeline. **The entire Grand Mesa spreads beneath you in every direction - there are steep drop-offs on either side but plenty of room for Seaman to traverse safely**. At the summit, to the east rises Leon Peak, the highest point on the mesa, scarcely 150 feet higher than your position.

After descending lightly through the alpine forest Seaman will be romping once again in meadows and swimming in Wolverine Lake and Forest Lake before wrapping up one of the best canine hikes in the Rockies.

GREAT SAND DUNES NATIONAL PARK

Mosca Pass Trail

MOSCA, COLORADO

Hiking Time: 3-4 hours

M △ $

It is only appropriate that the tallest sand dunes in North America stand side by side with the tallest mountains on the continent. These piles of sand - the 750-foot Star Dune is the champion - from ancient dry lake beds got trapped in a low curve of the Sangre de Cristo Mountains. Prevailing winds from the valley floor blow toward the mountains but frequent storm winds push the dunes back toward the valley so the sand grows high instead of flattening out.

There are no designated trails in the park sand and Seaman is invited to explore the main day use part of the 30-square mile dunefield. When climbing massive dunes use a zig-zag pattern to ascend to the ridgelines. From the main parking lot you'll see the imposing "High Dune" which affords a 360-degree view from its 650-foot summit. At the top Seaman will see what he can't experience - beyond the first ridge of dunes is out-of-bounds for dogs.

Your dog's day in this sand box will end when it gets too hot so start early and also consider night hikes. In the heat of the day the moist, cool sands of Medano Creek (actual water at times) make for a fun canine romp.

Across from the dunefield is *Mosca Pass Trail* that gains 1,400 feet in elevation in an easy 3.5 miles. There are no great destinations here (a grassy field) and even the views of the dunes are sparse but this will be a fun outing in the mountains for Seaman with no imperative to do the whole hike.

Pike National Forest - Pikes Peak

Barr National Recreation Trail

MANITOU SPRINGS, COLORADO
Hiking Time: 6-10 hours

S $

Pikes Peak, with its prominence on the Front Range that made it the first landmark settlers saw heading West, is the most-visited mountain in the United States. Half a million people make their way to the summit every year, most in their cars and more on the cog railroad. When it opened in the Fall of 1888, the 14-foot wide Pikes Peak Carriage Road was billed as the highest road in the world. The first automobile chugged 19 miles to the summit in 1901.

Others favor the trail up the eastern slope built by Fred Barr between 1914 and 1918 to accommodate his burro train business. It was pick-and-shovel duty, with an occasional dash of black powder for moving boulders and trees. The 13-mile route to the 14,110-foot summit gains nearly 8,000 feet in elevation - the biggest in Colorado. It is not overly steep however, with an average grade of 11%, and the *Barr Trail* is one of the Rocky Mountain State's most popular hikes.

Dogs are welcome to tackle the Barr Trail all the way to the Pikes Peak summit. There are three miles of canine hiking above the treeline and no natural water sources so head out prepared. Near the top are rock steps that most dogs can negotiate.

For those who want to manage a multi-day ascent dogs are welcome to stay overnight in Barr Camp (not in the main cabin or bunkhouse, though) that Fred constructed in the 1920s. Book Seaman's space well in advance.

Routt National Forest

Fish Creek National Recreation Trail #1102

STEAMBOAT SPRINGS, COLORADO
Hiking Time: 5-6 hours

S 🏊 $

James Crawford is the father of Steamboat Springs, having settled in a cabin on Soda Creek in 1874. Instead of becoming "Crawfordville" legend maintains the town was named for the rhythmic chugging of a hot spring that disgorged mineral water 15 feet into the air. The medicinal springs brought the first settlers to the valley and later this was "Ski Town U.S.A." with the arrival of Norwegian ski-jumping champion Carl Howelsen in 1913.

Your trail dog won't want to wait until the snows fall to enjoy Steamboat Springs. Just outside town Fish Creek makes a 283-foot plunge that is one of Colorado's most spectacular waterfalls. Also one of the most accessible. But Seaman won't be content with the easy trotting and multiple photo ops around Fish Creek Falls.

After crossing a bridge *Trail #1102* begins its own chugging up the canyon. **Seaman will know he is climbing on this one, stepping up rocks to gain 1,400 feet in under two steep miles to the Upper Fish Creek Falls**. Although not as tall, this water display framed in boulders is every bit as Instagram-worthy as its lower brother.

Return trips can begin here or canine hiking can continue three miles further to the grassy shorelines of Long Lake. Most of the hard work is over by the Upper Falls so this will be little more than an invigorating leg stretcher for Seaman through rolling forests and sub-alpine meadows that earn this trail its national recreation designation.

San Isabel National Forest

North Elbert Trail

LEADVILLE, COLORADO
Hiking Time: 6-8 hours

S 🚙

The highest mountain in America's Lower 48 is California's Mount Whitney at 14,505 feet. You can hike with your dog to the shadow of the summit but the final steps will be yours alone as you leave dog-friendly Inyo National Forest and travel into Sequoia National Park, where dogs are banned from the trails.

The highest spot in America where Seaman is legally allowed to go is Mount Elbert in Colorado, only 65 feet lower than Whitney. The first recorded summit of the peak was by Henry W. Stuckle in 1874. Mount Elbert is still not well known, despite its lofty position as the highest peak in the Rocky Mountains. Snobbish outdoor enthusiasts look at Mount Elbert with a degree of scorn because it is so "easy" to summit. There were even people who piled rocks on neighboring Mount Massive in an attempt to give it the extra twenty feet it would need to surpass Mount Elbert.

Of course, "easy" is relative and all prudent precautions for being on a 14,440-foot mountain must be taken. **But any trail dog accustomed to a ten-mile hike can scale Mount Elbert**. There are five routes to the top, the most popular being the *North Elbert Trail*. From trailhead to summit is 4.5 miles, the first two climbing through alpine forests. After the trail bursts above the treeline the route switches back twice before pulling straight to the summit. There is no rock scrambling or "mountain climbing" necessary. Views = amazing.

San Juan National Forest

Lizard Head Trail

AMES, COLORADO
Hiking Time: 6-7 hours

S ⛺

This one will put a bounce in any dog's step - Seaman will never start an alpine hike in a more gorgeous setting. The Lizard Head Wilderness takes its name for the most distinctive peak higher than 13,000 feet your dog will ever set eyes on. The early steps of this standout canine hike are through rolling meadows and Lizard Head Peak, with its 400-foot high spire, will soon be in front of you.

The easy, open grades continue for over a mile before switchbacks begin climbing through spruce-fir forests. Trout Lake can be spied through the trees. When Seaman bursts into the clear on the talus slopes he will have gained 1,400 feet in three miles.

He can catch his breath over the gentler ascent to tag the 12,147-foot summit of Black Face Mountain, the high point of the hike. Lizard Head is the star of the jagged San Miguel Range at this spot, including two of Colorado's fabled 14,000-foot peaks.

Some canine hikers turn around at this point, others continue across the high alpine meadows to complete an 11.7-mile loop that drops through a saddle of 600 feet before climbing back to over 12,000 feet below Lizard Head. The technical climb to the top of the volcanic spire of crumbling rock is considered one of the hardest in Colorado so Seaman will need no convincing to keep moving past on the *Cross Mountain Trail* before heading down to complete a grand day hike on the *Railroad Grade Trail* through open meadows again.

Santa fe National forest

Atalaya Mountain Trail

SANTA FE, NEW MEXICO
Hiking Time: 2-3 hours

M

Atalaya means "watchtower" in Spanish. In the early days of Santa Fe - and its early days are the oldest for any European community west of the Mississippi River - citizens would climb to the summit of the 9,121-foot high mountain on the east edge of town to watch out for fires. You can do the same today with Seaman.

Start by walking off the campus of St. John's College, drop into an arroyo with Seaman and, after about one mile, start the climb. There are 1,800-feet to tame on Atalaya Mountain and there is the choice of a steeper climb or an easier climb - the trail sign actually tells you that. The less strenuous route will add about two miles to the six-mile journey.

Either way Seaman will be on a wide, natural path bounding over rocks on the way to the top. The pinyon-juniper and Ponderosa pines rarely crowd the trail so you will likely be enjoying one of Santa Fe's 300+ days of sunshine.

This is not a back-to-nature canine hike. You start in the city and never dissolve totally from civilization. Plenty of close-up looks of Santa Fe's Pueblo Revival architecture pinball around the mountain and views to the west are outstanding panoramas of the capital city. That's the price you pay for convenience. On the positive side of the ledger the *Atalaya Trail* is a great winter mountain climb with easy trailhead access and an ascent that requires no special gear.

Santa fe National forest

McCauley Warm Springs Trail

JEMEZ SPRINGS, NEW MEXICO
Hiking Time: 1-2 hours

M ▲ ⚊

New Mexico does not get the pub that Yellowstone does for its geothermal activity but there is plenty of water bubbling under the five-million year-old magma in the state. Fissures in the earth allow the water to escape to the surface. Many of the hot springs have been tapped for commercial spas, some are too remote to reach easily and others are too easily accessed and crowded. McCauley Warm Springs, tucked into a naturalistic setting among old Ponderosa pines and steps down the stream in three beguiling pools, strikes a pleasing balance.

At 1.5 miles (west from the Jemez Falls Trailhead) or two miles (east from the Battleship Rock trailhead) through a tree-studded red rock canyon the canine hike requires just enough effort to deter the rabble. The springs pump out 99-degree water year-round.

The combination of rocky terrain and lack of understory conspire to give this hike with your dog a big feel. You will start with the goal of a hot soak but the enchanting trail will grab you on the way. It is uphill from Battleship Rock and downhill from Jemez Falls.

The McCauley pools are "clothing optional" so Seaman need not worry if he has forgotten swim trunks. The pools are ideal to sit in and small dogs may be able to paddle around in the crystal clear water. If you are at the Jemez Trailhead take the short hike to the observation of Jemez Falls that twists 70 feet down a rock face - the highest waterfall in the Jemez Mountains.

 SAWTOOTH
NATIONAL FOREST

Bald Mountain Trail
KETCHUM, IDAHO
Hiking Time: 5-6 hours

S 🏊

In 1935 Austrian Count Felix Schaff-gotsch was hired by the Union Pacific Railroad to scout the American West for the best site to build a European Alps-like ski resort. Schaffgotsch rejected Aspen, Jackson Hole, Yosemite - everywhere. He was prepared to report his failure when a railroad representative from Idaho asked him to check out Ketchum. Within three days, the Count reported: "Among the many attractive spots I have visited, this combines more delightful features of any place I have seen in the United States, Switzerland, or Austria for a winter sports resort." Eleven months later Sun Valley opened to international acclaim.

Ketchum features 40 miles of trails located within a 5-mile radius of town. The marquee canine hike is the 5-mile *Bald Mountain Trail* that crosses numerous ski trails on its way to the 9,151-foot summit. The packed dirt trail spends its lower elevations in wildflower-filled meadows along the Big Wood River before the switchbacks begin.

After gaining 3,400 feet in elevation Seaman will understand why Sun Valley is cherished for its long ski runs. The views of the Sawtooth Mountains become frequent until the treeline clears and the magnificent views become constant. **Not only are dogs allowed here, but halfway up the mountain, in a glade of giant fir trees, is a fountain with a perpetually-filled dog drinking bowl built right into the trail.** About the only place dogs are not allowed is on the ski lifts where tired human hikers hitch rides down.

 TRAVELERS' REST
STATE PARK

Lewis and Clark Loop
LOLO, MONTANA
Hiking Time: 1-2 hours

M 🏊 $

Some of the most harrowing decisions made by Meriwether Lewis and William Clark on their expedition to the Pacific Ocean took place in this idyllic patch of ground beside the free-flowing Lolo Creek. American Indian tribes had gathered in these meadows to camp and trade for centuries before the Corps of Discovery bunked down here, which they did coming and going. As a result this is the only site on the Lewis and Clark National Historic Trail that you can visit with your modern Seaman where physical evidence of historical Seaman has been found.

Heading west Lewis and Clark were unable to find a water passage all the way to the Pacific and it was here they regrouped and prepared for an arduous 200-mile overland trek across the Bitterroot Mountains on the Lolo Trail. While recuperating at Travelers' Rest on the way home it was decided, against all military precedent, to split the expedition in order to explore more territory. Lewis and Clark went their separate ways knowing it was likely the forces would never re-unite.

The *Lewis and Clark Loop* meanders easily through meadows and stands of cottonwoods around the Lolo Creek as it interprets the historic site. The explorers would likely recognize Travelers' Rest if they passed through today. **There is plenty of fun to be had for Seaman here, including swimming in the frisky rapids of the creek**. But one thing he can't do is camp - after hundreds of years camping is no longer allowed here.

UINTA-WASATCH-CACHE NATIONAL FOREST

Big Water Gulch/Little Water Gulch Trails

SALT LAKE CITY, UTAH
Hiking Time: 2-3 hours

M 🏊 **$**

The majestic peaks and rugged backcountry of the Uinta-Wasatch-Cache National Forest loom over the eastern shore of the Great Salt Lake, gobbling up more than two million acres and creating seven wilderness areas. **There are many wonderful canine hikes here but Seaman will raise his paw to vote for the hike to Dog Lake up Mill Creek Canyon**.

You will have to decipher some red tape concerning even and odd days; your dog is welcome any day but on odd days he can hike off-leash and no bikes are allowed on the trail. On summer odd days this hike will have the feel of a moving dog park.

Most canine hikers opt to head to Dog Lake on the three-mile *Big Water Gulch Trail*. Dog Lake is located at an elevation of about 8,745 feet; you gain about 1,440 feet but the uphills are spread out over three miles and Seaman won't be left resting by the side of the trail. Switchbacks aid the cause. The path is wide and well-worn.

Dog Lake is not visually stunning as alpine lakes tend to be but there is no prettier sight than watching dogs race happily into a cool mountain pond. The water is ringed only by flat dirt so nothing slows down a dog before jumping in. As hard as it is to believe, Dog Lake was named not for the many dogs who swim here (it is the only lake in Mill Creek Canyon where dogs are permitted to enjoy a doggie dip) but for its salamanders that are also known as "dog fish."

Color Country

Coconino National Forest

Soldier Pass-Jordan-Brins Mesa Trails

SEDONA, ARIZONA
Hiking Time: 2 hours

M

Sedona likes to calls itself "the day hike capital of the country" and your dog will not bark in disagreement. More than 300 miles of non-motorized trails traverse the Red Rock Ranger District that surrounds the resort community.

Scores of Sedona trails will set Seaman's tail to wagging and the *Soldier Pass-Jordan-Brins Mesa* loop is one that starts right on the north edge of town, just up the road from the dog park. Despite the proximity to civilization this canine hike will quickly immerse trail tramps in the deep green juniper forest and brilliant red and orange rock formations for which Sedona is famous.

The course pushes through the manzanita and velvet mesquite of the Red Rock Secret Mountain Wilderness before it bursts into the open. There are long, unobstructed views of noted landmarks - Coffee Pot Rock, Wilson Mountain, Steamboat Rock and others. If your journey follows a recent rain Seaman may be favored by water in the Seven Sacred Pools that have been carved out of ocher-colored sandstone.

The trail climbs some 500 feet to Brins Mesa, using a natural rock staircase in places, for more expansive vistas of Verde Valley red rock country. The mesa is covered in grasses facilitating those postcard-worthy views - the result of a devastating 2006 fire that burned away the trees from the 5,099-foot high flat-top promontory.

Coconino National Forest

West Fork Trail

SEDONA, ARIZONA
Hiking Time: 3 hours

M ≈ $

They say one million people a year come to hike the trails in Sedona - and this is the most popular trail in the Coconino National Forest. No doubt Seaman will want to see what all the fuss is about.

The *West Fork Trail* begins with a stroll through an historic apple orchard dating back to the 1880s. Then the level path visits the ruins of the Mayhew Lodge whose buildings were consumed in a fire in 1980. In its heyday Hollywood stars like Clark Gable, Jimmy Stewart, and Maureen O'Hara all frequented the rustic cabins here.

Shortly you reach the West Fork of the Oak Creek and canine hearts start to race. Oak Creek Canyon is a serpentine passageway under white limestone and red sandstone cliffs that soar over 1,000 feet high. **Seaman will no doubt love the 13 crossings of one of the few year-round streams in the Sedona high desert**. If you arrive after snow melt paws will likely get wet as well.

The canyon is 14 miles long but most people call it quits at three miles. The mostly level dirt trail rolls easily under stands of stately Ponderosa pines, cottonwood, and, of course, oak. The turn-around point is anti-climactic but as Harry Chapin once sang, "It's got to be the going, not the getting there that's good." The return trip out of Oak Creek Canyon is nearly as engaging as the way in as the stunning cliffs are encountered at entirely new angles and degrees of sunlight. Seaman may not even notice the crowds.

COLORADO RIVERWAY
RECREATION AREA

Fisher Towers Trail
CASTLE VALLEY, UTAH
Hiking Time: 2-3 hours

In a dazzling landscape of sandstone rock formations the pinnacles, fins, and spires of the Fisher Towers manage to stand out for sheer majesty. Legendary director John Ford began shooting Hollywood westerns on location here in 1949 after he went searching for a new desert location for his upcoming *Wagon Master* with Ben Johnson and Ward Bond in the leads. More than 50 feature films would be shot around Moab in the next 50 years. To John Wayne, this area always defined the West.

These days Seaman probably will encounter more world class rock climbers than movie cameras on this hike across slickrock and down into enchanting small canyons. The route works up close around the towers - at 900 feet tall Titan is billed as the highest free-standing natural tower in the United States - and out to promontories with long views of the surrounding Professor Valley.

The full hike through Fisher Towers covers 2.6 miles but stretches on narrow, exposed ledges and short ladders may abort this unique canine hike for some dogs before reaching its natural conclusion on a rocky knob atop Onion Creek Canyon. There is no shade out on the rocks here so take care to keep everyone hydrated.

 COLORADO RIVERWAY
RECREATION AREA

Grandstaff Canyon Trail
MOAB, UTAH
Hiking Time: 3 hours

There are more natural stone arches - over 2,000 - in Arches National Park than anywhere on earth. Your dog won't see any from beyond the parking lots, however. Luckily, just six miles from the park is **a tail-friendly hike to the world's sixth longest natural arch and America's third longest**.

This canine hike pushes into Grandstaff Canyon, cut into Navajo Rock by the ancient stream emptying into the Colorado River. Back in the 1870s William Granstaff ran cattle in the canyon while he split up possession of the Spanish Valley with his erstwhile partner, a French-Canadian trapper known only as "Frenchie." Granstaff hightailed out of the territory in 1881 when the law accused him of illegally selling liquor to local Indians. All he left behind was his name.

The packed-sand trail crosses the shallow-flowing stream many times as it works moderately uphill through the open canyon, especially in the last half-mile. This is a popular hike but if you've found an empty trail you may need to rely on Seaman's nose to stay on course through the abundant cottonwoods and willows thriving here.

A little more than two miles up into the canyon, pressed back against a rock wall, is multi-hued Morning Glory Natural Bridge that stretches 243 feet across a pool of water. Recent rains can transform the water hole under the arch into an ideal doggie swimming pool before retracing your steps back to the parking are at the Colorado River.

COLORADO RIVERWAY RECREATION AREA

Mary Jane Canyon

CASTLE VALLEY, UTAH
Hiking Time: 4 hours

E 🏊 🚙

Some canine hikes you just need to know about. There is no sign for Mary Jane Canyon off the main road northeast of Moab from UT Scenic Byway 128 ("Ranch Road Dead End"). There is no sign for the hike at the trailhead (across the parking lot from the *Sylvester Trail*). There are no trail markings (follow the path towards the sandstone rock formations known as the Priest and Nuns, which contribute to the area's designation as Castle Valley). That kind of stuff to know.

Shortly canine hikers reaches Professor Creek, named for early settler Dr. Sylvester Richardson. Point Seaman upstream and into Mary Jane Canyon, named for the doctor's wife.

Professor Creek flows year-round, although seldom above shoetop level. Fresh green vegetation dances against the exposed red rock canyon walls. **For the next four or so miles Seaman will be splashing happily through the cooling desert stream waters.** Eventually the winding canyon walls climb to over 100 feet and narrow to no more than 15 feet - if you haven't been hiking straight through the streambed the whole way you certainly will be here. The trail ends with a chokestone wedged into the canyon walls that produces an impressive 30-foot waterfall.

The way out of Mary Jane Canyon is the same as the way in. There are numerous dry slot canyons to poke into along the way. Seaman will absolutely agree - this is one hike you just need to know about.

CRACK CANYON WILDERNESS

Little Wild Horse Canyon-Bell's Canyon

MOAB, UTAH
Hiking Time: 4-5 hours

M ⛰ 🚙

This is the best slot canyon journey you can take with your dog in the West. Little Wild Horse Canyon and neighboring Bell's Canyon can be combined to form an eight-mile loop that provides an ideal introduction to the Southwestern phenomenon of slot canyon hiking.

Little Wild Horse Canyon is a classic slot canyon that narrows to single file passing for Seaman in places. Bell's Canyon is less claustrophobic but delivers gorgeous winding passages under high cliffs as well.

Expect obstacles and Seaman will likely need assistance in places: there are short rock scrambles and the occasional chokestone that blocks the canyon floor. Those floors are flat and mostly dry but count on cold brown water pooled dog-belly deep in spots as well.

Seaman can make the loop in either direction but clockwise (up Bell's Canyon to the the left first) seems to be the route of choice. A 1.5-mile jaunt along a wide jeep road links the two canyons through open desertlands and provides a refreshing break from the slots.

Saving Little Wild Horse Canyon for last negates a couple of the tougher rock scrambles and keeps the most exciting wiggles through the curvy passageways for last. The walls loom 300 feet high at this point. By this time, Seaman will realize he is on a hike like no other, one that will surely be talked about in the dog park back home.

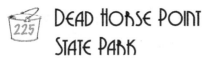

DEAD HORSE POINT STATE PARK

East Rim Trail/West Rim Trail
MOAB, UTAH
Hiking Time: 2-3 hours

M ⛺ $

There is a half-mile spur on the western side of the Dead Horse Point mesa that leads to an overlook of Shafer Canyon. You can see an open plain that was used to film the famous final scene in the movie *Thelma & Louise* when Susan Sarandon drives a 1966 Ford Thunderbird convertible over a cliff. **Some say the women were frustrated because they weren't able to hike with their dogs in any of Utah's famous national parks**.

You can hike with your dog at Dead Horse Point. Legend has it that cowboys once herded wild mustangs onto to the top of a mesa 2,000 feet above the Colorado River and blocked off their escape across a narrow neck of land with branches and brush, thus creating a natural corral. One time the horses in the corral were forgotten about and died of thirst while looking at the unaccessible river far below.

The *East and West Rim* trails form a four-mile loop around the rim of the mesa. Six short spur trails poke out to promontories overlooking the canyonlands to the east, west and south (most are unfenced and provide no protection for overcurious canines).

There is little elevation gain around the rim but the spur trails introduce inclines to Seaman's hiking day. Slickrock and desert terrain can be tricky under paw. The sparse sagebrush flats on top of Dead Horse Point mesa also are exposed and hot on a summer day.

DIXIE NATIONAL FOREST

Red Canyon Trail System
PANGUITCH, UTAH
Hiking Time: 3 hours

M ⛺

Disappointed you couldn't take your dog hiking in Bryce Canyon or Capitol Reef or Zion national parks? Get over it. Head 13 miles down the road from Bryce to the Red Canyon Visitor Center, which has been described as the "most photographed place in Utah."

Get the camera ready and point Seaman to the *Pink Ledges Trail* behind the center. You will soon be up close with the brilliant red rock formations and the accenting dark green conifers. Continue onto the aptly named *Hoodoo Trail* and across UT 12 to the equally apropos *Golden Wall Trail*.

The canine hike rambles through a wide valley, trading the bright red cliffs for golden colored rocks and crushed stone paths. To get closer to hoodoos again there is an option to jump onto the *Castle Bridge Trail*. The views become ever more spectacular as you climb out of the bowl to make a connection to the *Buckhorn Trail*.

Seaman may feel like he is on top of the red rock country world at this point - but there's more. Carefully step across a long narrow ledge 160 feet higher to trail's end at Buckhorn Point. Veterans of Angel's Landing at Zion National Park will recognize the trajectory of this hike. The amazing scenery keeps coming on the way back down until the shade of stately Ponderosa pines to finish your descent and complete the five mile loop.

Pink-gold-white-red, Seaman has seen all Color Country in southwest Utah has to offer - and without national park crowds.

 **FANTASY CANYON**

Loop Trail

VERNAL, UTAH
Hiking Time: 1 hour

E ▲ 🚙

When you call yourself Fantasy Canyon you had better deliver the goods. This patch of photogenic eroded rocks does just that, with the added bonus that no axle-breaking drive is required to reach this remote slice of Northeast Utah. The canyon is tucked on the north side of a low mesa in the otherwise featureless expanse of the Uinta Basin.

The gray-brown sandstone has eroded vertically and horizontally to fill a narrow ravine with fanciful delicate outcroppings. Fantasy Canyon earns its reputation as "nature's china shop" honestly. Someone has provided a name for 40 of nature's most intricate clay creations but you are likely to better enjoy seeing your own creatures in the formations.

A half-mile loop trail runs over and through Fantasy Canyon but Seaman likely won't give you time to find the faint traces of the dusty footpath as he races into the rocky wonderland to explore. This is Bureau of Land Management public land so your dog can roam while you snap photos of the complex pinnacles and spires.

There is some additional wandering available with Seaman in the washes and clay coulees beyond the small canyon but the surrounding area is filled with oil and gas fields so such explorations will be truncated.

 GLEN CANYON NATIONAL RECREATION AREA

Horseshoe Bend Trail

PAGE, ARIZONA
Hiking Time: 1 hour

E 🚙

OK, it is never promising for a canine hike when you pull into the parking lot and see tour buses. But sometimes the payoff is so incredible that you have to suck it up and join a couple of hundred of your newest friends on a hike.

Like most insanely popular hikes the journey to Horseshoe Bend is short and easy - less than one mile and up and down a gentle sandy hill interspersed with slick rock. The footpath is wide (it was once a sandy road) to maneuver through crowds and the surrounding desert is easily navigable if necessary.

Everyone is heading for an overlook of the Colorado River that is making a darn near perfect 270-degree horseshoe turn through the bare Navajo sandstone 1,100 feet below. The slow moving water at this point appears cobalt blue with a narrow ring of green vegetation along the shore. Horseshoe Bend from this vantage point is one of the most familiar photographs from the American Southwest. If you are going for one of those keepsake photos with Seaman aim for the morning when sunlight floods the canyon.

Don't be surprised if your naturally curious dog walks to the edge and peers over like everyone else. There is room to spread out on the mostly level slickrock around the rim to access uncrowded viewpoints. If you don't wish to join the parade back to the parking lot scramble with Seaman north for one mile to a side canyon known as Nine Mile Draw that is a popular photo subject in its own right.

 GOBLIN VALLEY
STATE PARK

Find your own trail

GREEN RIVER, UTAH
Hiking Time: 2-3 hours

E ⚠ $

You may have already seen the "goblins" yourself if you caught the outer space yuk-fest *Galaxy Quest*. The park was used to create the hostile planet Thermia where actors in a televised space drama were recruited to fight a real war.

After visiting Goblin Valley it is hard to believe that Hollywood did not arrive until 1999 to use the park as a backdrop for alien planets. Then again, the world didn't learn about this otherworldly place until the early 20th century when cowboys searching for cattle stumbled into the valley of weathered sandstone hoodoos and spires.

The bizarre gnome-like rock formations spread out across a barren valley beneath the parking lot. Just walk down into Goblin Valley with Seaman and head in any direction to start exploring the desert playground. **Curious dogs will exalt in bounding up and around the orbital stones populating the valley floor**. There are probably thousands of "goblins" living here. The edges of the valley feature intricately eroded cliffs and walls.

Pushing beyond the main valley, across intervening ridges, are more collections of hoodoos where the goblins are taller and more complex. Seaman will still be encountering goblins two miles from the parking lot.

For more challenging canine hiking steer your dog to the outsides of the valley into the surrounding badlands with sand dunes and mud hills. Formal trails also connect the campground and the goblins.

 GRAND CANYON
NATIONAL PARK

South Rim Trail

GRAND CANYON, ARIZONA
Hiking Time: several hours

E ⚠ $

Hiking into the Grand Canyon is on many an adventurer's bucket list. Your dog is prohibited from that once-in-a-lifetime experience but he can trot on the paved trail along the South Rim for many miles at "the one great sight which every American should see," as Theodore Roosevelt concluded. That includes the storied viewpoints like Mather Point and Grandview Point where even a sliver of the Colorado River a mile below can be spotted.

Seaman will also be trotting past such historical structures as Hopi House, the El Tovar Hotel, and Lookout Studio. Beyond the three-plus miles of canyonside trail in Grand Canyon Village the route goes another eight miles to the iconic Hermit's Rest, designed in 1914 by Mary Colter to resemble a mountain man's stone hovel. Dogs are not allowed on the shuttle buses that travel this far, however, so plan accordingly to get back.

One Grand Canyon attraction where you can escape the crowds with Seaman is Shoshone Point, a permit-only section of the national park that is reserved for weddings and the like. Check with the park office and **if there are no special events scheduled you can hike with your dog along the one-mile dirt road through majestic Ponderosa pines and through high country meadows to one of the most photographed edges of the Grand Canyon**.

Grand Staircase-Escalante National Monument

Devil's Garden

ESCALANTE, UTAH

Hiking Time: 1 hour

E 🚙

America's Canyon Country is peppered - seemingly randomly - with these pockets of crazy geological formations that demand to be explored. Some are turned into national parks (Bryce) and others state parks (Goblin Valley). The best for dog owners are the smaller obscure ones far from the casual crowds. Just open you car door and watch your trail dog race into the crazy rock formations.

Devil's Garden is such a place. It is off the beaten path, but not too far (12.3 miles from UT 12). It requires a trip down the notorious Hole-in-the-Rock Road but is passable by two-wheel vehicles to this point. And it delivers the multi-chromatic hoodoos, rock domes, and natural bridges all found in Utah's famous national parks, only in miniature. Devil's Garden has received a federal designation as an American Outstanding Natural Area.

There are no formal trails across the Navajo sandstone slickrock but there are many faded footpaths for Seaman to try. Explore the "garden" while keeping on the lookout for two signature arches, the delicate Metate Arch and the slab-like Mano Arch. Continue poking around until there are no more smoothed sandstone figurines and the garden tour is complete. **Don't hesitate to make a second trip through Devil's Garden to be certain you didn't miss anything the first time - Seaman will certainly not object to a second go-round**.

Grand Staircase-Escalante National Monument

Lower Calf Creek Falls Trail

BOULDER, UTAH

Hiking Time: 3-4 hours

M ⛺ 🏊 $

What is the perfect end to a hike with your dog? An unforgettable photo-op for you and a refreshing swim for him? If that's your definition of the ideal adventure denouement pull off of Scenic Byway Route 12 and jump on the trail to Lower Calf Creek Falls.

The footpath is sandy under paw and the going can be slow but you won't be in a hurry as you soak in the desert-varnished Navajo sandstone cliffs framing the open canyon. Oxidized iron and manganese paint the rocks black and orange and yellow.

The mostly level track climbs into the rocks for a spell, working around the marshy areas of Calf Creek. As the canyon begins to narrow and the gambel oaks and boxelder thicken shade is introduced to the canine hike. When Mormon tea takes over the streambed you are getting close.

After three miles the trail halts at the foot of Lower Calf Creek Falls - a desert oasis that could have come straight from a Hollywood western. A crystal clear perennial stream spills 126 feet down the mineral-streaked cliff walls. **While you angle your iPhone for the perfect photo angle Seaman will sprint into the generous plunge pool for a well-deserved swim**.

This can be your perfect ending - or not; there is also an Upper Calf Creek Falls. While Lower Calf Creek is one of the most popular hikes in Escalante if you want to dodge crowds try the short, strenuous hike from UT 12 down to the 88-foot upper falls with its own doggie swimming hole.

Grand Staircase-Escalante National Monument

Toadstool Trail

BIG WATER, UTAH

Hiking Time: 1-2 hours

E

Natural wonder and easy access are catnip for the traveling canine hiker. The *Toadstool Trail* checks both boxes big time. The canine hike starts from a parking lot directly on US 89 - the main road between Kanab, UT and Page, AZ - and leads into some of the most bizarre rock formations your dog will see in the American Southwest.

This easy-going trail traces a sandy wash inside a broad canyon of white cliffs highlighted by chocolate brown rocks. Stone cairns lead the route out of the wash when necessary. In just under one mile you will spot your first "toadstool" - spire-like formations with a boulder perched on top of a pedestal rock. This introductory giant brown guardian is a poster child for many area travel brochures.

This marks the end of the formal trail and Seaman is free to explore in this calcified fungal playground. Two types of sandstone, Dakota and Entrada, that erode at different rates are responsible for the fanciful boulders and caps. The harder Dakota (white) shelters the softer Entrada (brown) to form the toadstools.

But not all the balanced rocks feature this white-on-brown configuration. Some of the hoodoos near the back wall of the canyon display white Dakota pillars. Seaman will get a kick out of exploring the many alcoves in Toadstool canyon and be sure to climb high enough to soak in tail-wagging views of the Paria River Valley that is often blanketed in blooms of wild flowers.

Grand Staircase-Escalante National Monument

Willis Creek Canyon

CANNONVILLE, UTAH

Hiking Time: 1-3 hours

E A 🚙

What is it you are looking for in a hike with your dog? Fun? Come to Willis Creek Canyon. Aficionados of slot canyons encounter many obstacles when trying to share the experience with their dogs - ropes and ladders, technical climbs, problematic approaches, "no dogs allowed signs," etc. etc.

At Willis Creek all that is required is to lock your vehicle and walk into the slot canyon. There are no obstacles impeding your hike - save one, which can be bypassed - as the gorgeously sculpted walls close in down the creek. Those slickrock walls are streaked with desert varnish and will eventually grow to over 200 feet high deeper along.

The wash-route trail is sand and cobblestones and mostly flat, gaining a nearly imperceptible 300 feet. When Willis Creek can't be avoided the water level is rarely deeper than splashing through a puddle. (If the water is going to be too deep the access roads will likely be impasssable anyway.) The narrow walls provde shade on even the hottest summer days.

The dramatic twists and turns in Willis Creek slot canyon end after a little more than one mile as the wash yawns wider. Willis Canyon continues for another mile to the confluence of Sheep Canyon but it resembles more of a riparian desert hike. At whatever point you decide to turn Seaman around it is back through the slot - and keep an eye out for a tiny side waterfall pouring into the canyon - it's just more fun to be had in Willis Creek.

KODACHROME BASIN STATE PARK

Grand Parade Trail/Angels' Palace Trail

CANNONVILLE, UTAH
Hiking Time: 1-2 hours

M △ $

A visit to Kodachrome Basin State Park for Seaman is like pressing his nose against a fence looking at a park he's not allowed to visit. That park is Bryce Canyon National Park - Kodachrome Basin even has a campground called Bryce View.

Kodachrome Basin is not without its own unique pleasures, however. The beauty of the rocks here is so supreme that a National Geographic Society exploring party named the area after Kodak's industry standard Kodachrome color film.

The *Grand Parade Trail* travels easily across a wide, sandy path that moves past some of the park's 67 monolithic stone spires called sedimentary pipes. The pipes can soar up to 15 stories high and their origins are unknown; the best guess is that they are the solidified remains of ancient thermal geysers.

The big adventure for Seaman on the Grand Parade will be hiking into two box canyons wrapped by tall, multi-hued sandstone walls. Each box canyon includes heavily vegetated short ravines of mystery that lure your dog inside.

The neighboring *Angels' Palace Trail* - also about 1.5 miles long - crosses the Entrada sandstone cliffs that provide the background for the Grand Parade. The footpath is cut into the side of the cliff walls as it ascends to commanding views of the entire Kodachrome Basin. Also visible in the distance are the forbidden Pink Cliffs of that darned Bryce Canyon National Park.

McINNIS CANYONS NATIONAL CONSERVATION AREA

Rabbit's Ear Mesa Trail

LOMA, COLORADO
Hiking Time: 3 hours

M △ 🚙

The McInnis Canyons National Conservation Area in the high desert of western Colorado is stuffed with dinosaur fossils and natural arches but lacks the press agents who flog its more famous neighbors. You won't get the bones or the rock bridges on this wide open canine hike but there are unmatched vistas of the region's other star attraction, the Colorado River. And thanks to the low profile of these 122,000 acres off Interstate 70 you and Seaman are likely to have Rabbit's Ear Mesa entirely to yourself.

This balloon trail begins a steady climb up a dusty sandstone ridge to the mesa, passing rock formations and desert scrub of pinyon pines and juniper. After a mile-and-a-half the mesa top is conquered and ahead is a 3.6-mile loop and two hours of nearly flat hiking around the rim Seaman is sure to adore.

To this point your steady companion has been 50-mile long views of the American West. Things are just warming up. **On the far side of the loop the Colorado River first comes into view and for an amazing half hour Seaman will see the muddy waters snake through Horseshoe and Ruby canyons below**. The La Sal Mountains loom in the distant background.

This is a tail-wagging romp for Seaman all the way up and down but there are no water sources in the high desert so come prepared.

 Monument Valley
Navajo Tribal Park

Wildcat Trail
MONUMENT VALLEY, UTAH
Hiking Time: 1-2 hours

M $ 🚙

It will not take long after pulling into Monument Valley for movie buffs to recognize the isolated buttes and exquisitely carved rock formations scattered across the high plateau. Hollywood movie director John Ford was the first to film in the valley, making *Stagecoach* in 1939 that catapulted John Wayne to stardom. The action scenes were shot in open desert country known today as Stagecoach Wash. These movies defined the West in the American imagination.

Of all the eye-popping 1,000-foot high sandstone rock formations none are more recognizable than the Mitten Buttes, East and West. They appear in just about every oater ever filmed in Monument Valley - and are about the only two significant formations that the 17-mile auto road does not visit close up. Most people encounter the Mittens only from the observation deck of the visitor center.

Your dog can do better than that. The *Wildcat Trail*, a lasso loop of 3.2 miles, takes Seaman to the base of both towering buttes. As you start out on a packed red dirt footpath that drops to the valley floor you can be sure you are leaving 99% of visitors behind. **The buttes are in constant view, the only things that rise above Seaman's nose out here, save for an occasional mesquite bush that offers a semblance of shade**. On this hike you can easily imagine a movie camera on your shoulder filming scenes from the next great Western, starring your dog.

 Red Fleet
State Park

Dinosaur Trackway Trail
VERNAL, UTAH
Hiking Time: 1-2 hours

M 🏕 🏊

Northeast Utah and Northwest Colorado are ground zero for some of the most fertile dinosaur fossil hunting in the world. **Seaman can't visit places like Dinosaur National Monument so the Dinosaur Trackway in Red Fleet State Park is one of his best chances to walk in the footsteps of the prehistoric giant lizards**.

It was 200 million years ago that dinosaurs were tromping through the soft mud here that has hardened into Nugget sandstone. Today the trackway is a 30-degree slope on the shores of the stone-encrusted Red Fleet Reservoir. There are hundreds of dinosaur footprints on the trackway, three-toed prints in the stone from 10 to 15 inches wide - the finest collection of dinosaur tracks in Utah.

If truth be told, the dinosaur prints can be hard to find, especially if the light is not right or the water level is too high. But none of this will matter to Seaman who will enjoy the rambling 1.5-mile hike to the Trackway across slickrock and through sandy washes. Numbered signposts and dinosaur tracks painted on the rocks lead the way amidst the Utah Juniper and rabbitbrush-covered route but you may still need Seaman's nose to stay on the sometimes tricky trail.

Upon reaching the broad, slanted rock that is the Trackway Seaman will likely rush to jump into the reservoir for a swim while you are staring at the rock under your feet, trying to identify the three-toed footprints. It is a win-win hike for both of you.

Red Rock Canyon National Conservation Area

Calico Tanks Trail

LAS VEGAS, NEVADA
Hiking Time: 2 hours

M A ⚐ $

The Bureau of Land Management carved nearly 200,000 acres out of the iron-tinged mountains west of Las Vegas for the Red Rock Canyon National Conservation Area. A 13-mile serpentine scenic drive twists 1,000 feet into rocks for access. Seaman can try any of 26 trails that push away from the parking lots, most in the one-to-two hour range. Whichever ones you pick expect a bit of rock scrambling for your dog in the cracks of the Rainbow Mountain Wilderness.

High on the to-do list should be the *Calico Tanks Trail*, a 1.25-mile journey that ends with a full view of the Las Vegas skyline in the distance. **The trail begins conventionally before breaking down in a boulder-stuffed wash where Seaman can bound up a favored route of his choosing through the canyon.** Near the end are tinajas, pockets of water in the bedrock that may contain seasonal water; not enough for dog-paddling perhaps but plenty welcome in the harsh Mojave Desert. After a refreshing dip and a look at Sin City in the distance it is back to bouncing and scrambling 450 feet down the canyon.

With extra time and energy - and hospitable weather - the Sandstone Quarry trailhead here also hosts the *Turtlehead Peak Trail* that gains 2,000 feet to the 6,323-foot summit in a little more than two miles. Your purchase is an even clearer view of Las Vegas across the Calico Hills.

Valley of Fire State Park

Fire Wave Trail

OVERTON, NEVADA
Hiking Time: 1 hour

E A $

The red sandstone formations here look as if they actually melted and cooled in place. An American Automobile Club representative traveling on a primitive road through the area in the 1920s gave the valley its name. In 1934 it was a no-brainer to make the Valley of Fire Nevada's first state park. Seaman will have fun on the fine red sand and rock face trails across some 40,000 acres when the sun is not blazing overhead.

There are nine shortish trails leading into the desert rocks from the parking lots along the park's White Domes Road scenic drive. The go-to hike is the *Fire Wave Trail* that travels around a red rock wall and onto undulating rock hills of reds and yellows and pinks. **As you cross this rock color palette there is a suggested trail marked by cairns but really the entire desert landscape is open and beckoning to Seaman.** The out-and-back adventure concludes after 1.2 miles at an ice cream shop of swirling scoop-like confections.

The nearby *White Domes Loop Trail* offers both contrasting colors to the red rocks and a dab of cinematic history. *Star Trek* fans will no doubt recognize these Fire Canyon rocks. Lee Marvin also led his crew of hard-edged adventurers here to rescue a kidnapped Claudia Cardinale in the 1966 western, *The Professionals*. Some stone ruins from the movie are still in the rocks. The one-mile circuit also travels through a short slot canyon.

Desertlands

BOYCE THOMPSON ARBORETUM STATE PARK

Main Trail

SUPERIOR, ARIZONA
Hiking Time: 1-2 hours

E $

Boyce Thompson was born in Montana, educated in New England, and made his fortune trading mining stocks in New York City but it was the desert landscape of the American Southwest that captured his heart. After Thompson purchased the Magma Mine he moved to Arizona and built his Picket Post House, known locally as the "Castle on the Rock." For a guy living in the desert, Thompson still owned the world's second largest yacht. In the 1920s he established the arboretum to study the plants of desert countries and invited the public to share in the research.

Arizona's oldest and most inclusive botanical garden hosts 3,200 desert plants interspersed amidst two miles of winding paths, which Seaman is welcome to enjoy. **Don't be fooled - the hard-packed Thompson Arboretum paths skew more desert canine hike than garden stroll with rock formations and sporty inclines around Magma Ridge**.

The *Main Trail* travels for 1.5 miles but offers numerous offshoots into curated gardens and desert exhibits, including native Sonoran desert plants. Where water intrudes on the 323-acre garden in the form of a man-made Ayers Lake or trickling Queen Creek the impact is startling. Shade-giving eucalyptus trees share space with imperious 200-year old saguaro cacti, Chinese pistachio trees are neighbors to spiky palo-verdes and Mediterranean olive trees compete for attention with spiny-branched ocotillo.

 # CATALINA STATE PARK

Canyon Loop Trail

TUCSON, ARIZONA
Hiking Time: 1-2 hours

E ▲ $

Seaman won't be able to trot among the giant cacti in Saguaro National Park or in the Sonoran Desert in the expansive Tucson Mountain Park but he can experience this entrancing ecosystem nearby, nine miles north of Tucson, in Catalina State Park.

Before the Sutherland Wash became a refuge for canine hikers it was a small Hohokam Indian village 1,500 years ago. The community flourished for more than a millennia before being abandoned. Ranchers Francisco and Victoriana Romero ran cattle over 5,000 acres here but the enterprise did not survive two generations. Gradually the forgotten property came to the attention of scientists and historians. In 1983 Catalina State Park, sprawling across 5,483 acres, was established, including 34 distinct archeological sites.

Guide Seaman onto the 2.3-mile *Canyon Loop Trail* and enjoy the differing habitat types found in this beautiful desert terrain. The trail rolls gently up and down through riparian arroyos and past stands of mature saguaros. Keep an eye to the sky for a chance to see any of the more than 170 species of birds that call the park home. **The loop winds up with an unexpected hidden stream in the wash that just may contain a mirthful seasonal doggie swimming hole.**

CORONADO NATIONAL FOREST

Old Baldy Trail
TUCSON, ARIZONA
Hiking Time: 5-6 hours

S A $

The climb up 9,453-foot Mount Wrightson is Southern Arizona's favorite hike to escape the desert heat. Two routes conquer the highpoint of the Santa Rita Mountains - the *Super Trail* is less formidable but longer; *Old Baldy Trail* is more popular and spends more time in the cool and shady confines of the Ponderosa pines in Madera Canyon to offset the added difficulty.

The *Old Baldy Trail* tags the Mount Wrightson summit in 5.4 miles, although Seaman will be excused if he barks that it feels longer, especially with an elevation gain of 4,000 feet. You can also be forgiven if you forget you are in Arizona, especially when the ferns start proliferating on the forest floor. The trail name recalls the mountain's original moniker, given for its distinctive rocky peak. Seaman will reach those bare slopes below the summit at Baldy Saddle where you meet the canine hikers coming up the *Super Trail*.

The final mile takes it time switching up 700 more feet on the treeless, rocky path. **When you make the last twist shake paws with Seaman because you've earned a spot of congratulations**. There used to be a fire tower up here, built in 1928, and you can see why - the panoramic views extend to several other mountain ranges: the Huachucas, the Rincons, and the Sierra San Jose in Mexico. Only a concrete base remains today. It is a big summit with plenty of spots to sit with Seaman away from the crowds for a good spell before heading back down.

EL MALPAIS NATIONAL MONUMENT

El Calderon Trail
GRANTS, NEW MEXICO
Hiking Time: 1-2 hours

E A 🚙

The Spanish dubbed this volcanic field "Malpais," meaning "badlands" but it appears anything but when you begin this hike with your dog. The landscape is dotted with Ponderosa pines and some of America's oldest Douglas fir trees. Pygmy pine forests struggle atop the vulcanized rock. Even aspens, seldom found at these elevations, grow along the lava flow edges.

The dirt and crushed gravel trail soon reveals another story. The El Calderon Cinder Cone began shaping this landscape 115,000 years ago, spewing rivers of molten rock into lava trenches and tubes. Caves and sinks sculpted from grey-black basaltic rock quickly begin appearing on the 3.8-mile loop that explores the largest lava fields in New Mexico. The caves are free to explore with a permit but dogs aren't allowed - and wouldn't want to navigate the jagged rocks anyway.

The trail winds easily to the top of the cinder cone with views across the grasslands to the 400-foot high sandstone bluffs that frame the monument. Under paw are loose red and black cinders from the long-gone days when El Calderon was an active volcano.

Halfway into the *El Calderon Trail* the twisted lava features and craggy basaltic rock surrender the stage to airy woodlands. **Grasses and seasonal wildflowers fill in the corridors around the footpath as Seaman completes a fascinating circuit hike**. The final leg joins the *Continental Divide Trail* for one of its 3,100 miles.

HUMBOLDT-TOIYABE NATIONAL FOREST

Bristlecone Trail

LAS VEGAS, NEVADA
Hiking Time: 2-3 hours

M ⛰ 🚙

Sooner or later intrepid canine hikers will make their way to Humboldt-Toiyabe, the largest national forest in the Lower 48. The star of the Spring Mountains is Charleston Peak, the tallest mountain in Southern Nevada. Athletic dogs can tackle the 11,916-foot summit on a long hike but most folks will be better served on the less challenging *Bristlecone Trail* loop.

The Great Basin bristlecone pine in these mountains is the longest living tree species on the planet; the oldest documented bristlecone is believed to be over 5,000 years young. **The ancient pines grow in open stands so Seaman will be trotting through airy, open forests that surrender long views of the surrounding mountains**. Some of the oldest, twisted specimens are found in the upper stretches of this six-mile loop as the canine hike crests over 9,000 feet.

The bright green conifers stand out against the gray stone mountains. Color chasers will want to consider the fall months since the more than six million acres of forest are generously populated with quaking aspens as well. At any time this is a great escape-from-Las Vegas-hike.

Seaman will be trotting across all types of surfaces in the Spring Mountains, from foot paths to wide fire roads. To close the *Bristlecone Trail* loop most efficiently requires a hike a short ways on the main paved road linking the Upper and Lower trails.

LAKE MEAD NATIONAL RECREATION AREA

Historic Railroad Trail

BOULDER CITY, NEVADA
Hiking Time: 1-2 hours

E ⛰

Hikers are always suckers for abandoned railroad routes and this is one of the best. **The old roadbed goes through not one, not two, but five tunnels in the course of a little over two miles.** The tunnels were blasted in 1931 to bring supplies to the building site of the Hoover Dam. To accommodate the bulky equipment and large penstocks, the tunnels are each 25 feet in diameter and left unfinished, save for some wooden vertical supports at the entrances. The longest are the length of a football field - enough to enter near darkness. The railroad shut down in 1961.

The road grade was refinished with paw-friendly decomposed granite in 2017 making an extraordinary ramble even more pleasurable. With an elevation gain of only 11 feet, Seaman will enjoy some of the area's best views of Lake Mead for no purchase.

After the fifth tunnel the trail continues up to the Hoover Dam Parking Garage but dogs are not permitted there. The *Historic Railroad Trail* is outside the Lake Mead NRA entrance gate but to access campgrounds and additional trails admission is required. The best of that bunch for short explorations (usually the wise choice where temperatures can reach 120 degrees Fahrenheit) is the *Redstone Trail* that meanders among pockmocked red sandstone formations. For lake views from the stark eastern Mojave Desert try the *Callville Summit Trail* that features a scramble up 150 feet to the promontory.

LITTLE SAHARA RECREATION AREA

Rockwell Natural Area

EUREKA, UTAH
Hiking Time: 2 hours

E ⚠ $ 🚙

Lake Bonneville was a prehistoric lake that once covered most of present-day Utah and parts of Nevada and Idaho. At more than 1,000 feet deep the lake was as large as Lake Michigan today and much deeper. A bit south of the Great Salt Lake, deposits left by a Lake Bonneville feeder stream, the Sevier River, have been whipped around by prevailing winds to create the Little Sahara, billed as Utah's greatest sand play area.

The Little Sahara is a magnet for off-highway vehicles who roar in and out of dune bowls and up sand mountains as high as 700 feet. There are no designated trails out in the dunes so there is a chance you can encounter a motorized vehicle just about anywhere you hike, unless you make it across the dunes to Rockwell Natural Area which is a vehicle-free zone. Seaman will be sharing this massive sandbox with a unique plant species known as "Giant four-wing saltbush" that grows naturally in the dune fields of Little Sahara and nowhere else in the world.

But if you avoid popular holiday weekends there is a good chance to experience a solitary dune hike with your dog somewhere in the 124-square mile system of giant, free-moving sand dunes. **If Seaman tires of trotting through deep white quartz sand there are networks of dirt trails in the surrounding sagebrush flats to be had here as well**.

MECCA HILLS WILDERNESS

Sheep Hole Oasis Trail

MECCA, CALIFORNIA
Hiking Time: several hours

M ⚠ 🚙

Times have changed. Box Canyon Road, the two-lane paved road into the Mecca Hills Wilderness, was once Route 60, one of the main routes into Los Angeles. Now a lonely exit off I-10, the road feels like one of the most remote outposts in Southern California.

The hills themselves have not changed - at least in human experience. A product of the ornery San Andreas Fault, these badlands date back 600 million years. **Your dog can roam anywhere in these 26,356 Bureau of Land Management acres, romping across mesas and squeezing through narrow canyons.**

There is no imperative to interrupt Seaman's fun for a formal trail hike but the *Sheep Hole Oasis Trail* does sample most of the attractions of the Mecca Hills on its way to a somewhat reliable Mojave desert guzzler. The early steps cross a ridgeline deliver views of the Salton Sea in the distance and soon the oasis comes into view - a trio of fan palms in the wash below. Seaman can sniff for desert creatures around smoke trees and palo verdes.

The larger Hidden Springs Oasis is another mile down the increasingly challenging canyon. If continuing to a rock cave known as the Grottoes be prepared to crawl through dark spaces with a flashlight for you and maybe Seaman as well. Nearby Painted Canyon is the most popular destination in the Mecca Hills. The slot canyon is negotiated by 15-foot ladders but there is still plenty to explore with your dog as well.

MOJAVE DESERT PRESERVE

Teutonia Peak Trail

KELSO, CALIFORNIA

Hiking Time: 2 hours

M ▲

Dogs are not allowed on Joshua Tree National Park trails but no worries! **Here in the dog-friendly Mojave Desert Preserve the *Teutonia Peak Trail* spends more than half its 1.7-mile distance in the densest concentration of Joshua trees on the planet.** The oddly shaped member of the Yucca family, whose uplifted branches caused Mormon settlers to saddle the tree with its Biblical name, grows so thickly on the Cima Dome that it resembles an orchard.

The trail pushes pleasantly towards the foot of 5,755-foot Teutonia Peak. Before Seaman begins the 700-foot climb to the rocky summit the trail passes a silver mine that was worked in the 1890s before being abandoned. The mine shaft is covered by an iron grate. The path up the mountain uses switchbacks and soon the unique curvilinear horizon of the Cima Dome takes shape in the distance to the southwest. There is no shade, so plan your canine hike here accordingly.

Speaking of no shade, in the southern part of the preserve are the Kelso Dunes, the largest sand piles in the Mojave Desert. The main dune rises 650 feet and can be reached in 1.5 miles - all in soft sand. There are several neighboring dune summits for Seaman to aim for as well. To reach this giant sandbox for dogs requires navigation of a graded three-mile dirt road that is two-wheel drive friendly. Seaman's four-wheel leg drive will be welcome on the dunes.

PETRIFIED FOREST NATIONAL PARK

all paved trails

PETRIFIED FOREST, ARIZONA

Hiking Time: 2-3 hours

M ▲ $

"Please take your furry friends on trails, even backpacking in the wilderness area." That is not a misprint. That is straight from Petrified Forest park policy. Wow. It does not get any dog-friendlier at a national park than that. All 146 square miles of desert scrub and color-streaked badlands welcome your dog.

For canine hikers not quite that adventurous, Petrified Forest offers three intriguing paved trails, each about one mile long. The *Blue Mesa Trail* descends into an amphitheater surrounded by banded coulees of bluish clay called bentontite. Rainwater is the brush that creates streaky patterns in the barren porous hills.

The Atlantic and Pacific Railroad built though the Painted Desert in the 1880s and profiteers rode the trains to the nation's largest field of petrified wood. They carried off specimens lying in the desert and dynamited the largest logs in search of quartz and purple amethyst crystals. The *Crystal Forest Trail* meanders through the remains of obliterated petrified logs, whose preservation led to the creation of the Petrified Forest in 1906.

Some of those prehistoric trees can be seen on the *Long Logs Path*. Extinct conifers form the largest concentration of petrified wood left in the park. The *Agate House Trail* leads up a slight rise to a reconstructed Anasazi Indian Pueblo built entirely of colorful petrified wood sealed with mud.

PETROGLYPH
NATIONAL MONUMENT

Rinconada Canyon Trail
ALBUQUERQUE, NEW MEXICO
Hiking Time: 1-2 hours

E

Have you ever wondered what it would be like if your neighborhood dog walk included some of the country's most significant cultural heritage? That's what it is like at Petroglyph National Monument where the Rinconada Canyon trailhead is right across the street from hundreds of development homes. At the start of the hike are doggie bags and disposal cans like any neighborhood park.

The fact is folks have been living here for seven hundred years and in that time Native Americans and Spanish settlers whiled away the hours carving designs and symbols into the black volcanic rocks in the canyon. This natural desert hike loops for just over two miles on a mostly level natural sandy footpath. Expect short rises near the broad canyon walls and enjoy the wildflowers that peek through the blankets of sand sage.

Rinconada Canyon is one of the largest petroglyph sites in North America. Many of the 300 pictures in the rock field are best spotted with binoculars but plenty can be examined right next to the trail, including drawings that look like sheep and dogs.

The national monument offers three other hiking units scattered around western Albuquerque, two of which allow dogs. **The best for your trail dog is the Volcanoes Day Use Area - no petroglyphs here but wide open spaces and climbs into extinct cinder cones that afford panoramic views of the mini-volcanic valley and Albuquerque in the distance**.

 RHYOLITE
HISTORIC AREA

Town Tour
BEATTY, NEVADA
Hiking Time: 1-2 hours

E

When quartz - an indicator of gold - was found all over a hillside in 1904 there were soon 2,000 claims in a 30-mile radius of the town of Rhyolite. Soon the population approached 10,000; the railroad arrived and the town was electrified. There were hotels, a hospital, a school for 250 children, a stock exchange and even an opera. The financial Panic of 1907 decimated the town and by 1916 the lights and power were turned off forever in Rhyolite. The "Queen City" of Death Valley barely lasted a decade.

The old mining town fulfills every image Seaman has ever had of a ghost town in a stark, wind-whipped desert with the feeling that no dog has sniffed these streets in years. Aside from being remote Rhyolite is amazingly accessible - a paved road motors straight into town.

Rhyolite is in Death Valley but not part of the national park (verboten to trail dogs); it is on Bureau of Land Management land so when you pull up, open the door and just let Seaman out to run. **Hiking with your dog through the century-old street grid will reach a nearly intact train depot and the much-photographed rusticated stone walls of the three-story Cook Bank Building**. The highlight is The Bottle House, constructed by a miner from 50,000 beer and whiskey bottles - it was restored by Paramount Pictures in 1925. If Seaman hankers for a real trail in Rhyolite there are footpaths worn in the rocks east of this true American relic.

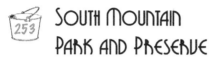

SOUTH MOUNTAIN PARK AND PRESERVE

National Trail

PHOENIX, ARIZONA
Hiking Time: several hours possible

M

For pure Sonoran desert hiking, this is the place to bring your dog. And many people do - more than three million hikers depart the 13 trailheads of America's largest municipal park each year. You'll get dusty footpaths, chiseled rocks and a look at more than 300 species of desert plants.

Prospectors poked around for riches on South Mountain in the early 1900s. The city of Phoenix struck the real gold, however, when 13,000 acres were acquired from the federal government in 1924 for only $17,000. The National Park Service also took care of most of the development work during the Great Depression.

The *National Trail* traces the spine of the park from one end to the other, a total of some 14 miles. That is a big ask for any dog in the desert environment but the wide, well-maintained trail can be used for any number of canine hiking loops. For that matter, when the temperature vaults over 100 degrees dogs are forbidden on the trails.

The *National Trail* tops out on Buena Vista Lookout at 2,700 feet and there are plenty of downtown Phoenix views to be had. When you want to put images of the country's sixth largest metropolis away there are long stretches of desert wilderness in the folds of the two mountain ranges in the park - the Ma Ha Range and Guadalupe Range. Add rock formations like the Tunnel and Fat Man's Pass into the canine hiking stew on South Mountain. Bring plenty of water for Seaman and a camera for the memory scrapbook.

WHITE MOUNTAIN WILDERNESS AREA

Argentina & Big Bonito Trails

RUIDOSO, NEW MEXICO
Hiking Time: 3-4 hours

M ▲ 🚙

The aspens and golden grasses of the high elevations - you'll reach 9,400 feet on this canine hike - will make Seaman forget the harsh desert in the surrounding lowlands. **As you climb, Bonita Creek may even offer pools deep enough for a doggie dip on this seven-mile loop**.

Take down this loop in either direction, up the *Argentina Canyon Trail* or the *Little Bonito Trail*, but the most important warning to remember is - DO NOT take the *Cut Across Trail* that links the two routes. Do so and Seaman will miss the wonders of the New Mexico high country. Instead, continue higher to the *Crest Trail* that is not that much further along anyway.

This will allow Seaman to romp through alpine meadows and deliver vast looks at the desert, including White Sands National Monument far to the southwest. Stop every now and then and look back for any views you may have missed.

Argentina Peak is a small outcropping off the *Crest Trail*. It will require some off-trail explorations to reach the best views of the Tularosa Basin but if you skip this side excursion Seaman will scarcely be the poorer for the decision.

Human intervention adds bonus interest to one of New Mexico's finest hikes with your dog. A rail fence in the montane grasslands helps protect the Argentina Spring seeps and a mineshaft near the trailhead will certainly pique Seaman's interest.

WHITE SANDS NATIONAL MONUMENT

Alkali Flat Trail

HOLLOMAN AFB, NEW MEXICO
Hiking Time: 3-4 hours

S △ $

Dogs have long been welcome on the glistening white sands of New Mexico. During America's nascent space age the Missile Dogs, Dingo, a Weimaraner, and Count, a German Shorthair, raced among the dunes sniffing out small missile parts from test launches to analyze success or failure. The Missile Dogs of White Sands amassed a peerless 96% recovery rate.

There are several ways to introduce your dog to this mystical place. A short boardwalk leads a half-mile into the dunes and the *Dune Life Nature Trail* pokes along the edge of the gypsum dunefield. For a total immersion in White Sands, however, head out to the *Alkali Flat Trail* with Seaman.

The first thing to know is that the Alkali Flat is that is the destination of this five-mile loop - the canine hike itself is *far* from flat. Seaman will be bounding across the park's biggest dunes with no vegetation in sight. Posts planted in the sand mark the way to the edge of the dry lakebed of Lake Otero for this otherworldly hike. And by all means put your shoes in your pack and join your dog bare-footed in America's whitest sands.

During the heat of summer, try a night hike - the desert cools off then and the white sands are especially haunting by moonlight. When the moon is full the park stays open until midnight.

Oh yes, no matter where you hike at White Sands with Seaman be on the lookout for unexploded ordinance that Dingo and Count may have missed.

WHITEWATER PRESERVE

Canyon View Loop Trail

WHITEWATER, CALIFORNIA
Hiking Time: 2 hours

M

Palm Springs and the Coachella Valley are a hiking hotbed but not so much for four-footed trail tramps. **Paws down, the best canine hiking in this desert oasis is at Whitewater Preserve**. That whitewater stream rushing through the property is no desert mirage - this slice of the San Gornonio Wilderness was once a now-defunct trout farm.

Before Seaman leads you off on this 3.5-mile journey pause and look at the rounded ridge across the back of the parking lot. That will be your destination. Push past the Visitor Center fish ponds (no swimming) and through a gateway of fan palms into the flat Whitewater River basin. The cottonwoods and sycamores and alders of the oasis quickly give way to Mojave desert conditions. After crossing the crystal clear stream (canine splashing allowed) the switchbacking trek up the ridge begins. You are using the celebrated *Pacific Crest Trail* at this point.

The long views of the meandering bleached landscape of the Whitewater arroyo against the barren folds of the surrounding mountain ranges are all around. If it has been a wet winter the footpath may pass through wispy grasses or a recent rain may have jostled the goldfields on the slopes to life. Once atop the ridge the route is freckled with Brittlebush and their profusion of yellow blooms in spring. Let Seaman soak in the always-satisfying look down at your vehicle before heading off the other side of the ridge and the switchbacking trot back down.

California

Alabama Hills Recreation and Scenic Area

Arch Loop

LONE PINE, CALIFORNIA
Hiking Time: 2-3 hours

E △ 🚙

"A fiery horse with the speed of light, a cloud of dust and a hearty 'Hi Yo Silver!'" Anyone who has seen the opening to the classic television series *The Lone Ranger* knows the Alabama Hills, a jumble of rounded, weathered granite boulders piled across a desert flatlands that form a vibrant contrast with the sharply sculptured ridges of the nearby Sierra mountains. These majestic backdrops and rugged rock formations began attracting the attention of Hollywood in the 1920s.

You can hike with your dog along dusty Movie Road, where pert near every major Western star galloped on horseback at one time or another. More than 400 films have been shot here including such recent fare as *Ironman*, *Gladiator* and *Django In Chains*.

There is only one formal hiking trailhead in the 30,000-acre Alabama Hills. The stone-lined *Arch Loop* here leads to the twisted Mobius Arch that provides a literal window to Mount Whitney, the tallest peak in the Lower 48. Stone steps tame the small arroyos along the way. Further along is the low, flat Lathe Arch with more photo-ops. A branch trail leads to the whimsical Eye of Alabama Arch and, yes, another frame of Mount Whitney.

There is plenty more for Seaman to explore. Grab a Movie Road film site locator brochure that leads you to side roads and lets you see how the Alabama Hills looked on the silver screen. You can also let Seaman romp into Lone Ranger Canyon - is that the *William Tell* Overture you hear playing?

Ancient Bristlecone Pine Forest

Methuselah Trail

BISHOP, CALIFORNIA
Hiking Time: 2-3 hours

M $ 🚙

When it comes to trees California has it all: the tallest trees, the biggest trees, and, here in Inyo National Forest, the oldest trees. Growing at altitudes of more than 10,000 feet, bristlecone pines have been surviving for more than 4,000 years on the harsh slopes of the White Mountains, east of Yosemite National Park and north of Death Valley. The cold temperatures, dry soil and short growing season cause the trees, whose dense wood is resistant to invasion by insects, to grow very slowly. *Very* slowly.

The *Methuselah Trail* leads to the very tree once identified as the planet's oldest living specimen. Core samples taken in 1957 led researchers to estimate the age of Methuselah to be 4,850 years old. Seaman will have to guess which one is Methuselah since the exact location is kept a secret to prevent vandalism - not that anyone should be messing with even the 2,000-year old youngsters and their fascinating twisting and colorful trunks. In 2013 researchers discovered an even older bristlecone but it remains unnamed as well as a secret.

This is also a sporty alpine hike for Seaman in the Schulman Grove with over 900 feet of elevation gain in 4.5 miles. The bristlecone pine forest is sparse, offering wonderful views above 10,000 feet. Take the balloon trail in a clockwise direction and latch onto the *Bristlecone Cabin Trail* to check out old cabins and mine entrances from the Mexican Mine where silver was uncovered in 1862.

BODIE STATE HISTORIC PARK

Ghost Town Tour

BRIDGEPORT, CALIFORNIA
Hiking Time: 1-2 hours

M $ 🚗

Bodie is the best preserved, most extensive ghost town where you can hike the streets with your dog. William Bodey dug gold out of these barren hills in 1859 but he died in a blizzard that winter and never saw the town his strike - one of the richest in California history - would spawn. By 1880 the town was bustling with 10,000 residents. It was reported that 65 saloons were operating in Bodie, to go along with brothels, gambling halls and opium dens. They say a man was killed in Bodie every day.

After the gold played out the town soldiered on, tapping into the timber resources in the nearby mountains. Electricity even came to Bodie in 1911. But avalanches and fires crippled the town and a slow death ensued. The State of California took over in 1962 to create an Historic Park, preserving the remains of the town in a state of "arrested decay."

This is no tourist trap - there are no re-creations in Bodie and no food and water for sale. The only business that intrudes on the ghost town aura is a small museum. You can walk Seaman into the gravelly streets of the townsite with 170 documented buildings, peering into store windows with shelves still stocked and pool halls with balls still racked on dusty, ornate tables. Bodie sits at 8,375 feet so Seaman will get a workout hiking into the hills on the outskirts of town to see the cemetery, the stamp mill, Bodey's possible cabin site, and many more historical curiosities.

CITY OF REDDING PARKS AND RECREATION

Sacramento River Trail

REDDING, CALIFORNIA
Hiking Time: 2-3 hours

E 🏊

Redding, which began life in 1872 as a temporary supply center for the California & Oregon Railroad and is named for the line's railroad agent, fancies itself as one of the country's trail meccas. It is not false bravado - there are 225 miles of trails within 15 miles of town and the National Trails Association keeps its headquarters here.

To find the crown jewel of the Redding trail system go no further than the town center. The *Sacramento River National Recreation Trail* winds merrily along both sides of California's longest river on a flat, 12-foot wide paved surface that covers 11 miles in total, with many options to shorten Seaman's hiking day.

The views are splendid, the weather almost always sunny, and the trotting easy but the lasting thrills of the *Sacramento River Trail* are its bridges. The Diestelhorst Bridge was the first automobile bridge to span the Sacramento River in 1915; it is a classic pier-and-girder structure with nine spans. You won't cross anything like the 420-foot Ribbon Bridge outside of central Europe.

But the star engineering marvel is the Sundial Bridge that was the first American project for revered Spanish bridge architect Santiago Calatrava. The focal point of his design is a 218-foot curved tower on the north bank of the river that doubles as support for the bridge's suspension cables and as the world's largest sundial. **And, yes, Seaman can swim under the glass decking**.

Del Monte Forest

Crawford Trail
PEBBLE BEACH, CALIFORNIA
Hiking Time: 1-2 hours

M ☚ $

Spanish explorers discovered and mapped the Monterey Peninsula in 1602 but it did not become a vacation destination until 1880 when railroad magnate Charles Crocker opened the Hotel Del Monte. Carriage roads were cleared for guests to enjoy the spectacular coastline or reach a secluded picnic spot; today they form the backbone of the famed 17-Mile Drive.

The 17-Mile Drive is awash with dog-hiking opportunities including the ocean boardwalk at Spanish Bay to the north and Carmel-by-the-Sea to the south. **Seaman will be chomping at the leash to get to Carmel Beach City Park. Here your dog can run unleashed on soft white sand**.

Inland, the S.F.B. Morse Botanical Reserve explores an ancient marine forest of bleached tree trunks and long-lived Monterey cypress. Samuel Finley Brown Morse developed the Pebble Beach resort in 1919 with world class golf courses but at the same time vowed to keep the natural wonder unspoiled.

On the *Crawford Trail* in the Reserve Seaman will be trotting on a cushion of conifer needles dropped by a diverse evergreen forest that features a pygmy grove of the endangered Gowen cypress that grows only here and over at Point Lobos. The trail rolls easily through the hills that reach 800 feet above the nearby sea with many options to extend your canine hike beyond the trail's 1.7 official miles into the adjoining Huckleberry Hill Natural Habitat Area.

Eaton Canyon Natural Area

Eaton Canyon Trail
PASADENA, CALIFORNIA
Hiking Time: 1-2 hours

M ☚

When hiking luminary John Muir visited Eaton Canyon, a place he called the Yosemite of the San Gabriel Mountains, he wrote, "The Fall, famous throughout the valley settlements as the finest yet discovered in the range, is a charming little thing, with a voice sweet as a songbird's, leaping some thirty-five or forty feet into a round, mirror pool. The cliff back of it and on both sides is completely covered with thick, furry mosses, and the white fall shines against the green like a silver instrument in a velvet case."

This is Seaman's destination. For a wildly popular trail hard by America's second largest metropolis that heads into a dead-end canyon this canine hike manages to not feel completely claustrophobic. The first mile travels on a wide, crusty road over open chaparral and native woodlands that strings out the many Eaton Canyon pilgrims.

After 1.2 miles the trail leaves the natural area and ducks under a concrete bridge of the Mount Wilson Toll Road. The entire personality of this canine hike changes as you enter the canyon. **The last half mile will be pure joy for Seaman on the canyon floor, crossing the creek or scrambling over rocks**. The plunge pool at Eaton Falls should be deep enough for doggie paddling.

For a full canine hiking day that former toll road climbs 1,300 feet in less than four miles to an historic tree nursery at Henninger Flats for inspiring views of the San Gabriel foothills.

Empire Mine State Historic Park

Hardrock Trail

GRASS VALLEY, CALIFORNIA
Hiking Time: 1-2 hours

The Empire Mine was the richest hard-rock mine in California, operating for 106 years and producing almost six million ounces of gold. But it never came easy. Logger George Roberts discovered a quartz outcropping glistening with gold near the present-day parking lot shortly after the 1849 Gold Rush began. Miners swarmed but most quickly sold their claims when they saw the hard work at hand. A consortium consolidated the claims into the Empire Mine. Even then it would not be until the 1880s that the mine would turn a profit.

Seaman will be hiking on top of 367 miles of tunnels, some over one mile deep, that were excavated at the Empire Mine - the distance between Los Angeles and San Francisco. The *Hardrock Trail* pushes away from the mining exhibits in airy woodlands and past rusty souvenirs from the Orleans Stamp Mine. Pilings of tailings give clues to the vast catacomb below.

The easy canine hiking turns more spirited with a turn onto the one-mile loop that climbs Osborn Hill. This exploration through gold mining history visits four more mine sites and foundations before descending back to the more easy-going *Hard Rock Trail* with its varied forest and crossing of Little Wolf Creek. More mine relics signal the impending end of this three-plus mile canine hike through history, concluding in the shadow of mine owner William Bourn Jr.'s fabulous Richardsonian Romanesque-styled stone manor house.

Golden Gate National Recreation Area

Funston Trail

SAN FRANCISCO, CALIFORNIA
Hiking Time: 1-2 hours

This is the most confounding place for dog owners in the United States. The Golden Gate National Recreation cobbles together over 20 separate parcels into one of the world's largest and most popular urban parks. Each location has its own regulations for dogs, there are regulations within parcels and there are regulations within trails. But once you decipher the well-defined "yes" and "no" designations this is one of the best places to bring your dog in the national park system.

That is because Seaman can often go off-leash when allowed to explore the cliffs and forests around San Francisco Bay. **At Fort Funston, an old army installation on the headlands of the Pacific Ocean, your dog is likely to only hear "Fort Fun" before racing off towards one of the Bay Area's prettiest beaches**. Don't be surprised if dogs outnumber people (not counting the hang gliders) when Seaman visits this network of trails around Battery Davis.

The footpath atop the 200-foot bluffs starts out paved but becomes sandy as it snakes its way through low-growing ice plant down to the beach. A satisfying canine hiking loop can be forged by the *Coastal Trail* (thank you sand ladder) and the *Funston Beach Trail*. The Pacific Ocean waves are stick fetching heaven but harness your powerful Roberto Clemente throwing arm here - the current offshore is considered too strong for safe swimming.

M

If there was one essential canine hike of Americana it would have to be the hike to the Hollywood sign, wouldn't it? What was erected in 1923 as a billboard for selling houses and intended to stand for only 18 months is now the most recognizable icon of American culture to the rest of the world.

There are several choices to hike to the Hollywood sign atop Mt. Lee but the *Canyon Drive Trail* is special because at its beginning Seaman can pay homage to another Hollywood legend - the campy 1960s *Batman* television series. A short hike from the trailhead in the opposite direction leads to Bronson Caves, best known to Adam West fans as the entrance to the Batcave.

The trip to the Hollywood sign will cover 3.25 miles and gain nearly 1,000 feet in elevation, most on a steady climb. **Canyon Drive Trail is more drive than trail, wide and level which will come in handy for all the other unleashed dogs Seaman will likely encounter on this hike**. There is almost no shade as you put the City of Angels further and further beneath you.

It is illegal to hike to the sign, perched safely behind restrictive fences, with or without your dog. Instead, the final steps to the summit wind behind the 50-foot high letters to the famous DOOWYLLOH view - Hollywood spelled backwards. Even without the sign, the panorama of Los Angeles and the Pacific Ocean from 1,708-foot Mt. Lee is amazing. A true American classic of a canine hike.

M △ ⚊ $

With all the mind-bending views available of Lake Tahoe it is saying something when the overlook of Emerald Bay at Inspiration Point claims to be the most photographed spot in America. Most people just park and point their smartphones but your dog can do better at one of the world's largest alpine lakes.

Across the street from Inspiration Point is a one-mile trip to Cascade Falls that gains scarcely 100 feet in elevation on the trip. This is absolutely wonderful canine hiking terrain with widely dispersed Jeffrey pines and rocks that appear to have been interjected for decoration rather than obstacles. You never actually get a full-on look at the 200-foot falls but the final steps across open granite slopes will bring Seaman to the side of the water display which can be powerfully impressive during late spring snow melts.

A full day of canine hiking with a car shuttle can incorporate Eagle Falls from the Baypoint Trailhead but most likely it will require a short drive north to its separate trailhead. The stone stairway cut into a rockwall is a tip-off that more challenging canine hiking fare is on tap. The trek to the falls is scarcely a half-mile but Seaman will urge you to continue two more fun miles after crossing the cascades into the Desolation Wilderness. Here the scenery stars change from the blue lake to the craggy gray mountains. **Your destination is Eagle Lake, as enchanting a canine swimming pool as Seaman will find in California**.

Lake Tahoe Basin Management Unit

Mt. Tallac Trail

SOUTH LAKE TAHOE, CALIFORNIA
Hiking Time: 6-8 hours

S △ ☂ $

Many people consider the Tahoe Basin the best place to hike with your dog in America and the ascent up Mt. Tallac may well be the best day hike in Tahoe. **It is a rugged five-mile canine hike with an elevation gain of 3,255 feet and this journey is so special that if you decide to turn around before summiting it could still be Seaman's favorite Tahoe hike**.

Mt. Tallac is the monarch of the Lake Tahoe shoreline, with 3,000 of its 9,735 feet above the water. The first half of Seaman's climb is moderately paced with pretty alpine lakes coming at a steady clip - Fallen Leaf (1 mile), Floating Island (1.6 miles), and Cathedral Lake (2.4 miles).

Then the going gets rougher as Seaman grinds his way up the mountain face on open scree slopes. The trail is well-maintained but still expect loose rocks under paw. As the summit nears the only vegetation to accompany you are lichens on the rocks.

There are no competing peaks in Mt. Tallac's immediate neighborhood so the views will start coming well before tagging the summit. Once atop the wide, jagged promontory there won't be much that escapes Seaman's eyes. There is Lake Tahoe, of course; the other alpine lakes; and the surrounding Desolation Wilderness. Even the casinos across the state line in Nevada all reveal themselves on Mt. Tallac. *Mt. Tallac Trail* is in the Desolation Wilderness that requires access by permit for canine day hikers - fill one out at the trailhead.

Los Padres National Forest

Pfeiffer Beach Trail

BIG SUR, CALIFORNIA
Hiking Time: 1-2 hours possible

E ☂ $

The Big Sur coastline south of the Monterey Peninsula is a must-see for any itinerary in central California. This stretch of oceanside cliffs is best accessed through a series of California state parks, including Point Lobos State Reserve, once described famously as the "greatest meeting of land and water in the world." Unfortunately, dogs are not allowed on any trails here.

Thanks to Pfeiffer Beach Seaman does not have to settle with seeing Big Sur only from the car window. **Pfeiffer Beach is a place where the word "magical" is tossed around as easily as "good dog" at a puppy training class**. To get here takes less than ten minutes on a sandy trail through a maritime forest (unless the parking lot is full - not an uncommon finding - in which case a 1.5-mile walk to the beach is required).

The sand is wrapped in spectacular rock formations making Pfeiffer Beach a very secluded place indeed. Offshore, Keyhole Rock, a natural arch where surf blasts through, frames an evening sunset. The rocky coves make for firsky waves and exciting play in the waves for dogs. Less adventurous canine swimmers can enjoy a small freshwater stream feeding into the beach. Canine beach hiking is available to the north, tides permitting. Take note of Pfeiffer's famous purple-tinged sands, tinted by the manganese, quartz and garnet rocks in the cliffs. This will certainly be one of your most memorable trips to the beach with your dog anywhere - short hike or no.

Marshall Gold Discovery State Historic Park

Monroe Ridge Trail

COLOMA, CALIFORNIA
Hiking Time: 2-3 hours

If you were able to assemble all the gold ever mined in the history of the earth it would fit comfortably in two Olympic swimming pools. And about 1% of all the above-ground gold ever mined was found in the first five years of the California Gold Rush. Those first shining flecks of gold were spotted in a tailrace for a sawmill James Marshall was building for himself and John Sutter here alongside the South Fork American River in 1848.

Seaman's prospecting begins on the *Gold Discovery Loop Trail* that visits a replica of that mill, a mining exhibit, and some of the park's 20 historic buildings. **Your dog can splash in the waters of the exact discovery site, one of the most consequential spots in America**.

The *Monument Trail* shoots off into riparian black oak woodlands and begins switching one-half mile up to Marshall's hilltop gravesite. The carpenter never made any money from the Gold Rush but he was honored with an impressive statuary bronze, pointing towards the discovery site, after his death in 1888. It is the oldest monument in the California park system.

The three-mile *Monroe Ridge Trail* begins here for serious canine hiking, climbing steadily for views of the gold camp and evidence of hard rock mining. The ridge is populated with the steel-hard red manzanita that spice up this woodland ramble as it works down directly into the parking lot where Seaman can cool off in the stony-bottomed American River.

 San Bernadino National Forest

Castle Rock Trail

BIG BEAR LAKE, CALIFORNIA
Hiking Time: 1-2 hours

M

For decades, whenever Hollywood needed a stunning Western location Big Bear Lake is where movie makers came. *Gone With the Wind* may have been set in the Civil War South but was shot at Big Bear Lake. The Ponderosa may have been in Virginia City, Nevada but this is where the action for *Bonanza* took place. *Old Yeller* filmed here and Lassie got the star treatment in Big Bear Lake. And on and on.

Among the canine day hikes around Big Bear Lake the *Castle Rock Trail* stands out for its beauty and caloric burn. From a small parking lot overlooking the water the hike heads uphill across the road in a hurry. The incline is over 30 percent in places but the footpath is solid and dusty which helps since at nearly 7,000 feet this area, even in Southern California, can see snow any month other than July or August.

As Seaman climbs through the rounded boulders and scattered pines and cedars you can almost feel the presence of movie crews as this cinematic terrain feels so familiar. After a half-mile of serious panting the trail moves more inland than upward until reaching the jumble of rounded boulders known as Castle Rock. **There is plenty here to test Seaman's acumen in figuring a way to the top**.

The views of Big Bear Lake are astounding but you may have seen them before - D.W. Griffith hauled his movie cameras to this exact spot in 1915 for scenes in the first great American motion picture, *The Birth of a Nation*.

 # San Bernadino National Forest

Ernie Maxwell Scenic Trail
IDYLLWILD, CALIFORNIA
Hiking Time: 2-3 hours

E **$**

Every time you head to the mountains for a canine hike you don't have to always test your dog's mettle with a lung-crushing climb. **Sometimes it is enough to be out on a fun ramble with your dog through gorgeous alpine scenery without planning on your next rest stop**. One of the best for that is the *Ernie Maxwell Scenic Trail*. Which is fortunate since it is also one of the few hikes Seaman can enjoy in the rugged San Jacinto Mountains.

Ernie Maxwell, founder of the Idyllwild *Town Crier*, was still a horse-rider in the 1950s as auto traffic was increasing in the San Jacintos. His trusty steeds would get spooked on the main roads so he convinced the Forest Service to build an equine route from Humber Park, at the edge of the San Jacinto Wilderness, into town. Local convict work crews cut a meandering level path across the slopes to create the 2.6-mile trail.

Today's *Ernie Maxwell Scenic Trail* is used mainly by canine hikers - Idyllwild prides itself on being a dog-friendly town. From Humber Park the trail eases down 300 feet, ducking in and out of large rock formations jutting from the mountainside. There is scarcely a root under paw on this joyful footpath. Jeffrey pines, Coulter pines, and Ponderosa pines scent the trail. There is no grand destination - just a town street - so turn around whenever. The views are different and grand in both directions: Suicide Rock, Tahquitz Rock, Marion Mountain and more that Seaman can see but not touch.

 # Santa Monica Mountains National Recreation Area

Solstice Canyon Loop
MALIBU, CALIFORNIA
Hiking Time: 1-2 hours

M

The expansive Santa Monica Mountains National Recreation Area is an amalgamation of 150,000 private, city, county, state and federal acres knitted into a single entity with 500 miles of trails. It is not quite the canine hiker's nirvanna it might seem, however, as those governing bodies all have their own regulations for dogs on trails. This will also not be a solitary, contemplative hike with your dog as one in every 17 Americans lives within an hour's drive of the Santa Monica Mountains.

The mighty San Andreas Fault has folded peaks and canyons into the highlands above the Pacific Ocean that attract athletic dogs. Solstice Canyon is the poster child for the beauty of these coastal crevasses.

The easy-going *Solstice Canyon Trail* uses dirt and paved paths to trace - and cross - a year-round stream through the shaded canyon. That old road leads to the brick and stone ruins of Tropical Terrace, a hideaway retreat of supermarket mogul Fred Roberts designed by America's foremost African American architect Paul Revere Williams. The nearby waterfall is out of bounds for dogs - one of those niggling bits of canine red tape here.

The 3.2-mile loop closes on the sporty *Rising Sun Trail*, a dirt scrape that travels through open sage scrub and delivers panoramic views of the Pacific Ocean. Seaman will have gained nearly 700 feet in elevation on this ridge in the rare Mediterranean climate of the Santa Monicas that make this a hot, dry canine hike most of the year.

SEQUOIA NATIONAL FOREST

Boole Tree Trail
VISALIA, CALIFORNIA
Hiking Time: 1-2 hours

The only way Seaman will see the world's largest concentration of giant sequoia trees in Kings Canyon National Park is through a car window. But **five miles north of the famous General Grant Grove your dog can lift his leg on the eighth largest tree in the world, the Boole Tree**.

Converse Basin is a giant sequoia graveyard - it was once quite possibly the finest sequoia grove that ever was. Massive trees over 300 feet high were enthusiastically felled by loggers - often for little more than shingles. One 285-foot sequoia known as the General Noble Tree was cut in 1893 to display at the Columbian Exposition in Chicago and the Chicago Stump can still be seen in the woods today.

The *Boole Tree Trail* is a 2.5-mile loop that quickly puts Seaman on the edge of Kings Canyon. Open, sweeping views greet you as switchbacks begin up the ridge. With the climb completed a short side trail leads into a depression containing the Boole Tree. No one knows why this great tree was spared when equally large neighbors were brought down with relish.

Surrounded by dense growth, it is actually possible to not immediately recognize the Boole Tree. It is related to its brothers in landscaped Kings Canyon National Park like the wolf is to your dog. But once you see Seaman up against its massive trunk - its ground perimeter of 113 feet is the greatest of all giant sequoias - there is no mistaking this special tree, the largest specimen in our national forest system.

SHASTA-TRINITY NATIONAL FOREST

McCloud River Falls Trail
MT. SHASTA, CALIFORNIA
Hiking Time: 1-2 hours

Mt. Shasta, a potentially active volcano with a prominence of nearly 10,000 feet, dominates this area in ways seen and unseen. Such is the case with the McCloud River, one of the jewels of California's waters. The basaltic canyons of the watercourse were shaped by ancient Shasta eruptions and the river's impressive waterfalls are swelled by a steady infusion of subterranean water flowing outward from the massive volcano.

There are three waterfalls of note in the river, linked by a waterside trail of just under two miles. Most canine hikers work upstream from a national forest campground or an angler's access further downstream that adds another mile to the walk. Moving under a shady old growth forest, the trail gains 300 feet in elevation with steps and switchbacks to help out any level of canine hiker. The trail is paw-friendly and even uses a bit of pavement. **Seaman will hear the McCloud River the entire hike and can easily jump in most of the way**.

The plunge pool beneath the 15-foot cataract at the Lower Falls is particularly inviting. The Middle Falls is the diva of the national forest, sending the 80-foot wide river thundering down a 50-foot cliff. After spending most of the canine hike at stream level the trail climbs to Upper Falls that is punching its way through a basaltic amphitheater. If Seaman is hankering for yet another swim, a well-defined rogue trail picks it way down to the water's edge.

 ## SIERRA
NATIONAL FOREST

Shadow of the Giants Trail

OAKHURST, CALIFORNIA

Hiking Time: 1-3 hours

M △ ⌐⊙⊙

Seaman can't get on the trail through the famous Mariposa Grove that inspired Abraham Lincoln to launch America's love affair with conservation in 1864 but he can walk among giant sequoias five miles south of Yosemite National Park in the Nelder Grove. Naturalist John Muir discovered this stand of giant sequoias homesteaded by miner John Nelder in 1875. Muir was not, however, able to prevent heavy logging in the grove.

The *Shadow of the Giants Trail* is a self-guiding interpretive hike with exhibits built in 1965. **Unlike sequoias in national parks, the 100 or so giants here remain in a natural setting and your dog can walk right up to the largest trees**. Nelder Grove is known as much for the beauty of its lush forest as for its scattering of giant sequoias.

The largest arboreal giants in Nelder Grove are located along fire roads that radiate from the tail-friendly campground. The most popular is Bull Buck, a pinkish-bark survivor that is reached on a half-mile loop trail. Bull Buck is 250 feet tall, 99 feet around at its distinctive flared base and probably 2,700 years old.

The dirt road in the opposite direction leads three gentle miles past an increasingly impressive array of giant sequoias until you happen upon Old Granddad and the Kids. The understory - stuffed with dogwoods, sugar pines, firs, and cedar - is so rich here it is possible to miss this all-star tree and its famed massive upper branches.

 ## SMITH RIVER NATIONAL
RECREATION AREA

Craig's Creek Trail

CRESCENT CITY, CALIFORNIA

Hiking Time: 3-4 hours

M △ ⌐⊙⊙

There are no stands of old growth forest on the planet more spectacular than the redwoods of California's northern coast. Sporting bark impervious to insects and having no known diseases, coastal redwoods can live 2,000 years, grow over 350 feet tall and weigh 500 tons. Your dog, unfortunately, can experience the grandeur of the coastal redwoods only in picnic areas, overlooks and campgrounds. Dogs are not allowed on any trails in Redwood National Park or Jedediah Smith Redwoods State Park or Del Norte Coast Redwoods or, well, you get the idea.

The great groves begin to thin out away from the moisture-laden coast in Smith River NRA, where trail dogs are welcome. *Craig's Creek Trail*, with Seaman trotting in the hoofprints of mules that help blazed this old prospector path, takes him to the big trees. The lively Smith River - California's last free-flowing river - is the star of this slice of Six Rivers National Forest but it is more often heard than seen. The redwood groves you brought your dog for are typically spotted when the trail dips into narrow stream beds.

Picturesque views of the South Fork of the Smith River start coming in 1.75 miles, about halfway through this moderately paced canine hike. **The trail then picks up Craig's Creek and joins it for the big climax - maybe more so for your swimming trail companion - where the creek spills into the river**. Then it's back through the towering redwoods.

Vasquez Rocks Natural Area and Nature Center

Pacific Crest Trail

SANTA CLARITA, CALIFORNIA
Hiking Time: 2-3 hours

M A

The Vasquez Rocks are billed as "one of California's most famous geological wonders." Those Famous Rocks - slanted at 45 degrees and more - come courtesy of seismic activity along the San Andreas Fault. The rocks have provided a dramatic backdrop for many a Hollywood scene, most notably as the rocky planet in the original *Star Trek* where Captain Kirk fights a lumbering reptilian Gorn extratrerrestial.

The rocks are named for Tiburcio Vásquez, one of California's most notorious stage coach robbers of the 1800s who used the sloping rocks as an effective hideout. Appropriately, on film two of dogdom's greatest cinematic heroes, Rin Tin Tin and Lassie, brought bad guys to justice here.

The *Pacific Crest Trail* (PCT) slices through this Los Angeles County park for 2.75 miles before ducking through a tunnel under the Antelope Valley Freeway. Starting out on the PCT the surroundings are uninspiring, actually leading away from the namesake rocks. **Things quickly pick up for Seaman, however, with canyons to bound through and rocks to explore**.

There are several options to close your canine hiking loop after a junction at 1.4 miles, whether you choose to follow the entire PCT in the park or not. You will travel through the main movie star rock formations and past archeological highlights like centuries-old petroglyph pictographs and grinding bowls. And keep an eye out for movie crews. Your dog may be the next big canine action star.

 Whiskeytown National Recreation Area

James K. Carr Trail

WHISKEYTOWN, CALIFORNIA
Hiking Time: 2-3 hours

M A ⚊ $

How does a 220-foot waterfall remain unknown in America's most populous state until 2004?

The Whiskeytown community digs its roots out of the California Gold Rush. The town supposedly got its name when a mishap-prone miner named Billie Peterson lost a whiskey barrel while hauling supplies. The keg tumbled down the hillside and broke on the rocks, spilling into what became known as Whiskey Creek.

Miners knew of the jaw-dropping falls and so did loggers but no one spread the word. After these 42,000 acres became federal property in the 1960s there were no funds to protect the natural treasure. It was left off maps and eventually forgotten. An aerial survey rediscovered the three-tier plunge.

Now there is a 1.7-mile trail to Whiskeytown Falls, named for James Carr, a local who became Secretary of the Interior and lobbied for the park. The hard-packed trail, wide enough - barely - for old log trucks, starts out in an open conifer forest and climbs... and climbs...and climbs. **There aren't many downhill pawfalls before reaching the Wintu View overlook**.

The canine hike transitions to a footpath entering a shady box canyon to the base of the falls. Stone steps move up the cliff to multiple vista points. Sculpted granite, deep green mosses, fern blankets, and fallen logs enliven the waterfall canvas. Now you know why there was a conspiracy of silence around Whiskeytown Falls for all those years.

Pacific Northwest

BRUNEAU DUNES STATE PARK

The Dunes 6-Mile Hiking Trail
MOUNTAIN HOME, IDAHO
Hiking Time: 3-4 hours

M ▲ 🏊 $ 🚙

The tallest single-structured sand dune in North America unexpectedly lives in southwestern Idaho. Sands started piling up in a natural basin here about 15,000 years ago during the prehistoric Bonneville Flood. Prevailing winds blow in opposite directions about equal amounts of time and so, unlike most dunes, these sands rock back and forth instead of drift.

The *Dunes 6-Mile Hiking Trail* kicks off behind the Visitor Center, heading through semi-wilderness desert scrub and past marshland. Soon enough you reach open dunes and Seaman begins the slow ascent to the crest of the 470-foot Big Dune. The trail crosses the crest of the dune, passing over the impressive Vortex Crater, a 300-foot bowl of sand.

The volcanic Owyhee Mountains are visible to the west and the peaks of the Boise Mountains jut out from the horizon to the north. A unique feature of the Bruneau Dunes are the lakes which formed at the foot of the sand-piles in the 1950s when the building of a nearby reservoir raised the water table. **A doggie dip in the lake after a workout on the sand will be a tail-wagging highlight of this trek in Bruneau**.

When Seaman is sufficiently played out in the water and sand it is time to complete the loop. If the Bruneau Lakes do not do a sufficient job of cooling the hike down this part of the trail is sprinkled with shady Russian Olive trees along the route back to the parking lot.

CAPE DISAPPOINTMENT STATE PARK

Cape Disappointment Trail
ILWACO, WASHINGTON
Hiking Time: 1-2 hours

M ▲ 🏊 $

If British fur trader John Meares had been able to sail just a few miles further south in 1788 before a storm forced him to turn around he would have gone down in history as the European discoverer of the mouth of the Columbia River. Instead George Vancouver garnered the honor four years later. Hence, Cape Disappointment.

It was anything but disappointment in 1805 when Seaman and his fellow Lewis & Clark explorers saw the Pacific Ocean for the first time at these headlands, culminating a 4,133-mile journey that had begun three years earlier in St. Louis on the Mississippi River.

Canine hiking at Cape Disappointment stuffs art, history, old growth forests, a lighthouse, an old army battery, and stunning scenery into a small daypack. Start with some first-rate swimming and fetching in a sandy, driftwood-strewn cove known as Waikiki Beach. Then follow a series of art trails created by Maya Lin of Vietnam Memorial fame for the Confluence Project in 2006. An inscribed boardwalk recounts the expeditioners' adventures with quotes from journals.

The trail makes a sporty ascent of the Sitka spruce-covered headlands with views of the Pacific and the Columbia from grassy outcroppings. The destination is the Cape Disappointment Lighthouse that was built 200 feet above the surf in 1856. The light was hard to see for ships approaching from the south and a second light tower had to be built on the North Head. Just another disappointment.

City of Rocks National Reserve

Creekside Towers-South Fork-Stairways Trails

ALMO, IDAHO

Hiking Time: 1-2 hours

M A

Pioneers on the California Trail wrote in reverence about the towering granite pinnacles and fins that they passed traveling through this stretch of the Albion Mountains in Southern Idaho. Many left names and messages scrawled in axle grease on the rocks. One, James F. Wilkins, tagged this stop on the trail *City of Rocks*.

Today adventurers head *to* City of Rocks instead of passing through. Many are climbers testing themselves on routes up the rocks that reach over 600 feet high. Seaman will be clambering across the granite surfaces as well on over 22 miles of trails. The *Creekside Towers Trail* immerses canine hikers into one of the most congested sections of the Preserve known as the "Inner City."

The route maneuvers through tall spires for half-a-mile with plenty of side nooks and crannies for Seaman to investigate. Branches of Circle Creek percolate into the "city" to provide welcome refreshment as Seaman ambles happily along.

The 2.5-mile loop through the Inner City is closed by the *South Fork Trail* that bursts out onto the open rocks for long views of the Reserve. Unlike many rock jumble landscapes, the City of Rocks offers diverse habitats including woodlands and meadows.

The Reserve also permits dogs into the backcountry so there is ample opportunity to stretch eager canine legs across the sculpted Circle Creek Basin landscape.

Columbia River Gorge National Scenic Area

Eagle Creek Recreation Trail

CASCADE LOCKS, OREGON

Hiking Time: 2-6 hours

M A 🏊

Can moss be the star of a canine hike? The *Eagle Creek Recreation Trail* is the most popular hike in the Columbia Gorge and most people come for the jaw-dropping waterfalls. The water displays deliver on the hype but it is the rain forest mosses that slowly work their magic during this visit. Moss is everywhere from dead tree snags to rocks to wooden bridges.

Between the crowds and the walking paths carved into basaltic cliffs, Eagle Creek is for experienced, easy-to-control trail dogs only. There are sheer drop-offs with no guard rails, although a guide cable is bolted into cliff walls at strategic spots.

The destination for canine day hikers is often Tunnel Falls, where a rock passage is carved behind the thundering 175-foot cataract. It is impossible to oversell the wonder of this moss-covered amphitheater. This journey gains over 1,100 feet in elevation in six miles.

An even taller waterfall lies another half-mile up the trail but only a portion of Twister Falls is visible from the main trail. The potholes in the pock-marked rock surface become even more treacherous and the drop-offs higher for Seaman after Tunnel Falls so use sound judgement in tackling "The Vertigo Mile."

Less ambitious trail hikers can still get the full wonder from Eagle Creek by making the exhilarating Punch Bowl Falls at two miles in as the destination. A short spur leads Seaman down to the cylindrical grotto for a swim in the pool.

171

COLUMBIA RIVER GORGE NATIONAL SCENIC AREA

Multnomah Falls Loop #2

TROUTDALE, OREGON
Hiking Time: 2-3 hours

M 🏊

Created by a cataclysmic blast of glacial lake water 15,000 years ago, the Columbia River flows through one of the few east-west canyons in the world. Some 77 waterfalls tumble off ridges and sheer walls that soar 2,000 feet above the river. Included in this hydrospectacular bounty is the largest concentration of high waterfalls in North America. No wonder the Columbia River Gorge between Oregon and Washington was designated America's first National Scenic Area.

Multnomah Falls is the emperor of Columbia Gorge waterfalls with a year-round plunge of 620 feet in two sheer drops. This is the biggest natural attraction in the Pacific Northwest with two million visitors. Most won't venture past the overlook at Multnomah Falls Lodge. Many will go to the historic Benson Bridge across the middle and some will even follow the switchbacking paved path for 1.2 miles to the very top of the iconic cataract.

But Seaman will want more. Continue on the *Larch Mountain Trail* (#441) into the lush old growth forest, passing more waterfalls. In less than one mile, link into the *Wahkeena Trail* (#420) for the walk back down. Fairy Falls, a lovely fan-style waterfall, highlights this leg of the canine hike. Near the bottom of the 4.8-mile loop the natural surface trail passes hard by the 242-foot Wahkeena Falls that squeezes through a moss-covered volcanic cliff. **That will give Seaman over 1,000 feet of waterfalls for only a few hours purchase**.

DECEPTION PASS STATE PARK

Lighthouse Point Loop / Lottie Point Loop

OAK HARBOR, WASHINGTON
Hiking Time: 1-2 hours

M ⛺ 🏊 **$**

More dogs come to Deception Pass, so named because early explorers mistook the narrow gap between Whidbey and Fidalgo islands as the mouth of a river, than any other state park in Washington. These twin loops, that diverge from a single point on the south shore of Bowman Bay, highlight much of the reason for the park's popularity. **Seaman will bound up a small cliff to start the *Lighthouse Point Loop* but it will take a good while for swim-loving dogs to get this hike underway - there is a sandy beach a few steps to the right and a rockier beach a few steps to the left**. The 1.5-mile balloon trail immerses your dog in an intriguing mix of ancient Douglas firs and cinnamon-barked Pacific madrone on the headlands above the rocky cove. Tamper down expectations of a grand payoff as the "lighthouse" is only the strictest sense of the term of a lightbulb housed in a small steel navigational tower on an offshore island. In this gorgeous setting the lack of grandeur is scarcely missed.

The *Lottie Point Loop* is more of the same, also about 1.5 miles with minimal elevation change and that peeling red bark of madrone trees. This payoff is even closer views of Deception Pass, Canoe Pass, and the 180-foot high cantilever bridges that link the islands and have inspired photographers for over 80 years. Before returning to the trailhead you can walk Seaman across the Deception Bridge for tail-wagging views of the entire storied passage.

ECOLA STATE PARK

Indian Beach/Cannon Beach Trails

CANNON BEACH, OREGON

Hiking Time: 2-3 hours

M ▲ ≈ $

JOHN DAY FOSSIL BEDS NATIONAL MONUMENT

Carroll Rim Trail

MITCHELL, OREGON

Hiking Time: 1-2 hours

M 🚙

There are 363 miles of tail-friendly coastline in Oregon - every bit of it - and this chunk on top of Tillamook Head may be the most popular. It was even on Lewis and Clark's radar when the Corps of Discovery chased down rumors of a beached whale here in 1806. "The grandest and most pleasing prospects which my eyes ever surveyed," wrote Captain William Clark.

Modern day Seaman will see two of Oregon's most photographed subjects from the Tillamook Head Trails. From the main parking lot at Ecola Point the *Cannon Beach Trail* drifts through an old growth Sitka spruce forest to the northern end of Crescent Beach and its collection of sea stacks in the surf, including the 235-foot tall Haystack Rock that is one of the largest free-standing rocks in the world. At low tide Seaman can trot right up to the monolith and smell the sea creatures clinging to its sides.

Indian Trail skirts the conifer-shrouded cliffs to the north. Many rogue side trails lead down to the secluded sandy beach. Your destination is an Oregon Coast Trail Hiking Camp and beyond it a spur to breathtaking views of the Pacific. Clinging to a speck of solid basalt rock a mile offshore is Tillamook Rock Lighthouse. Conditions on "Terrible Tilly" were so harsh keepers were given three weeks off after purposely shortened shifts. Construction required 17 months and just weeks before completion the three-masted barque *Lupatia* wrecked in heavy fog. The only survivor was the crew's dog.

The deep ravines and eroded formations of northeast Oregon's Blue Mountains display one of the longest and most continuous records of evolutionary change in the United States. Fossils of land plants and animals date back as many as 54 million years.

There are three units to the John Day Fossil Beds and the star is the Painted Hills, one of the 7 Wonders of Oregon. The *Carroll Rim Trail* climbs steadily up the side of a claystone hill, reaching the top after 400 feet and one mile. From here the picturesque panorama confirms the Painted Hills place in the Beaver State's scenic pantheon.

The yellows, golds, blacks, and reds that stripe the naked claystone hills are always changing with the light and moisture. **Hike back down with Seaman and then back up and everything is likely to look different over on Painted Ridge**.

From the Carroll Rim you can also scout the park's short trails including the vibrantly red *Painted Cove Trail* below. The *Red Scar Knoll Trail* at the park edge is also worth Seaman's time.

And who was John Day? He was an unfortunate fur trader who became separated from his expedition party along a tributary of the Columbia River in 1810. Day was robbed by Indians who took all his possessions, including his clothes. Subsequent travelers would point out the spot where the incident took place and eventually the river, the longest undammed tributary of the Columbia, became named for the man who had his worst day here.

LEWIS & CLARK
NATIONAL HISTORICAL PARK

Fort to Sea Trail
ASTORIA, OREGON
Hiking Time: 5-6 hours

M 🏊 $

 MINERAL RIDGE
SCENIC AREA

Mineral Ridge National Recreation Trail
COEUR D'ALENE, IDAHO
Hiking Time: 2 hours

M 🏊

The most famous travelers in American history were Meriwether Lewis and William Clark, who journeyed from St. Joseph, Missouri to the Pacific Ocean to map out just what Thomas Jefferson had bought in his Louisiana Purchase from France. When the original Seaman reached the Pacific at this spot, he became the first dog to travel the breadth of America.

After venturing more than 4,000 miles to reach the Pacific Ocean the Corps of Discovery did not camp there but set up winter quarters at Fort Clatsop six miles inland. In the 1950s when a replica of the fort was built volunteers also began planning a trail along a route likely used to reach the surf. It took the celebration of the Lewis & Clark Bicentennial 50 years later to get it built.

The *Fort to Sea Trail* begins in thick rain forest with abundant wetlands, looking much like it would have from December 1805 to March 1806. **But it soon encounters many things Seaman would never have seen when he ran this way over 200 years ago that add considerable interest to this canine hike: bridges, boardwalks, cattle farms, fences, golfers, and even U.S. Highway 101 which the trail tunnels under**.

The ground under paw turns sandy for the last mile through pine thickets before the climax in the dunes at Sunset Beach. If you haven't used a car shuttle it is now necessary to make a sea-to-fort canine hike back to your vehicle.

Lake Coeur d'Alene has placed highly on lists of the world's most beautiful lakes since Fort Sherman was built on its shores in 1878. By the time the military outpost shuttered in 1901, tourism was already entrenched along the lake. So many vacationers arrived by steamship that Lake Coeur d'Alene - whose literal translation from French is the meaningless "heart of the awl" - was America's busiest inland port west of the Mississippi River.

The best place for Seaman to purchase views of this stunning body of water is at the east end in the Mineral Ridge Scenic Area. When the BLM began developing recreation sites in Idaho in 1962 this was the place they chose to start.

The *Mineral Ridge Trail* switches lustily up 660 feet to the 2,800-foot summit through decadent stands of Ponderosa pine and Douglas fir. It also passes old mining pit excavations that date to the 1890s when hard rock mining for lead and zinc flourished.

Long-remembered views will be uncovered of Wolf Lodge Bay to the north and Beauty Bay to the west. Spur trails extend Seaman's exploration in the Mineral Ridge forests and lead to more photo ops of the lake. If it is wintertime the skies will contain some 200 bald eagles who migrate here each year. While there is no swimming along the trail, tempting Lake Coeur d'Alene waters are only steps from the parking lot.

Moran
State Park

Mount Constitution Loop
OLGA, WASHINGTON
Hiking Time: 3-4 hours

M A 🏊 **$**

Most people will arrive at Ellsworth Storey's 52-foot replica of a Russian medieval stone watchtower atop Mount Constitution by car. **Seaman will no doubt prefer to summit the Lower 48's second highest ocean island mountain with paw power**. If you catch a clear day on Orcas Island Victoria is to the west, Vancouver to the north, Mount Baker to the east and Mount Rainier to the south.

Start this 6.7-mile loop at Mountain Lake and begin switchbacking on the dirt scar that scrapes through an old growth forest towards Little Summit. You could also start at Little Summit but that would put the hardest grind on this circuit canine hike at the end rather than the beginning. Don't turn past Little Summit without making the short detour to start collecting some of the finest maritime views anywhere.

The Douglas fir and Western hemlock surrender to ridge views as you close in on the 2,409-foot summit. After begrudgingly sharing the 360-degree views on top of Mount Constitution with the car tourists continue across the parking lot for a delightful descent through the park's dark green forested interior.

In short order Seaman is at Twin Lakes with easy access for dog paddling. If he is reluctant to leave promise him that the last mile of this all-star canine hike will be completely along Mountain Lake. Seaman will even find diving docks to complete a memorable tour of Seattle shipbuilder Robert Moran's old stomping grounds.

Mount Hood
National Forest

Old Salmon River Trail
WELCHES, OREGON
Hiking Time: 1-2 hours

E A 🏊 **$**

Sometimes you just want to take an easy, scenic hike with your dog. Welcome to the *Old Salmon River Trail*.

Most of the magnificent old growth forests of the Pacific Northwest are not easy for canine hikers to get to - their inaccessibility is why they were never logged in the first place. Somehow the giant trees along the Salmon River survived, even after a road was built into the area. All the more remarkable when a single 10-foot thick Western red cedar tree can yield $10,000 worth of lumber.

This quintessential Oregon canine hike is almost completely level on a generous needle-infused path. When there is a slight incline a set of steps usually accompanies the slope. When there is a small stream to cross a bridge shows up. The Salmon River is your constant companion and side trails scoot down to pockets of sandy beach and deep pools perfect for doggie dips.

This mossy green cathedral is so easy to get to there are five access points in the first 1.9 miles of the out-and-back footpath. There is no great climax to the *Old Salmon Trail*, the thrill is just being among these marvelous trees in this setting. Even the trunks of fallen cedars are alive with new growth in their role as "nurse logs" for future generations.

You can turn Seaman around at any time - or continue on past the Green Canyon Campground. If you can convince your dog to leave this special place at all.

MOUNT HOOD NATIONAL FOREST

Umbrella Falls Loop Trail

HOOD RIVER, OREGON
Hiking Time: 2-3 hours

M ▲ 🏊 $

Mount Hood lords over the state of Oregon with one of the largest prominences of any peak in the continental United States. With over one million acres the national forest surrounding the 11,250-foot summit is is a canine hiker's paradise. Mount Hood was slated to become a national park in 1940 but World War II intervened. Campaigns to elevate the status of the mountain are still active, as is this volcano. So these splendid trails could one day go off limits to dogs.

In the meantime you will want to get Seaman to Mount Hood to experience Oregon's wonderfully long wildflower season. The *Umbrella Falls Loop* in Hood River Meadows is the place to do just that.

The circuit hike wanders around Nordic ski runs and cross-country trails as it climbs 840 feet in two easy-to-swallow miles. The destination is Umbrella Falls that plunges through a gap in the conifer forest into an enticing woodland pool. The trail continues higher up the southeast side of Mount Hood but for this loop guide Seaman back to the junction with the *Sahale Falls Trail*.

There are more creek crossings and more meadows and plenty of huckleberries to gobble in season. **There is an observation point for 60-foot Sahale Falls but Seaman will want to scramble down for a leap into the plunge pool**. The four-mile loop closes with a downhill ramble through the towering trees and one last look up Mount Hood and its meadows.

MT. BAKER-SNOQUALMIE NATIONAL FOREST

Horseshoe Bend Trail

GLACIER, WASHINGTON
Hiking Time: 1-2 hours

E ▲ 🏊 $ 🚙

When producers wanted to film a movie version of Jack London's adventure yarn *Call of the Wild* in 1934 the Nooksack River is where they came. The *Horseshoe Bend Trail* hugs the banks of the North Fork its entire length but does not mimic the unruly white glacial waters mere feet away. **The worst Seaman can expect on this easy-going footpath is mud and the occasional root**.

The trail passes through towering Douglas Fir, Western hemlock and Western red cedar that have been protected in this area since 1937. The Nooksack Indians who lived here were known as People of the Ferns and fronds and mosses certainly dominate the forest understory at Seaman's eye level throughout this exploration.

The non-technical canine hiking season can be short around Mount Baker that is one of the snowiest places on earth - a world record 1,140 inches fell in 1999 - but the *Horseshoe Bend Trail* is far enough down the mountain to be accessible almost year-round.

The Nooksack's hypnotic theatrics reach a crescendo after a little more than a half mile; a stone bench to watch the performance stood here until it was washed away. Many canine hikers turn around at the remains but the trail moves uphill from the river and continues for another couple of miles before becoming completely overgrown. The river's climactic show comes downstream in an 88-foot twin plunge just off Highway 542.

Olympic National Forest

Quinault Rain Forest Trail System
QUINAULT, WASHINGTON
Hiking Time: 2-3 hours

E ▲ ⚊ $

As you hike with your dog through some of America's tallest and greenest trees in the Quinault Rain Forest, think about this: the first car to make it to Quinault arrived in 1912 - two years before they had built any roads here. That's how badly folks want to see this special place.

Lake Quinault bills itself as the "Valley of the Rain Forest Giants" and Exhibit A is the Worlds' Largest Sitka Spruce Tree. This monster soars 191 feet high with a circumference only a few whiskers shy of 56 feet around. **On the North Shore a half-mile trail leads to a gnarled big cedar believed to be over 1,000 years old. You can easily stand inside the ancient arboreal wonder with Seaman**.

Short, interconnected trails fill out the four-mile *Quinault Rain Forest Trail System*, leading to a cedar bog, waterfalls, and the lakeshore for a doggie dip. Clubmoss draping branches and thick canopies suffocate the light on the forest floor of this four-mile canine hike.

The *Rain Forest Nature Trail* interprets the creation of this lush arboreal paradise in a half-mile loop. At one magical turn Seaman can stand beneath all four titans of the Pacific rain forest - Western red cedar, Sitka spruce, Douglas fir and Western hemlock - growing in a row. Giant trees often growing in such orderly procession since they propagate on the mossy safety of ancestors fallen on the forest floor. The nurse logs decay and their thriving wards are left to carry on the legacy.

Olympic National Park

Ruby Beach Trail
FORKS, WASHINGTON
Hiking Time: 1-2 hours

E ▲ ⚊

You are never going to hike with your dog on another beach like Kalaloch (CLAY-lock). When the sea gets angry it disgorges massive logs onto the shores of the most remote northwestern part of the country. Thousand upon thousands of logs.

Seven ocean beaches feature short jaunts through the coastal rain forest from adjoining Highway 101 - six with numbers and Ruby Beach. Seaman will take less than ten minutes to reach the sand from the bluffs but this won't be any ordinary beachcombing expedition - there is plenty of stepping to be done on and around these piles of bleached elephantine driftwood in the soft sand.

Ruby Beach is a bit pebblier under paw than its cousins but also features more dramatic sea stacks in the surf. Seaman can hike right up to the rock formations and little Abbey Island at low tide - the only time you want to enjoy these beaches since the waves can crash right up to the bluffs in places. Long beachcombing canine hikes are possible north and south if you know the tides. Keep an eye out offshore for whales and Seaman can sniff sea stars in the pools of rocky outcroppings where Cedar Creek flows into the Pacific Ocean at Ruby Beach.

After coming all this way to the corner of the United States, you won't want to leave in a hurry - and you won't have to. Dogs are allowed to stay in the cabins at Kalaloch Lodge, constructed from milled driftwood that washed up on shore, naturally.

OREGON DUNES
NATIONAL RECREATION AREA

Tahkenitch Dunes/Threemile Lake North Trails

REEDSPORT, OREGON

Hiking Time: 2-3 hours

M ⛺ 🏊 $

This is the Super Bowl of doggie sand play with 40 miles of tail-friendly beach. The mountains of sand at Oregon Dunes are the tallest on the Pacific Coast and extend inland for 2.5 miles. Where those dunes end is where the *Tahkenitch Dunes* and *Threemile Lake North* Trails, a combined 6.5-mile loop, begin. Seaman will probably be better served to head out on the dunes trail first when everyone is fresh and save the lake trail that travels through an old conifer forest for most of its length for last. **Either way Seaman will be off on the best seaside dunes hike he will ever tackle**.

The trail crosses open oblique dunes, pristine interdune lakes, and beautiful tree islands. When Seaman bounds to the top of a dune there are long views through the intermittent forest out to the Pacific Ocean, the ultimate destination on this spectacular canine hike.

Two short spur trails lead to a wide chunk of isolated beach. For hiking with your dog you can usually hop through the mouth of Tahkenitch Creek to the north but not the mouth of the Umpqua River a couple miles to the south. Dogs are not welcome on the beach during snowy plover nesting season.

Heading back, the trail meanders along the edge of the namesake Threemile Lake as it takes it time in a thick spruce forest. There is more dog-paddling here and in the picturesque Elbow Lake before reaching the trailhead and campground on the Oregon Coast Highway.

PORT ORFORD HEADS
STATE PARK

Headland/Nellies Cove Trails

PORT ORFORD, OREGON

Hiking Time: 1-2 hours

M

The Oregon coast is one of the great sights in America and Port Orford Heads is an easy way for your dog to experience one of Oregon's Seven Wonders. Spectacular, but also dangerous. So many ships wrecked off these 280-foot headlands that one of Oregon's first lifeboat stations was built here in the 1930s. The U.S Coast Guard surfmen monitored a 40-mile stretch of Pacific Ocean and when duty called hurried down a 504-foot staircase to an unsinkable 36-foot lifeboat (now on display outside the defunct station-turned museum) waiting in Nellies Cove.

Seaman need not make that arduous climb today. The canine hiking is all on top of the headlands and begins in a thick Sitka spruce forest, amidst many impressive specimens. The *Nellies Cove Trail* spends much of its time in this delicious forest with overlooks of a trio of sea stacks and the remains of the boathouse that burned in 1970.

After a stop at the remains of the old 37-foot observation tower you will connect with the *Headland Trail* that picks its way through low-growing conifers and blankets of the leathery-leaved shrub known as Western salal. On the headlands nothing grows high enough that a golden retriever can't see above. The northfacing views are to Cape Blanco Lighthouse, Oregon's oldest and tallest. The sea stacks in the surf include the unusual pyramidal Klooqueh Rock. And don't be surprised to spot a pod of grey whales before completing the 1.2-mile loop.

Ross Lake National Recreation Area

Thunder Knob Trail

DIABLO, WASHINGTON
Hiking Time: 1-2 hours

M △

Despite its imposing name, Thunder Knob is one of the smallest and easiest peaks to conquer in the rugged North Cascades, a land of busy glaciers. Thunder Knob is also one of the rare summits Seaman is permitted to tag in the North Cascades.

The *Thunder Knob Trail* kicks off with a heavy plank bridge across the energetic waters of Colonial Creek (taken down in the winter for protection) and then deposits Seaman on one of the best groomed trails he will ever hike on in a national forest. **Wide and level with nary a root in sight, this footpath is so pleasant your dog will scarcely notice the nearly 500 feet in elevation gain on this 1.8-mile out-and-back hike**.

What demands notice is how impossibly green this stretch of hemlock forest is. The spellbinding greenery continues into the higher and drier elevations of lodgepole pine. As the forest opens up Thunder Knob begins to yield views of the ragged granite peaks all around you.

The *Thunder Knob Trail* is a four-star canine hike even without its payout at the end - your purchase of the spectacular view of Diablo Lake. The deep turquoise colors are the result of fine glacial silt washed into the water. But this is no souvenir of a distant ice age; Diablo Lake is a reservoir created after the construction of a hydroelectric dam in 1930. Stay as long as you want atop Thunder Knob - there is a log bench on the overlook to sit with Seaman.

San Juan Island National Historic Park

Young Hill Trail

FRIDAY HARBOR, WASHINGTON
Hiking Time: 1-2 hours

M 🏊

San Juan is the most popular of the hundreds of islands that dot the waters between the United States and Canada. In the 19th century the international border was disputed and this achingly scenic island was divided. Things went well enough until a rooting pig was killed in an American garden in 1859. Turned out to be a British swine and tensions escalated. The Pig War was averted but an "American Camp" and "English Camp" were established until possession of the island was arbitrated in the American's favor in 1871.

Hopefully when you bring your trail dog to San Juan Island you'll have enough time that you won't have to choose sides. If you have to pick, take Seaman to the English Camp with its craggy outcroppings and lush forest headlands surrounding Bell Point. **The trip to 650-foot Young Hill is a sporty walking trail of under one mile past the old English Camp Cemetery that culminates in a panoramic view into Canada**. The former British Royal Marine garrison has been crisply restored with post buildings and a formal garden. Start a shady canine stroll around Bell Point here or even jump onto a ranger-led guided tour - dogs are welcome.

If your dog prefers a swim, swap the English Camp for the American Camp and the hike along South Beach to Grandma's Cove. While Seaman is splashing in the Strait of Juan de Fuca waves, keep an eye out for passing pods of orcas from the driftwood-studded sands.

179

SUISLAW
NATIONAL FOREST

St. Perpetua Trail

YACHATS, OREGON

Hiking Time: 2-3 hours

S A

When you boast that you have the "Best View on the Oregon Coast," as Cape Perpetua Scenic Area does, you had better bring more than a knife to that gunfight. For your dog to weigh in on that debate he must negotiate an elevation gain of 700 feet on a pine straw-covered, switchbacking trail for 1.2 miles (you could drive him to the overlook like everyone else but there's no fun in that). The destination for the *St. Perpetua Trail* is the highest point you can reach by car on the Oregon Coast at 803 feet.

Seaman won't have to wait until the top to enjoy Pacific Ocean views as the lush spruce forest breaks into wildflower-sprinkled meadows and overlooks along the way. Catch a clear day on Cape Perpetua and the views stretch 70 miles up and down the Oregon Coast and 37 miles across the Marine Garden shoreline and out into the Pacific.

Before heading back on this out-and-back canine hike stroll around the short *Whispering Spruce Trail* loop. The stone parapet at the ocean overlook is the handiwork of the Civilian Conservation Corps in the 1930s.

Down below, take the 0.8-mile spur trail in the opposite direction to meet a 500-year old Sitka Spruce. Seaman will no doubt appreciate the paw-friendly, mostly level path along Cape Creek. He also can slip inside the woody cave at the base of the monster conifer for a photo op as a souvenir of this memorable canine outing.

WILLAMETTE
NATIONAL FOREST

Opal Creek Trail

DETROIT, OREGON

Hiking Time: 3-4 hours

E A ⚊ $ 🚙

There are other places to hike with your dog to see 800-year old Douglas firs and Western red cedars but none where you'll see a used car show room straight out of *The Untouchables*.

When the first settlers arrived in the Opal Creek Valley in 1859 it was not the 200-foot trees they were after; it was gold. There wasn't so much gold but the miners out at Jawbone Flats found enough lead, zinc, copper, and silver to keep the Shiny Rock Mining Co. going until 1992. When the operations ended more than 150 acres were gifted to the Friends of Opal Creek who preserve not only the magnificent trees but the mining camp as well.

The *Opal Creek Trail* follows an old prospecting road into Jawbone Flats - active population of 11, give or take. Along the way Seaman can poke his head into an old mine, cross half-bridges, and pass rusting mining artifacts that includes old cars and hauling equipment in the outdoor museum.

As jaw-dropping as the old growth forest is in Opal Creek the startling turquoise waters of the Little North Santiam River go toe-to-toe with the arboreal oldsters for "wow" moments on this canine hike. The road takes about three miles to reach the former company town and there are a variety of traditional trails to explore beyond before heading back. The must-check-off for your dog is the hop over to Opal Pool Falls where emerald green water pours over a small chasm at the head of the creek.

INDEX OF PARKS